Chanting from the Heart

THICH NHAT HANH

and the

MONKS AND NUNS

OF PLUM VILLAGE

PARALLAX PRESS

BERKELEY, CALIFORNIA

Parallax Press ▪ P.O. Box 7355
Berkeley, California 94707 ▪ www.parallax.org

Parallax Press is the publishing division of Unified Buddhist Church, Inc.

Discourses translated from Pali retain Pali spellings. Those translated from Chinese retain Sanskrit spellings.

Calligraphy by Thich Nhat Hanh.
Cover design by Charles Woods and Ayelet Maida.
Text design by Gopa & Ted2, Inc.

Library of Congress Cataloging-in-Publication Data

Nghi thúc tung niêm. English.
  Chanting from the heart : Buddhist ceremonies and daily practices
/ Thich Nhat Hanh and the monks and nuns of Plum Village. — [Rev. ed.].
    p. cm.
  Previously published: Plum village chanting and recitation book, 2000.
  Includes bibliographical references and index.
  ISBN 1-888375-63-9 (pbk. : alk. paper)
  1. Buddhism—Prayer-books and devotions—English. 2. Village des pruniers
(Buddhist community) I. Nhât Hanh, Thích. II. Title.

BQ9800.T536N4513 2006
294.3'4433—dc22

                                                                2006031571

1 2 3 4 5 / 11 10 09 08 07

Contents

Introduction

C HANTING From the Heart is a collection of verses, chants, practices, ceremonies, and discourses developed and used regularly by the monks, nuns, and laypeople at the monasteries and lay retreat centers established by Vietnamese Buddhist Zen Master Thich Nhat Hanh and his community. These centers are Plum Village, Deer Park Monastery, Maple Forest Monastery, and Green Mountain Dharma Center. The book was first published in the year 2000. Because it records a practice that is both centuries old and also very alive today, *Chanting From the Heart* is a living book that grows like a tree, with new branches but the same solid base. This book is the first paperback edition and the first revision since the book's initial publication. It contains a number of new discourses and recitations as well as some changes in the wording of items in the original edition to reflect more accurately their original meaning and the way they are recited today.

When we chant, we chant from the heart. We are not "performing," either for a deity or for anyone else. We are not just carrying out a ritual, our mouths going through the motions while our minds are elsewhere. These words and music have been composed to serve as Dharma instruments helping us come back to the deepest place in ourselves, the place where we are most awake and alive. Chanting is often the most direct and immediate way to reconnect us with these places.

Let us give ourselves over to the Buddha inside of us, not holding anything back. Let us surrender all notions of ourselves and others, our projects and agendas, and put our entire being into our chanting and daily practice. Every time we do this, we taste a joy as sweet and clear as the purest spring water, and as boundless as the great blue sky.

At Plum Village, chants and recitations are part of everyday life and are also important for special occasions. They help to strengthen our practice of mindfulness, nourishing the wholesome seeds of love and understanding within us and renewing our determination to be aware and awake to the present moment. These practices are made available to you in this book. They may be performed with your community of fellow practitioners, your family, or on your own.

Chanting From the Heart does not require any special knowledge. Sanskrit and Pali words and other Buddhist terms are defined in the glossary in the back. With the exception of the "c" in Sanskrit words (which is pronounced "ch"), words are usually pronounced phonetically. You are invited to use this book creatively, adapting the contents to fit your own practice and that of your community. Please enjoy these practices with a relaxed and gentle attitude, with an open mind and receptive heart.

చ

Chanting From the Heart begins with some basic exercises and then is divided into four primary sections. The first section, Daily Practice, includes a suggested daily practice session; silent meal practice; gathas (mindfulness verses) for everyday use; and a section of additional practices and recitations.

The second section, Ceremonies, presents over twenty ceremonies created for the many events and occasions in life, from supporting someone who is sick to blessing a new practice center.

The third section, Discourses, contains twenty-two of the most fundamental teachings presented by the Buddha and his enlightened disciples. They come from both Pali and Chinese sources. Some have been shortened so that you can recite them in your daily practice sessions. From time to time, you may want to study these discourses and discuss them with your practice community. Any discourse read at any time is beneficial, though some are particularly helpful on certain occasions. On special days, New Year's Day for example, you might like to read the Discourse on Happiness. When someone you care for is sick or has passed away, you can read the Anuradha Discourse, the Discourse on the Teachings to Be Given to the Sick, or the Discourse on the Middle Way.

The fourth section, Music, includes musical notation for a number of the chants, verses, and recitations in this book. A ♪ symbol indicates which sections in the text have a musical version. Finally, there is both a glossary and an index of titles.

చ

We hope you discover some of the many ways that this book can be useful to you in your life. We offer *Chanting From the Heart* with the wish that it may be of benefit to you, your family, your community, and all beings.

—Thich Nhat Hanh
and the monks and nuns of Plum Village
October, 2006

Basic Exercises

~

THERE ARE MANY different ways to cultivate mindfulness in our lives. In Plum Village, we use several practices, such as sitting meditation, walking meditation, inviting the bell, reciting gathas, touching the Earth or bowing, deep relaxation, and hugging meditation. Following are brief descriptions of each of these. Some exercises also list suggestions for further reading.

SITTING MEDITATION

Sitting meditation is a way of returning home to give full attention and care to ourselves. Like the peaceful image of the Buddha on the altar, we too can radiate peace and stability. The purpose of sitting meditation is to enjoy. Don't try to attain anything!

At Plum Village, we practice mindfulness of breathing. Whether you sit on a cushion, a blanket, a chair, or directly on the floor, sit in a way that feels comfortable. If possible, inhale through your nostrils, and notice your abdomen expand. Then, as you exhale, notice your abdomen return to normal size. One way to help maintain awareness of breathing is to recite a gatha. When you breathe in, say silently, "In." As you breathe out, say silently, "Out." After doing this for a while, you might like to try a guided meditation.

Sitting meditation periods can be ten, twenty, or thirty minutes — or however long you like. Sitting is for your pleasure, so relax. If your posture is causing you too much pain, feel free to adjust your position, moving slowly and attentively, following your breathing and every movement of your body so you will not lose your concentration. You can even stand up slowly and mindfully if necessary, and when you feel ready, sit down again. At the end of the period, allow a few minutes to massage your legs and feet before standing up again.

WALKING MEDITATION

Walking meditation indoors or outdoors is a very precious practice. Walking meditation means that we know we are walking. We walk just for walking, no longer in a hurry. There are families and communities who walk together every day, and it brings them a lot of peace and joy.

To practice, walk slowly, in a relaxed way, with your head upright and a light smile on your lips. Simply keep in touch with both your breathing and your steps. When you practice indoors, take one step as you breathe in and another as you breathe out. Outdoors, you can walk more quickly, allowing your lungs as much time and air as they need, and simply noticing how many steps you take as your lungs fill up and how many as they empty. The link is the counting, using a word, a phrase, or a gatha. If you see something along the way that you want to touch with your mindfulness — the blue sky, the hills, a tree, or a bird — just stop, but while doing so, continue to breathe mindfully.*

INVITING THE BELL

It can be very helpful to have a beautiful bell to support us in the practice. With the sound of the bell, we can relax and return to the present moment.

For our daily practice and during ceremonies, a bell master (yourself, if you are alone) is often called upon to invite the bell to sound. Before doing so, he or she may wish to recite this gatha, either silently or aloud, according to the circumstances:

> Body, speech, and mind held in perfect oneness,
> I send my heart along with the sound of the bell.
> May the hearers awaken from forgetfulness
> and transcend all anxiety and sorrow.

---

* See Thich Nhat Hanh, *The Long Road Turns to Joy: A Guide to Walking Meditation* (Berkeley, CA: Parallax Press, 1996).

To invite the bell, the bell master first wakes it up by lightly but firmly placing the wooden stick on the rim of the bell and holding it there so that everyone hears a short sound. This prepares the bell and everyone present for the full sound of the bell that will follow a second or two later. The bell can then be sounded.

As soon as you hear the bell, follow your breathing. If you like, repeat this verse silently:

> Listen, listen.
> This wonderful sound
> brings me back
> to my true home.

Before inviting the bell again, allow enough time for three in- and out-breaths. At the end of a period of sitting meditation, the bell master wakes up the bell lightly, then wakes it up again a little more loudly, and then invites one full sound of the bell.*

Reciting Gathas

Gathas are short poems or verses we can recite to help us dwell in mindfulness during whatever activity we are undertaking. While reciting gathas, we become deeply aware of the action we are engaged in, and this helps us to perform that action with understanding and love. The gathas presented in the first section of this book are easy to remember and to practice during our daily activities. They can be memorized and repeated, written out and placed in key locations in your life where you will see them daily, or kept with you in a pocket or a bag for any time you need a little reminder to return to yourself.†

Touching the Earth

The practice of "Touching the Earth," also known as bowing deeply or prostrating, helps us return to the Earth and to our roots, and to recognize that we are not alone but connected to a whole stream of spiritual and blood an-

---

* An audiotape, *Plum Village Meditations* (Louisville, CO: Sounds True, 1997), presents the way the bell is invited at Plum Village. It is available from Parallax Press.
† See also Thich Nhat Hanh, *Present Moment Wonderful Moment: Mindfulness Verses for Daily Living*, Revised Edition (Berkeley, CA: Parallax Press, 2006).

cestors. We touch the Earth to let go of the idea that we are separate and to remind ourselves that we are the Earth and part of Life.

To begin this practice, join your palms in front of your chest in the shape of a lotus bud. Then gently lower yourself to the ground so that all four limbs and your forehead are resting comfortably on the floor. While touching the Earth, turn your palms face up, showing your openness to the Three Jewels — the Buddha, Dharma, and Sangha. Breathe in all the strength and stability of the Earth, and breathe out to release your clinging to any suffering. This is a wonderful practice.

DEEP RELAXATION

The following is an example of how to guide yourself or others in Deep Relaxation. Allowing your body to rest is very important. When your body is at ease and relaxed, your mind will be at peace as well. The practice of Deep Relaxation is essential for your body and mind to heal. Please take the time to practice it often. Although the following guided relaxation may take you thirty minutes, feel free to modify it to fit your situation. Use the time you have. Just five to ten minutes when you wake up in the morning, before going to bed in the evening, or during a short break in the middle of a busy day will relax your body and mind. You can also make it longer and more in-depth. The most important thing is to enjoy it.

Lie down comfortably with your back on the floor or a bed. Close your eyes. Allow your arms to rest gently on either side of your body and let your legs relax, turning outwards.

As you breathe in and out, become aware of your whole body lying down. Feel all the areas of your body that are touching the floor or bed you are lying on: your heels, the backs of your legs, your buttocks, your back, the backs of your hands and arms, the back of your head. With each out-breath, feel yourself sinking deeper and deeper into the floor, letting go of tension, letting go of worries, not holding on to anything.

As you breathe in, feel your abdomen rising; as your breathe out, feel your abdomen falling. For several breaths, just notice the rise and fall of your abdomen.

Now, as you breathe in, become aware of your two feet. As you breathe out, allow your two feet to relax. Breathing in, send your love to your feet; breathing out, smile to your feet. As you breathe in and out, know how wonderful it is to have two feet that allow you to walk, run, play sports, dance, drive, and do so many other activities throughout the day. Send your gratitude to your two feet for always being there for you wherever you need them.

Breathing in, become aware of your right and left legs. Breathing out, allow all the cells in your legs to relax. Breathing in, smile to your legs; breathing out, send them your love. Appreciate whatever degree of strength and health is there in your legs. As you breathe in and out, send them your tenderness and care. Allow them to rest, sinking gently into the floor. Release any tension you may be holding in your legs.

Breathing in, become aware of your two hands lying on the floor. Breathing out, completely relax all the muscles in your two hands, releasing any tension you may be holding in them. As you breathe in, appreciate how wonderful it is to have two hands. As you breathe out, send a smile of love to your two hands. Breathe in and out and be in touch with all the things your two hands allow you to do: cook, write, drive, hold someone's hand, hold a baby, wash your own body, draw, play a musical instrument, type, build and fix things, pet an animal, hold a cup of tea. So many things are available to you because of your two hands. Just enjoy the fact that you have two hands, and allow all the cells in your hands to really rest.

Breathing in, become aware of your two arms. Breathing out, let your arms fully relax. As you breathe in, send your love to your arms; as you breathe out, smile to them. Take the time to appreciate your arms and whatever strength and health are there in them. Send them your gratitude for allowing you to hug someone, to swing on a swing, to help and serve others, to work — cleaning the house, mowing the lawn, doing so many things throughout the day. Breathing in and out, allow your two arms to let go and rest completely on the floor. Feel the tension leaving your arms. As you embrace them with your mindfulness, feel joy and ease in every part of your two arms.

Breathing in, become aware of your shoulders. Breathing out, allow any tension in your shoulders to flow out into the floor. As you breathe in, send your love to your shoulders; as you breathe out, smile with gratitude to them. Breathing in and out, be aware that you may have allowed a lot of tension and stress to accumulate in your shoulders. With each exhalation, allow the tension to leave your shoulders, and feel them relaxing more and more deeply. Send them your tenderness and care, knowing that you do not want to put too much strain on them, you want to live in a way that will allow them to be relaxed and at ease.

Breathing in, become aware of your heart. Breathing out, allow your heart to rest. With your in-breath, send your love to your heart. With your out-breath, smile to your heart. As you breathe in and out, get in touch with how wonderful it is to have a heart still beating in your chest. Your heart allows your life to be possible, and it is always there for you, every minute of every day. It never takes a break. Your heart has been beating since you were a four-week-old fetus in your mother's womb. It is a marvelous organ that allows you to do everything you do throughout the day. Breathe in and know that your heart also loves you. Breathe out and commit to live in a way that will help your heart to function well. With each exhalation, feel your heart relaxing more and more. Allow each cell in your heart to smile with ease and joy.

Breathing in, become aware of your stomach and intestines. Breathing out, allow your stomach and intestines to relax. As you breathe in, send them your love and gratitude. As you breathe out, smile tenderly to them. Breathing in and out, know how essential these organs are to your health. Give them the chance to rest deeply. Each day they digest and assimilate the food you eat, giving you energy and strength. They need you to take the time to recognize and appreciate them. As you breathe in, feel your stomach and intestines relaxing and releasing all tension. As you breathe out, enjoy the fact that you have a stomach and intestines.

Breathing in, become aware of your eyes. Breathing out, allow your eyes and the muscles around your eyes to relax. Breathing in, smile to your eyes; breathing out, send them your love. Allow your eyes to rest and sink back into your head. As you breathe in and out, know how precious your two eyes are. They allow you to look into the eyes of someone you love, to see a beautiful sunset, to read and write, to move around with ease, to see a bird flying in the sky, to watch a movie — so many things are possible because of your two eyes. Take the time to appreciate the miraculous gift of sight, and allow your eyes to rest deeply. You can gently raise your eyebrows to help release any tension you may be holding around your eyes.

Here you can continue to relax other areas of your body, using the same pattern as above.

Now, if there is a place in your body that is sick or in pain, take this time to become aware of it and send it your love. Breathing in, allow this area to rest; breathing out, smile to it with great tenderness and affection. Be aware that there are other parts of your body that are still strong and healthy. Allow these strong parts of your body to send their strength and energy to the weak or sick area. Feel the support, energy, and love of the rest of your body penetrating the weak area, soothing and healing it. Breathe in and affirm your own capacity to heal; breathe out and let go of the worry or fear you may be holding in your body. Breathing in and out, smile with love and confidence to the area of your body that is not well.

Finally, breathing in, become aware of the whole of your body lying down. Breathing out, enjoy the sensation of your whole body lying down, very relaxed and calm. Smile to your whole body as you breathe in, and send your love and compassion to your whole body as you breathe out. Feel all the cells in your whole body smiling joyfully with you. Feel gratitude for all the cells in your whole body. Return to the gentle rise and fall of your abdomen.

If you are guiding other people, and if you are comfortable doing so, you can now sing a few relaxing songs or lullabies.

To end, slowly stretch and open your eyes. Take your time to get up, mindfully and lightly. Practice to carry the calmness and attentiveness you have generated here into your next activity, and throughout the day.

HUGGING MEDITATION

When we hug, our hearts connect and we know that we are not separate beings. Hugging with mindfulness and concentration can bring reconciliation, healing, understanding, and much happiness.

You can practice hugging meditation with a friend, a child, your parents, your partner, or even a tree. To practice, first bow to each other and recognize each other's presence. Then, enjoy three deep conscious breaths to bring yourself fully into the present moment. Next, open your arms and begin hugging, holding each other for three in- and out-breaths. With the first breath, become aware that you are present in this very moment and feel happy. With the second breath, become aware that the other person is present in this moment and feel happy as well. With the third breath, become aware that you are here together, right now on this Earth. We can feel deep gratitude and happiness for our togetherness. Finally, release the other person and bow to each other to show your thanks.

Daily Practice

Daily Practice Session

YOU MIGHT LIKE to practice each day following the Daily Practice Session presented here. It includes the many elements that we often use at Plum Village. A daily practice session commonly begins with a period of sitting meditation, followed by slow walking meditation (kinh hanh), and then a session of chanting and recitation. The first sitting period can be a guided meditation. During a shorter practice session, you may wish to practice sitting for only twelve minutes. Or if you do not wish to practice chanting and recitation, simply replace the chanting and recitation with a second period of sitting meditation. For instructions on these practices, see pages 15–22.

It is not necessary to chant and recite everything on this schedule. Reciting The Heart of Perfect Understanding (*Prajñaparamita*) and reading one of the basic discourses is enough to inspire and guide your practice. You may also replace the sections given here with others of your choice. What is most important is to create a daily practice that you will enjoy as part of your own daily life and that of your practice community.

1. VERSES FOR SITTING MEDITATION
[CHANTED BY BELL MASTER AS BELL IS INVITED TO SOUND]

Morning Chant ♪
The Dharma body is bringing morning light.
In concentration, our hearts are at peace,
a half-smile is born upon our lips.
This is a new day. We vow to go through it in mindfulness.
The sun of wisdom has now risen, shining in every direction.
Noble Sangha, diligently bring your mind into meditation.
Namo Shakyamunaye Buddhaya
Namo Shakyamunaye Buddhaya
Namo Shakyamunaye Buddhaya

Evening Chant Version One ♪
Stably seated under the Bodhi tree.
Body, speech, and mind are one in stillness, free from views
of right and wrong.
When we are focused in perfect mindfulness, the path is illumined.
The shore of confusion is left behind.
Noble Sangha, diligently bring your mind into meditation.
Namo Shakyamunaye Buddhaya
Namo Shakyamunaye Buddhaya
Namo Shakyamunaye Buddhaya

Evening Chant Version Two ♪
With posture upright and stable, we are seated at the foot of the Bodhi tree.
Body, speech, and mind are one in stillness; there is no more thought
of right and wrong.
Our mind and body dwell in perfect mindfulness.
We rediscover our original nature, leaving the shore of illusion behind.
Noble Sangha, diligently bring your mind into meditation.
Namo Shakyamunaye Buddhaya
Namo Shakyamunaye Buddhaya
Namo Shakyamunaye Buddhaya

2. INCENSE OFFERING *Version One* ♪

[BELL, BELL, BELL]

In gratitude, we offer this incense
throughout space and time
to all Buddhas and Bodhisattvas.
May it be fragrant as Earth herself,
reflecting careful efforts,
wholehearted awareness,
and the fruit of understanding,
slowly ripening.
May we and all beings
be companions of Buddhas and Bodhisattvas.
May we awaken from forgetfulness
and realize our true home.
[BELL]

Incense Offering Version Two ♪
[BELL, BELL, BELL]
The fragrance of this incense
invites the awakened mind
to be truly present with us now.
The fragrance of this incense
fills our practice center,
protects and guards our mind
from all wrong thinking.
The fragrance of this incense
collects us and unites us.
Precepts, concentration, and insight
we offer for all that is.
Namo Bodhisattvebhyah
Namo Mahasattvebhyah
[BELL]

3. TOUCHING THE EARTH ♪

Opening Gatha
The one who bows and the one who is bowed to
are both, by nature, empty.
Therefore the communication between them
is inexpressibly perfect.
Our practice center is the Net of Indra
reflecting all Buddhas everywhere.
And with my person in front of each Buddha,
I go with my whole life for refuge.
[BELL]

Prostrations
[TOUCH THE EARTH AT EACH SOUND OF THE BELL]

Offering light in the Ten Directions,
the Buddha, the Dharma, and the Sangha,
to whom we bow in gratitude.
[BELL]

Teaching and living the way of awareness
in the very midst of suffering and confusion,
Shakyamuni Buddha, the Fully Enlightened One,
to whom we bow in gratitude.
[BELL]

Cutting through ignorance, awakening our hearts and our minds,
Manjushri, the Bodhisattva of Great Understanding,
to whom we bow in gratitude.
[BELL]

Working mindfully, working joyfully for the sake of all beings,
Samantabhadra, the Bodhisattva of Great Action,
to whom we bow in gratitude.
[BELL]

Listening deeply, serving beings in countless ways,
Avalokiteshvara, the Bodhisattva of Great Compassion,
to whom we bow in gratitude.
[BELL]

Fearless and persevering through realms of suffering and darkness,
Kshitigarbha, the Bodhisattva of Great Aspiration,
to whom we bow in gratitude.
[BELL]

Seed of awakening and loving kindness
in children and all beings,
Maitreya, the Buddha to-be-born,
to whom we bow in gratitude.
[BELL]

Showing the way fearlessly and compassionately,
the stream of all our Ancestral Teachers,
to whom we bow in gratitude.
[BELL, BELL]

4. OPENING VERSE ♪
[BELL, BELL, BELL]

Namo Tassa Bhagavato Arahato Samma Sambuddhassa
Namo Tassa Bhagavato Arahato Samma Sambuddhassa
Namo Tassa Bhagavato Arahato Samma Sambuddhassa
[BELL]

The Dharma is deep and lovely.
We now have a chance to see, study, and practice it.
We vow to realize its true meaning.
[BELL]

5. THE HEART OF PERFECT UNDERSTANDING ♪

The Bodhisattva Avalokita,
while moving in the deep course of Perfect Understanding,
shed light on the Five Skandhas and found them equally empty.
After this penetration, he overcame ill-being.
[BELL]

Listen, Shariputra,
form is emptiness, and emptiness is form.
Form is not other than emptiness, emptiness is not other than form.
The same is true with feelings, perceptions, mental formations,
and consciousness.
[BELL]

Listen, Shariputra,
all dharmas are marked with emptiness.
They are neither produced nor destroyed,
neither defiled nor immaculate,
neither increasing nor decreasing.
Therefore in emptiness there is neither form, nor feelings, nor perceptions,
nor mental formations, nor consciousness.
No eye, or ear, or nose, or tongue, or body, or mind.
No form, no sound, no smell, no taste, no touch, no object of mind.
No realms of elements (from eyes to mind consciousness),

no interdependent origins and no extinction of them
(from ignorance to death and decay).
No ill-being, no cause of ill-being, no end of ill-being, and no path.
No understanding and no attainment.
[BELL]

Because there is no attainment,
the Bodhisattvas, grounded in Perfect Understanding,
find no obstacles for their minds.
Having no obstacles, they overcome fear,
liberating themselves forever from illusion, realizing perfect nirvana.
All Buddhas in the past, present, and future,
thanks to this Perfect Understanding,
arrive at full, right, and universal enlightenment.
[BELL]

Therefore one should know
that Perfect Understanding is the highest mantra, the unequaled mantra,
the destroyer of ill-being, the incorruptible truth.
A mantra of Prajñaparamita should therefore be proclaimed:

Gate gate paragate parasamgate bodhi svaha
Gate gate paragate parasamgate bodhi svaha
Gate gate paragate parasamgate bodhi svaha
[BELL, BELL]

6. SUTRA RECITATION
[AT THIS POINT IN THE CEREMONY, RECITE A SUTRA FROM PAGES 269–348.]

7. INVOKING THE BODHISATTVAS' NAMES ♪

We invoke your name, Avalokiteshvara. We aspire to learn your way of listening in order to help relieve the suffering in the world. You know how to listen in order to understand. We invoke your name in order to practice listening with all our attention and openheartedness. We will sit and listen without any prejudice. We will sit and listen without judging or reacting. We will sit and listen in order to understand. We will sit and listen so attentively that we will be able to hear what the other person is saying and also

what is being left unsaid. We know that just by listening deeply we already alleviate a great deal of pain and suffering in the other person.
[BELL]

We invoke your name, Manjushri. We aspire to learn your way, which is to be still and to look deeply into the heart of things and into the hearts of people. We will look with all our attention and openheartedness. We will look with unprejudiced eyes. We will look without judging or reacting. We will look deeply so that we will be able to see and understand the roots of suffering, the impermanent and selfless nature of all that is. We will practice your way of using the sword of understanding to cut through the bonds of suffering, thus freeing ourselves and other species.
[BELL]

We invoke your name, Samantabhadra. We aspire to practice your vow to act with the eyes and heart of compassion, to bring joy to one person in the morning and to ease the pain of one person in the afternoon. We know that the happiness of others is our own happiness, and we aspire to practice joy on the path of service. We know that every word, every look, every action, and every smile can bring happiness to others. We know that if we practice wholeheartedly, we ourselves may become an inexhaustible source of peace and joy for our loved ones and for all species.
[BELL]

We invoke your name, Kshitigarbha. We aspire to learn your way of being present where there is darkness, suffering, oppression, and despair, so we can bring light, hope, relief, and liberation to those places. We are determined not to forget about or abandon those in desperate situations. We will do our best to establish contact with those who cannot find a way out of their suffering, those whose cries for help, justice, equality, and human rights are not being heard. We know that hell can be found in many places on Earth. We will do our best not to contribute to creating more hells on Earth, and to help transform the hells that already exist. We will practice in order to realize the qualities of perseverance and stability, so that, like the Earth, we can always be supportive and faithful to those in need.
[BELL]

We invoke your name, Sadaparibhuta. We aspire to learn your way of never disparaging or underestimating any living being. With great respect, you

say to all you meet, "You are someone of great value, you have Buddha nature, I see this potential in you." We will look with a wise, compassionate gaze, so we are able to hold up a mirror where others can see their ultimate nature reflected. We will remind people who feel worthless that they too are a precious wonder of life. We vow to water only the positive seeds in ourselves and in others, so that our thoughts, words, and actions can encourage confidence and self-acceptance in ourselves, our children, our loved ones, and in everyone we meet. Inspired by the great faith and insight that everyone is Buddha, we will practice your way of patience and inclusiveness so we can liberate ourselves from ignorance and misunderstanding, and offer freedom, peace, and joy to ourselves, to others and to our society.
[BELL, BELL]

8. The Three Refuges ♪

I take refuge in the Buddha,
the one who shows me the way in this life.
I take refuge in the Dharma,
the way of understanding and of love.
I take refuge in the Sangha,
the community that lives in harmony and awareness.
[BELL]

Dwelling in the refuge of Buddha,
I clearly see the path of light and beauty in the world.
Dwelling in the refuge of Dharma,
I learn to open many doors on the path of transformation.
Dwelling in the refuge of Sangha,
shining light that supports me, keeping my practice free of obstruction.
[BELL]

Taking refuge in the Buddha in myself,
I aspire to help all people recognize their own awakened nature,
realizing the Mind of Love.
Taking refuge in the Dharma in myself,
I aspire to help all people fully master the ways of practice
and walk together on the path of liberation.
Taking refuge in the Sangha in myself,
I aspire to help all people build Fourfold Communities,

to embrace all beings and support their transformation.
[BELL, BELL]

9. SHARING THE MERIT ♪

Reciting the sutras, practicing the way of awareness
gives rise to benefits without limit.
We vow to share the fruits with all beings.
We vow to offer tribute to parents, teachers, friends, and numerous beings
who give guidance and support along the path.
[BELL, BELL, BELL]

Silent Meal Practice

FROM TIME TO TIME, you might enjoy having a silent meal at home with your family or friends. Eating in silence allows us to see the preciousness of the food and our friends, and also our close relationship with the Earth and all species. Every vegetable, every drop of water, every piece of bread contains in it the life of our whole planet and the sun. With each bite of food, we can taste the meaning and value of our life. We can meditate on the plants and animals, on the work of the farmer, and on the many thousands of children who die each day for lack of food. Sitting silently at the table with others, we also have the opportunity to see them clearly and deeply, and to smile to communicate real love and friendship.

The first time you eat in silence, it may seem awkward, but after you get used to it, silent meals can bring a lot of peace, joy, and insight. These gathas, recited sielntly to yourself, help you look deeply into all that is.

1. LOOKING AT YOUR EMPTY PLATE OR BOWL

My plate (bowl), empty now,
will soon be filled with precious food.
I see how fortunate I am
to have enough to eat
to continue the practice.

2. SERVING FOOD

In this food
I see clearly
the entire universe
supporting my existence.

3. SITTING DOWN
Sitting here
is like sitting under a Bodhi tree.

My body is mindfulness itself,
free from all distraction.

4. Looking at the Plate of Food before Eating

Beings all over the Earth
are struggling to live.
I aspire to practice deeply
so that all may have enough to eat.

5. Contemplating the Food

This plate of food,
so fragrant and appetizing,
also contains much suffering.

6. Introducing the Five Contemplations

The Buddha advises us to eat in mindfulness,
establishing ourselves in the present moment
so that we can be aware of the food in front of us and
the community surrounding us.
We eat in a way that makes peace, joy, brotherhood,
and sisterhood possible
during the whole time of eating.
Brothers and sisters, when you hear the bell,
please meditate on the Five Contemplations.

7. The Five Contemplations

[READ ALOUD BY ONE PERSON BEFORE BEGINNING TO EAT]

This food is a gift of the earth, the sky, numerous living beings, and
much hard and loving work.
May we eat with mindfulness and gratitude so as to be worthy to
receive this food.
May we recognize and transform unwholesome mental formations,
especially our greed.
May we take only foods that nourish us and keep us healthy.

We accept this food so that we may nurture our sisterhood and brother-hood, build our Sangha, and nourish our ideal of serving living beings.

8. BEGINNING TO EAT
[RECITED SILENTLY WHILE CHEWING THE FIRST FOUR MOUTHFULS]

With the first mouthful, I practice the love that brings joy.
With the second mouthful, I practice the love that relieves suffering.
With the third mouthful, I practice the joy of being alive.
With the fourth mouthful, I practice equal love for all beings.

9. WHEN THE PLATE OR BOWL IS EMPTY

My plate (bowl) is empty.
My hunger is satisfied.
I am determined to live for the benefit of all beings.

10. DRINKING TEA ♪

This cup of tea in my two hands,
mindfulness held perfectly.
My mind and body dwell
in the very here and now.

11. WASHING THE DISHES

Washing the dishes is like bathing a baby Buddha.
The profane is the sacred.
Everyday mind is Buddha's mind.

Gathas

GATHAS, also called mindfulness verses, help us to dwell in the present moment and to be deeply aware of the action we are doing so that we can perform it with understanding and love. The gathas here can be used as part of your daily practice. They are easy to remember and to use.*

ENTERING THE MEDITATION HALL ♪

Entering the meditation hall,
I see my true self.
As I sit down,
I vow to cut off all disturbances.

INVITING THE BELL *Version One* ♪

Body, speech, and mind held in perfect oneness,
I send my heart along with the sound of the bell.
May the hearers awaken from forgetfulness
and transcend all anxiety and sorrow.

INVITING THE BELL *Version Two*

May the sound of this bell penetrate deeply into the cosmos.
In even the darkest places, may living beings hear it clearly
so their suffering will cease,
understanding arises in their hearts,
and they can transcend the path of anxiety and sorrow.
Namo Shakyamunaye Buddhaya

---

* These and many other gathas for daily living are included in Thich Nhat Hanh, *Present Moment Wonderful Moment* Revised Edition (Berkeley, CA: Parallax Press, 2006); as well as in Thich Nhat Hanh, *Stepping Into Freedom* (Berkeley, CA: Parallax Press, 1997).

INVITING THE BELL *Version Three*

May the sound of this bell
penetrate deeply into the cosmos,
so that beings even in those dark places
may hear it and be free from birth and death.
May all beings realize awakening
And find their way home.
Namo Shakyamunaye Buddhaya

LISTENING TO THE BELL *Version One*

Listening to the bell,
I feel my afflictions begin to dissolve.
My mind is calm, my body relaxed.
A smile is born on my lips.
Following the bell's sound,
my breathing guides me back
to the safe island of mindfulness.
In the garden of my heart,
the flower of peace blooms beautifully.
Namo Shakyamunaye Buddhaya

LISTENING TO THE BELL *Version Two*

Listen, listen,
this wonderful sound
brings me back to my true home.

LISTENING TO THE BELL *Version Three* ♪

Hearing the bell, I let go of all my afflictions.
My heart is calm, my sorrows ended.
I am no longer bound to anything.
I learn to listen to my suffering
and the suffering of the other person.
When understanding is born in me,
compassion is also born.

LIGHTING A CANDLE ♪

Lighting this candle,
offering the light to countless Buddhas,
the peace and joy I feel,
brighten the face of the Earth.

PRAISING BUDDHA

As refreshing as a lotus flower,
as bright as the North Star,
to the Buddha, I go for refuge.

SITTING DOWN

Sitting here
is like sitting under a Bodhi tree.
My body is mindfulness itself,
free from all distraction.

FINDING A STABLE SITTING POSTURE

In the lotus position,
the human flower blooms.
The udumbara flower is here
offering its true fragrance.

CALMING THE BREATH

Breathing in, I calm my body.
Breathing out, I smile.
Dwelling in the present moment,
I know this is a wonderful moment.

BREATHING *Version One*

Going back to the island of self,
I see Buddha is my mindfulness
shining near, shining far.

Dharma is my breathing
guarding body and mind.
Sangha is my Five Skandhas
working in harmony.

Breathing in, breathing out.
Flower, fresh.
Mountain, solid.
Water, reflecting.
Space, free.

BREATHING *Version Two*

Breathing in, I know I'm breathing in.
Breathing out, I know I'm breathing out.
As my in-breath grows deep,
my out-breath grows slow.
Breathing in, I feel calm,
breathing out, I feel at ease.
Breathing in, I smile,
breathing out, I release.
Dwelling in the present moment,
I know this is a wonderful moment.

BREATHING *Version Three*

I have arrived, I am home
in the here, in the now.
I am solid, I am free,
in the ultimate, I dwell.

Arrived, arrived,
at home, at home,
dwelling in the here,
dwelling in the now.

Solid as a mountain,
free as the white clouds.

The door to no-birth, no-death has opened,
free and unshakable I dwell.

BREATHING *Version Four*

In, Out.
Deep, Slow.
Calm, Ease.
Smile, Release.
Present moment, Wonderful moment.

ADJUSTING MEDITATION POSTURE

Feelings come and go
like clouds in a windy sky.
Conscious breathing
is my anchor.

CLEANING THE MEDITATION HALL

As I clean this fresh, calm room,
boundless joy and energy arise.

SWEEPING ♪

As I carefully sweep
the ground of enlightenment,
a tree of understanding
springs up from the Earth.

GREETING SOMEONE
[WITH PALMS JOINED]

A lotus for you,
a Buddha-to-be.

Exercises and Recitations

Y OU CAN USE these practices and recitations at any time as part of your daily practice or for special occasions. Many can be done on their own; others you might like to substitute for those offered earlier in the Daily Practice Session [see pages 25–33]. Some can be included as part of group practice or even as guided meditations.

LOVE MEDITATION*

[WE BEGIN PRACTICING THIS LOVE MEDITATION FOCUSING ON OURSELVES ("I"). UNTIL WE ARE ABLE TO LOVE AND TAKE CARE OF OURSELVES, WE CANNOT BE OF MUCH HELP TO OTHERS. NEXT, WE CAN PRACTICE TOWARDS OTHERS (SUBSTITUTING "HE," "SHE" OR "THEY"), FIRST WITH SOMEONE WE LOVE, NEXT WITH SOMEONE WE LIKE, THEN WITH SOMEONE NEUTRAL TO US, AND FINALLY TOWARD SOMEONE WHO HAS MADE US SUFFER.]

May I be peaceful, happy, and light in body and spirit.
May I be safe and free from injury.
May I be free from anger, fear, and anxiety.

May I learn to look at myself with the eyes of understanding and love.
May I be able to recognize and touch the seeds of joy and happiness
in myself.
May I learn to identify and see the sources of anger, craving, and
delusion in myself.

May I know how to nourish the seeds of joy in myself every day.
May I be able to live fresh, solid, and free.
May I be free from attachment and aversion, but not be indifferent.

* Adapted from the Visuddhi Magga. For other practices to nourish love, see Thich Nhat Hanh, *Teachings on Love* Revised Edition (Berkeley, CA: Parallax Press, 2007).

Fourteen Verses on Meditation

1. Just as a bird has two wings,
the practice of meditation has "stopping" and "deep looking."
The two wings depend on each other.
Stopping and deep looking go in tandem.

2. Stopping means to be still,
in order to recognize, to be in contact,
to nourish, to heal,
to calm, to soothe, and to focus the mind.

3. Deep looking means to regard in depth
the true nature of the Five Skandhas,
so that understanding may arise
to transform all sadness and pain.

4. The breath and the footstep
generate the source of mindfulness,
which enables one to recognize,
to be in touch with the wonders of life.

5. To calm, to relax the body and mind,
to nourish, to heal,
to protect the six senses,
and to maintain right concentration.

6. Looking deeply into reality
to see the true nature of all dharmas,
meditation helps us to let go
of all seeking, wishing, and fears.

7. To dwell in the present moment,
to transform all habit energies,
to give rise to understanding,
liberating ourselves from all afflictions.

8. Impermanence is nonself.
Nonself is interdependence,

is emptiness, is conventional designation,
is the Middle Way, is interbeing.

9. Emptiness, signlessness, and aimlessness
unravel all sadness and pain.
In the daily practice
one is not caught in conceptual knowledge.

10. Nirvana means non-attainment.
Immediate and gradual enlightenment are not separate.
Realizing this, one lives with freedom
right in this present life.

11. The basic meditation sutras
such as the mindfulness of breathing
and the Four Establishments of Mindfulness,
show us step by step
how to transform the body and the mind.

12. The Mahayana sutras and shastras
open more grand doors
to help us see the depth
of the original meditation current.

13. There should be no discrimination
between the Buddha and the patriarch school of meditation.
The Four Noble Truths must be based on one another
to make the foundation of transmission and reception.

14. With the support of the Sangha,
one can practice successfully, with ease,
and accomplish quickly
the great aspiration to help all beings.

The Five Earth-Touchings

I

In gratitude, I bow to all generations of ancestors in my blood family.
[BELL]
[ALL TOUCH THE EARTH]

I see my mother and father, whose blood, flesh, and vitality are circulating in my own veins and nourishing every cell in me. Through them, I see my four grandparents. Their expectations, experiences, and wisdom have been transmitted from so many generations of ancestors. I carry in me the life, blood, experience, wisdom, happiness, and sorrow of all generations. The suffering and all the elements that need to be transformed, I am practicing to transform. I open my heart, flesh, and bones to receive the energy of insight, love, and experience transmitted to me by all my ancestors. I see my roots in my father, mother, grandfathers, grandmothers, and all my ancestors. I know I am only the continuation of this ancestral lineage. Please support, protect, and transmit to me your energy. I know wherever children and grandchildren are, ancestors are there, also. I know that parents always love and support their children and grandchildren, although they are not always able to express it skillfully because of difficulties they themselves encountered. I see that my ancestors tried to build a way of life based on gratitude, joy, confidence, respect, and loving kindness. As a continuation of my ancestors, I bow deeply and allow their energy to flow through me. I ask my ancestors for their support, protection, and strength.
[THREE BREATHS]
[BELL]
[ALL STAND UP]

II

In gratitude, I bow to all generations of ancestors in my spiritual family.
[BELL]
[ALL TOUCH THE EARTH]

I see in myself my teachers, the ones who show me the way of love and understanding, the way to breathe, smile, forgive, and live deeply in the present moment. I see through my teachers all teachers over many generations and traditions, going back to the ones who began my spiritual family thousands of years ago. I see the Buddha or Christ or the patriarchs and matriarchs as my teachers, and also as my spiritual ancestors. I see that their energy and that of many generations of teachers has entered me and is creating peace, joy, understanding, and loving kindness in me. I know that the energy of these teachers has deeply transformed the world. Without the Buddha and all these spiritual ancestors, I would not know the way to practice to bring peace and happiness into my life and into the lives of my family and society. I open my heart and my body to receive the energy of understanding, loving kindness, and protection from the Awakened Ones, their teachings, and the community of practice over many generations. I am their continuation. I ask these spiritual ancestors to transmit to me their infinite source of energy, peace, stability, understanding, and love. I vow to practice to transform the suffering in myself and the world, and to transmit their energy to future generations of practitioners. My spiritual ancestors may have had their own difficulties and not always been able to transmit the teachings, but I accept them as they are.

[THREE BREATHS]

[BELL]

[ALL STAND UP]

III

In gratitude, I bow to this land and all of the ancestors who made it available.

[BELL]

[ALL TOUCH THE EARTH]

I see that I am whole, protected, and nourished by this land and all of the living beings who have been here and made life easy and possible for me through all their efforts. I see Chief Seattle, Thomas Jefferson, Dorothy Day, Cesar Chavez, Martin Luther King, Jr., and all the others known and unknown.* I see all those who have made this country a refuge for people of so many origins and colors, by their talent, perseverance, and love — those who have worked hard to build schools, hospitals, bridges, and roads, to protect human rights, to develop science and technology, and to fight for freedom and social justice. I see myself touching my ancestors of Native American origin who have lived on this land for such a long time and known the ways to live in peace and harmony with nature, protecting the mountains, forests, animals, vegetation, and minerals of this land. I feel the energy of this land penetrating my body and soul, supporting and accepting

* Substitute the names of ancestors appropriate for the country in which you are practicing.

me. I vow to cultivate and maintain this energy and transmit it to future generations. I vow to contribute my part in transforming the violence, hatred, and delusion that still lie deep in the collective consciousness of this society so that future generations will have more safety, joy, and peace. I ask this land for its protection and support.

[THREE BREATHS]

[BELL]

[ALL STAND UP]

IV

In gratitude and compassion, I bow down and transmit my energy to those I love.

[BELL]

[ALL TOUCH THE EARTH]

All the energy I have received I now want to transmit to my father, my mother, everyone I love, all who have suffered and worried because of me and for my sake. I know I have not been mindful enough in my daily life. I also know that those who love me have had their own difficulties. They have suffered because they were not lucky enough to have an environment that encouraged their full development. I transmit my energy to my mother, my father, my brothers, my sisters, my beloved ones, my husband, my wife, my daughter, and my son, so that their pain will be relieved, so they can smile and feel the joy of being alive. I want all of them to be healthy and joyful. I know that when they are happy, I will also be happy. I no longer feel resentment towards any of them. I pray that all ancestors in my blood and spiritual families will focus their energies toward each of them, to protect and support them. I know that I am not separate from them. I am one with those I love.

[THREE BREATHS]

[BELL]

[ALL STAND UP]

V

In understanding and compassion, I bow down to reconcile myself with all those who have made me suffer.

[BELL]

[ALL TOUCH THE EARTH]

I open my heart and send forth my energy of love and understanding to everyone who has made me suffer, to those who have destroyed much of my life and the lives of those I love. I know now that these people have themselves undergone a lot of suffering and that their hearts are overloaded with pain, anger, and hatred. I know that anyone who suffers that much will make those around him or her suffer. I know they may have been unlucky, never having the chance to be cared for and loved. Life and society have dealt them so many hardships. They have been wronged and abused. They have not been guided in the path of mindful living. They have accumulated wrong perceptions about life, about me, and about us. They have wronged us and the people we love. I pray to my ancestors in my blood and spiritual families to channel to these persons who have made us suffer the energy of love and protection, so that their hearts will be able to receive the nectar of love and blossom like a flower. I pray that they can be transformed to experience the joy of living, so that they will not continue to make themselves and others suffer. I see their suffering and do not want to hold any feelings of hatred or anger in myself toward them. I do not want them to suffer. I channel my energy of love and understanding to them and ask all my ancestors to help them.

[THREE BREATHS]

[BELL]

[ALL STAND UP]

THE THREE EARTH-TOUCHINGS

I

Touching the Earth, I connect with ancestors and descendants of both my spiritual and my blood families.

[BELL]

[ALL TOUCH THE EARTH]

My spiritual ancestors include the Buddha, the Bodhisattvas, the noble Sangha of Buddha's disciples, [INSERT NAMES OF OTHERS YOU WOULD LIKE TO INCLUDE], and my own spiritual teachers still alive or already passed away. They are present in me because they have transmitted to me seeds of peace, wisdom, love, and happiness. They have woken up in me my resource of understanding and compassion. When I look at my spiritual ancestors, I see those who are perfect in the practice of the mindfulness trainings, understanding, and compassion, and those who are still imperfect. I accept them all because I see within myself shortcomings and weaknesses. Aware that my practice of the mindfulness trainings is not always perfect, and that I am not always as understanding and compassionate as I would like to be, I open my heart and accept all my spiritual descendants. Some of my descendants practice the mindfulness trainings, understanding, and compassion in a way which invites confidence and respect, but there are also those who come across many difficulties and are constantly subject to ups and downs in their practice.

In the same way, I accept all my ancestors on my mother's side and my father's side of the family. I accept all their good qualities and their virtuous actions, and I also accept all their weaknesses. I open my heart and accept all my blood descendants with their good qualities, their talents, and also their weaknesses.

My spiritual ancestors, blood ancestors, spiritual descendants, and blood descendants are all part of me. I am them, and they are me. I do not have a separate self. All exist as part of a wonderful stream of life which is constantly moving.

[THREE BREATHS]

[BELL]

[ALL STAND UP]

II

Touching the Earth, I connect with all people and all species that are alive at this moment in this world with me.

[BELL]

[ALL TOUCH THE EARTH]

I am one with the wonderful pattern of life that radiates out in all directions. I see the close connection between myself and others, how we share happiness and suffering. I am one with those who were born disabled or who have become disabled because of war, accident, or illness. I am one with those who are caught in a situation of war or oppression. I am one with those who find no happiness in family life, who have no roots and no peace of mind, who are hungry for understanding and love, and who are looking for something beautiful, wholesome, and true to embrace and to believe in. I am someone at the point of death who is very afraid and does not know what is going to happen. I am a child who lives in a place where there is miserable poverty and disease, whose legs and arms are like sticks and who has no future. I am also the manufacturer of bombs that are sold to poor countries. I am the frog swimming in the pond and I am also the snake who needs the body of the frog to nourish its own body. I am the caterpillar or the ant that the bird is looking for to eat, and I am also the bird that is looking for the caterpillar or the ant. I am the forest that is being cut down. I am the rivers and the air that are being polluted, and I am also the person who cuts down the forest and pollutes the rivers and the air. I see myself in all species, and I see all species in me.

I am one with the great beings who have realized the truth of no-birth and no-death and are able to look at the forms of birth and death, happiness and suffering, with calm eyes. I am one with those people — who can be found a little bit everywhere — who have sufficient peace of mind, understanding and love, who are able to touch what is wonderful, nourishing, and healing, who also have the capacity to embrace the world with a heart of love and arms of caring action. I am someone who has enough peace, joy, and freedom and is able to offer fearlessness and joy to living beings around themselves. I see that I am not lonely and cut off. The love and the happiness of great beings on this planet help me not to sink in despair. They help me to live my life in a meaningful way, with true peace and happiness. I see them all in me, and I see myself in all of them.

[THREE BREATHS]

[BELL]

[ALL STAND UP]

III

Touching the Earth, I let go of my idea that I am this body and my life span is limited.

[BELL]

[ALL TOUCH THE EARTH]

I see that this body, made up of the four elements, is not really me and I am not limited by this body. I am part of a stream of life of spiritual and blood ancestors that for thousands of years has been flowing into the present and flows on for thousands of years into the future. I am one with my ancestors. I am one with all people and all species, whether they are peaceful and fearless, or suffering and afraid. At this very moment, I am present everywhere on this planet. I am also present in the past and in the future. The disintegration of this body does not touch me, just as when the plum blossom falls it does not mean the end of the plum tree. I see myself as a wave on the surface of the ocean. My nature is the ocean water. I see myself in

all the other waves and I see all the other waves in me. The appearance and disappearance of the form of the wave does not affect the ocean. My Dharma body and spiritual life are not subject to birth and death. I see the presence of myself before my body manifested and after my body has disintegrated. Even in this moment, I see how I exist elsewhere than in this body. Seventy or eighty years is not my life span. My life span, like the life span of a leaf or of a Buddha, is limitless. I have gone beyond the idea that I am a body that is separated in space and time from all other forms of life.
[THREE BREATHS]
[BELL]
[ALL STAND UP]

THE FIVE REMEMBRANCES ♪
[THESE FIVE REMEMBRANCES HELP US TO IDENTIFY AND LOOK
DEEPLY AT THE SEEDS OF FEAR. THEY CAN BE RECITED DAILY, READ
ALOUD AS A GUIDED MEDITATION, OR USED AS A SILENT MEDITATION
BY INDIVIDUAL PRACTITIONERS.]

I am of the nature to grow old.
There is no way to escape growing old.
[BELL]

I am of the nature to have ill-health.
There is no way to escape having ill-health.
[BELL]

I am of the nature to die.
There is no way to escape death.
[BELL]

All that is dear to me and everyone I love are of the nature to change.
There is no way to escape being separated from them.
[BELL]

I inherit the results of my actions of body, speech, and mind.
My actions are my continuation.
[BELL, BELL]

THE FIVE AWARENESSES

[THESE VERSES ARE USED IN THE WEDDING CEREMONY, SEE PAGE 167 .
THEY ARE ALSO TO BE RECITED BY COUPLES ON THE FULL-MOON AND
NEW-MOON DAYS.]

We are aware that all generations of our ancestors
and all future generations are present in us.
[BELL]

We are aware of the expectations that our ancestors, our children,
and their children have of us.
[BELL]

We are aware that our joy, peace, freedom, and harmony
are the joy, peace, freedom, and harmony
of our ancestors, our children, and their children.
[BELL]

We are aware that understanding is the very foundation of love.
[BELL]

We are aware that blaming and arguing can never help us
and only create a wider gap between us;
that only understanding, trust, and love
can help us change and grow.
[BELL, BELL]

REPENTANCE GATHA

All wrongdoing arises from the mind.
When the mind is purified, what trace of wrong is left?
After repentance, my heart is light like the white clouds
that have always floated over the ancient forest in freedom.
[BELL, BELL]

GATHA ON IMPERMANENCE ♪

The day is now ended.
Our lives are shorter.

Let us look carefully.
What have we done?

Noble Sangha, with all our heart,
let us be diligent,
engaging in the practice.
Let us live deeply,
free from our afflictions,
aware of impermanence
so that life does not
drift away without meaning.
[BELL, BELL]

VISUALIZING BUDDHA

The Buddha is a flower of humanity
who practiced the Way for countless lives.
He appeared on this Earth as a prince who left his royal palace
to practice at the foot of the Bodhi tree.
He conquered illusion.
When the morning star arose,
he realized the great path of awakening
and turned the wheel of the Dharma.

With single-mindedness, all species aspire to experience the path free
from birth.
With single-mindedness, all species will experience a path free from birth.

Namo Tassa Bhagavato Arahato Samma Sambuddhassa
Namo Tassa Bhagavato Arahato Samma Sambuddhassa
Namo Tassa Bhagavato Arahato Samma Sambuddhassa
[BELL]

PRAISING THE THREE JEWELS

The Buddha jewel shines infinitely.
He has realized perfect enlightenment for countless lifetimes.
The beauty and stability of a Buddha sitting
can be seen in the mountains and rivers.

How splendid is the Vulture Peak!
How beautiful the light that shines forth from Buddha's third eye,
illuminating the six dark paths.
The Nagapushpa Assembly will be our next appointment
for the continuation of the true teachings and practices.
We take refuge in the Buddha ever-present.

The Dharma jewel is infinitely lovely.
It is the precious words spoken by the Buddha himself,
like fragrant flowers floating down from the heavens.
The wonderful Dharma is plain to see.
It is recorded luminously in three transparent baskets,
handed down from generation to generation in the Ten Directions,
so that today we can see our way.
We vow to study it with all our heart.
We take refuge in the Dharma ever-present.

The Sangha jewel is infinitely precious,
a field of merit where good seeds can be sown.
The three robes and the bowl are symbols of freedom.
Mindfulness trainings, concentration, and insight
support each other.
The Sangha dwells in mindfulness day and night,
providing the foundation for us to realize the fruit of meditation.
With one heart, we come home to the Sangha,
and take refuge in the Sangha ever-present.
[BELL, BELL]

PRAISING THE BUDDHA

The Buddha is like the fresh, full moon
that soars across the immense sky.
When the river of mind is truly calm,
the moon is reflected perfectly
upon the surface of the deep waters.
The countenance of the World-Honored One,
like the full moon or like the orb of the sun,
shines with the light of clarity,
a halo of wisdom spreading in every direction,

enveloping all with love, compassion, joy, and equanimity.

The inexhaustible virtues of the World-Honored One
cannot be adequately praised.
We in the [NAME] practice center, on this day
gather as a Fourfold Sangha, come to the altar, meditate and chant,
praise the virtuous actions of the Buddha, and offer this prayer:

May the path of the Buddha grow brighter.
May the Dharma become clearer.
May wind and rain be favorable.
May this country be at peace in the cities and rural areas.
May all follow the way of right practice.
May nature be safe. May people in society be free and equal.
May the refreshing breeze of compassion enter into this world of heat,
allowing the sun of wisdom to shine clearly in the cloudy sky
so that the path of liberation is appreciated everywhere
and the Dharma rain falls, benefiting all species.

May the Sangha that is present here practice diligently,
showing concern and love for each other
as they would for their own family,
transforming their consciousness.
We aspire to follow the example
of the Bodhisattvas Samantabhadra and Avalokiteshvara
and all other Bodhisattva Mahasattvas,
and the Great Perfection of Wisdom.
[BELL]

CHANT OF PRAISE AND ASPIRATION

A flower held up speaks wonderfully.
Its five petals have a special fragrance.
The Dharma Treasure is transmitted from India
and continued in the Mind-Seal school in China.
May all generations of Ancestral Teachers,
residing in the nirvana of the Wonderful Mind,
seated high on the precious Dharma Throne,
with the Awakened Understanding which transcends the world,

please look down on all your descendants.
With love please be witness to our aspiration:
all generations of Ancestral Teachers have developed widely the path
of stability and freedom.
They are the example and source for all future generations.

PRAISING THE BODHISATTVA OF COMPASSION ♪

The nectar of compassion is seen on the willow branch held
by the Bodhisattva.
A single drop of this nectar is enough to bring life
to the Ten Directions of the Cosmos.
May all afflictions of this world disappear totally and
may this place of practice be completely purified
by the Bodhisattva's nectar of compassion.

Homage to the Bodhisattva Who Refreshes the Earth.

From the depths of understanding, a flower of great eloquence blooms:
The Bodhisattva stands majestically
upon the waves of birth and death, free from all afflictions.
Her great compassion eliminates all sickness,
even that once thought of as incurable.
Her wondrous light sweeps away all obstacles and dangers.
Her willow branch, once waved,
reveals countless Buddha Lands.
Her lotus flower blossoms a multitude of practice centers.
We bow to her. We see her true presence in the here and the now.
We offer her the incense of our hearts.
May the Bodhisattva of Deep Listening embrace us all
with Great Compassion.

Namo'valokiteshvaraya
[Homage to Bodhisattva Avalokiteshvara]
[BELL]

Verses of Consecration

This water's shape is round or square
according to the container that holds it.
In the spring warmth, it is liquid; in the winter cold, it is solid.
When its path is open, it flows.
When its path is obstructed, it stands still.
How vast it is, yet its source is so small it is difficult to find.
How wonderful it is in its streams, which flow endlessly.
In the jade rivulets, the footprints of dragons remain.
In the deep pond, water holds the bright halo of the autumn moon.
On the tip of the king's pen, water becomes
the compassion of clemency.
On the willow branch, it becomes
the clear fresh balm of compassion.
Only one drop of the water of compassion is needed,
and the Ten Directions are all purified.
[BELL]

May the Day Be Well ♪
[CHANT FOR CIRCUMAMBULATION]

May the day be well and the night be well.
May the midday hour bring happiness too.
In every minute and every second,
may the day and night be well.
By the blessing of the Triple Gem,
may all things be protected and safe.
May all beings born in each of the four ways
live in a land of purity.
May all in the Three Realms be born upon Lotus Thrones.
May countless wandering souls
realize the three virtuous positions of the Bodhisattva Path.
May all living beings, with grace and ease,
fulfill the Bodhisattva Stages.

The countenance of the World-Honored One, like the full moon
or like the orb of the sun, shines with the light of clarity.
A halo of wisdom spreads in every direction,

enveloping all with love and compassion,
joy and equanimity.

Namo Shakyamunaye Buddhaya
Namo Shakyamunaye Buddhaya
Namo Shakyamunaye Buddhaya
[BELL, BELL]

WE ARE TRULY PRESENT ♪

With hearts established in mindfulness, we are truly present
for sitting and walking meditation, and for reciting the sutras.
May this practice center, with its Fourfold Sangha,
be supported by the Three Jewels and Holy Beings,
well-protected from the eight misfortunes
and the three paths of suffering.

May parents, teachers, friends, and all beings within the Three Realms
be filled with the most divine grace,
and may it be found that in the world there is no place at war.
May the winds be favorable, the rains seasonable,
and the peoples' hearts at peace.
May the practice of the noble community, diligent and steady,
ascend the Ten Bodhisattva Stages with ease and energy.
May the Sangha body live peacefully, fresh and full of joy,
a refuge for all, offering happiness and insight.

The wisdom of the Awakened Mind shines out like the full moon.
The body of the Awakened One is pure and clear as crystal.
In the world the Awakened One relieves bitterness and suffering.
In every place the Awakened Mind reveals love and compassion.

Namo Shakyamunaye Buddhaya
Namo Shakyamunaye Buddhaya
Namo Shakyamunaye Buddhaya
[BELL, BELL]

The Four Recollections ♪

The Blessed One is worthy and fully self-awakened.
I bow before the Buddha.
[BELL]

The teaching is well expounded by the Blessed One.
I pay homage to the Dharma.
[BELL]

The community of the Blessed One's disciples has practiced well.
I pay respect to the Sangha.
[BELL]

The Noble Teacher in whom I take refuge
is the One who embodies and reveals the Ultimate Reality,
is the One who is worthy of all respect and offerings,
is the One who is endowed with perfected wisdom,
is the One who is endowed with right understanding and
compassionate action,
is the One who happily crossed to the shore of freedom,
is the One who looked deeply to know the world well,
is the highest charioteer training humankind,
teaching gods and humans,
the Awakened One, the World-Honored One.
[BELL]

The Teaching given by my Noble Teacher
is the path I undertake, the Teaching well-proclaimed,
is the Teaching that can be realized right here and right now,
is the Teaching that is immediately useful and effective,
is the Teaching inviting all to come and see directly,
is the Teaching that is leading to the good, the true, the beautiful,
extinguishing the fire of afflictions;
it is a teaching for all sensible people to realize for themselves.
[BELL]

Practicing the Teachings, the Noble Community in which I take refuge
is the Community that goes in the direction of goodness,

in the direction of truth,
in the direction of beauty,
in the direction of righteousness;
is the Community that is composed of four pairs and eight kinds
of holy people;
is the Community that is worthy of offerings, worthy of great respect,
worthy of admiration, worthy of salutation;
is the Community standing upon the highest fields of merit in all
of the world.
[BELL]

The Mindfulness Trainings, the wholesome way of living taught by my
Noble Teacher,
is the wonderful practice that remains unbroken,
that remains harmonious, that remains flawless, that remains refined;
is the wonderful practice that has the capacity to prevent wrongdoing and
to prevent danger;
is the wonderful practice that has the capacity to protect self and others
and to reveal beauty;
is the wonderful practice that is leading to concentration, leading to
peacefulness, leading to insight, leading to non-fear;
is the wonderful practice that shows us the way to total emancipation and
long-lasting happiness.
[BELL]

THE REFUGE CHANT ♪

Incense perfumes the atmosphere.
A lotus blooms and the Buddha appears.
The world of suffering and discrimination
is filled with the light of the rising sun.
As the dust of fear and anxiety settles,
with open heart, one-pointed mind,
I turn to the Three Jewels.
[BELL]

The Fully Enlightened One, beautifully seated, peaceful and smiling,
a living source of understanding and compassion,
to the Buddha I go for refuge.
[BELL]

The path of mindful living,
leading to healing, joy, and enlightenment, the way of peace,
to the Dharma I go for refuge.
[BELL]

The loving and supportive community of practice,
realizing harmony, awareness, and liberation,
to the Sangha I go for refuge.
[BELL]

I am aware that the Three Gems are within my heart.
I vow to realize them,
practicing mindful breathing and smiling,
looking deeply into things.
I vow to understand living beings and their suffering,
to cultivate compassion and loving kindness,
to practice joy and equanimity.
[BELL]

I vow to offer joy to one person in the morning,
to help relieve the grief of one person in the afternoon,
living simply and sanely with few possessions,
keeping my body healthy.
I vow to let go of all worries and anxiety
in order to be light and free.
[BELL]

I am aware that I owe so much
to my parents, teachers, friends, and all beings.
I vow to be worthy of their trust, to practice wholeheartedly
so that understanding and compassion will flower,
helping living beings be free from their suffering.
May the Buddha, the Dharma, and the Sangha
support my efforts.
[BELL, BELL]

Nourishing Happiness

Sitting here in this moment, protected by the Sangha,
my happiness is clear and alive.

What a great fortune to have been born a human,
to encounter the Dharma,
to be in harmony with others,
and to water the Mind of Love
in this beautiful garden of practice.
[BELL]

The energies of the Sangha and mindfulness trainings
are protecting and helping me not make mistakes
or be swept along in darkness by unwholesome seeds.
With kind spiritual friends, I am on the path of goodness,
illumined by the light of Buddhas and Bodhisattvas.

Although seeds of suffering are still in me
in the form of afflictions and habit energies,
mindfulness is also there, helping me touch
what is most wonderful within and around me.

I can still enjoy mindfulness of the six senses:
my eyes look peacefully upon the clear blue sky,
my ears listen with wonder to the songs of birds,
my nose smells the rich scent of sandalwood,
my tongue tastes the nectar of the Dharma,
my posture is upright, stable, and relaxed,
and my mind is one with my body.

If there were not a World-Honored One,
if there were not the wonderful Dharma,
if there were not a harmonious Sangha,
I would not be so fortunate
to enjoy this Dharma happiness today.

My resources for practice are my own peace and joy.
I vow to cultivate and nourish them with daily mindfulness.
For my ancestors, family, future generations,
and the whole of humanity, I vow to practice well.

In my society I know that there are countless people suffering,
drowned in sensual pleasure, jealousy, and hatred.

I am determined to take care of my own mental formations,
to learn the art of deep listening and using loving speech
in order to encourage communication and understanding
and to be able to accept and love.

Practicing the actions of a bodhisattva,
I vow to look with eyes of love and a heart of understanding.
I vow to listen with a clear mind and ears of compassion,
bringing peace and joy into the lives of others,
to lighten and alleviate the suffering of living beings.

I am aware that ignorance and wrong perceptions
can turn this world into a fiery hell.
I vow to walk always upon the path of transformation,
producing understanding and loving kindness.
I will be able to cultivate a garden of awakening.

Although there are birth, sickness, old age, and death,
now that I have a path of practice, I have nothing more to fear.
It is a great happiness to be alive in the Sangha
with the practice of mindfulness trainings and concentration,
to live every moment in stability and freedom,
to take part in the work of relieving others' suffering,
the career of Buddhas and Bodhisattvas.

In each precious moment, I am filled with deep gratitude.
I bow before the World-Honored One.
Please bear witness to my wholehearted gratitude,
embracing all beings with arms of great compassion.
[BELL, BELL]

TURNING TO THE TATHAGATA

I touch the Earth deeply, turning to the Tathagata,
the lighthouse that shines over the ocean of dust and suffering.
Lord of Compassion, embrace us with your love,
for today we are determined to return to our true home.
[BELL]

We, your spiritual children, still owe so much gratitude
to our parents, teachers, friends, and all other beings.
Looking over the Three Realms and across the Four Quarters,
we see all species drowning in an ocean of misfortune.
It wakes us with a start.
Although we have turned in the right direction,
the shore of awakening still lies very far away.
Fortunately, we see the hands of the Compassionate One
bringing relief to every corner of the world.
[BELL]

With one-pointed mind, we return, taking refuge.
We aspire to be the spiritual children of the Tathagata.
We unify our body and mind before the Buddha's throne,
releasing all attachment and negativity.
With great respect, we now aspire to receive the wonderful teachings.
We shall always practice diligently and carefully,
our mindfulness trainings and concentration nourished to maturity,
for the fruit of understanding to be ripened in the future.
We ask the Bodhisattvas to protect us day and night.
May the Buddha, Dharma, and Sangha show us their compassion.
[BELL]

We know that the fruits of our past actions are still heavy,
that the merit from our virtues is still frail,
that we are often full of wrong perceptions,
that our capacity to understand is poor,
that the impurities of our mind still arise very easily,
that our practices of listening and contemplation are not firm.
In this moment we entrust ourselves to the Lotus Throne,
and, with our five limbs resting gently on the Earth, we now pray.
Infinite loving kindness, please expand and envelop us
so that we too may open our hearts.
[BELL]

We, your spiritual children for countless past lives,
have chased after worldly things,
unable to recognize the clear, pure basis of our True Mind.
Our actions of body, speech, and mind have been unwholesome.

We have drowned in ignorant cravings, jealousy, hatred, and anger.
But now the sound of the great bell has caused us to awaken
with a heart that is determined to renew our body and our mind.
Please help us completely remove the red dust of all
wrongdoings, mistakes, and faults.
[BELL]

We, your spiritual children in this moment,
make the vow to leave all our habit energies behind,
and for the whole of our life to go for refuge to the Sangha.
Awakened One, please place your hand over us in protection,
so that loving kindness and compassion will guide and assist us.
We promise that when we practice meditation,
when we take part in Dharma discussion,
when we stand, walk, lie, or sit,
when we cook, wash, work, or play,
when we recite the names of the Buddhas and Bodhisattvas,
when we offer incense or when we touch the Earth,
every step will bring peace and joy to the world,
every smile will be resplendent with freedom.
We will live mindfully in each and every moment
to demonstrate the way of liberation from suffering.
We vow to touch the Pure Land with every step.
We promise in every contact
to be in touch with the ultimate dimension,
taking steps on the soil of reality, breathing the air of true emptiness,
lighting up wisdom to make resplendent the wonderful True Mind,
drawing aside the dark curtain of ignorance,
with our body and mind peaceful and happy,
free and at leisure until the moment when we leave this life,
our heart with no regrets, our body without pain,
our thoughts unclouded by ignorance,
our mindfulness clear and bright, and our six senses calm
as when entering meditative concentration.
[BELL]

If necessary to be reborn, we will always do so
as the spiritual children of the Tathagata.
We will continue in the work of helping other beings,

bringing them all over to the shore of awakening.
Realizing the Three Bodies and the Four Wisdoms,
using the Five Eyes and the Six Miracles,
manifesting thousands of appropriate forms,
being present at the same time in all the Three Worlds,
coming in and going out in freedom and with ease,
we will not abandon anyone, helping all beings to transform,
bringing all to the shore of no regression.
[BELL]

Space is without limit. There are infinite living beings,
and the same is true with afflictions and results of past actions.
We pray that our aspirations will also become infinite.
We bow to the Awakened One as we make this vow.
We will maintain virtue, sharing the merit with countless others
in order to fully repay the gratitude that we owe
and to teach the practice everywhere within the Three Realms.
May we, alongside all species of living beings,
fully realize the Great Awakened Understanding.
[BELL, BELL]

PROTECTING AND TRANSFORMING

We, your disciples, who from beginningless time
have made ourselves unhappy out of confusion and ignorance,
being born and dying with no direction,
have now found confidence in the highest awakening.
However much we may have drifted on the ocean of suffering,
today we see clearly that there is a beautiful path.
We turn toward the light of loving kindness to direct us.
We bow deeply to the Awakened One and to our spiritual ancestors
who light up the path before us, guiding every step.
[BELL]

The wrongdoings and sufferings that imprison us
are brought about by craving, hatred, ignorance, and pride.
Today we begin anew to purify and free our hearts.
With awakened wisdom, bright as the sun and the full moon,
and immeasurable compassion to help humankind,

we resolve to live beautifully.
With all our heart, we go for refuge to the Three Precious Jewels.
With the boat of loving kindness,
we cross over the ocean of suffering.
With the torch of wisdom, we leave behind the forest of confusion.
With determination, we learn, reflect, and practice.
Right View is the ground of our actions, in body, speech, and mind.
Right Mindfulness embraces us,
walking, standing, lying down, and sitting,
speaking, smiling, coming in, and going out.
Whenever anger or anxiety enter our heart,
we are determined to breathe mindfully and come back to ourselves.
With every step, we will walk in the Pure Land.
With every look, the Dharmakaya is revealed.
We are careful and attentive as sense organs touch sense objects
so mindfulness will protect us all day,
so all habit energies can be observed and easily transformed.
May our heart's garden of awakening
bloom with hundreds of flowers.
May we bring the feelings of peace and joy into every household.
May we plant wholesome seeds on the ten thousand paths.
May we never have the need to leave the Sangha body.
May we never attempt to escape the suffering of the world,
always being present wherever beings need our help.
May mountains and rivers be our witness in this moment
as we bow our heads and request the Lord of Compassion
to embrace us all.
[BELL, BELL]

LOVING SPEECH AND DEEP LISTENING

Here, I can come back to myself.
Looking up with admiration, I observe
the spiritual characteristics which clearly
shine from the face of the Tathagata.
The Tathagata is the morning light
and the immense space of the firmament,
calm and stable like the moon,
carrying us along

on our journey home
from the world of confusion
to a land of freedom and inclusiveness.

For so many past lifetimes,
we have made mistakes
which have brought about much suffering.
All of us hold onto internal formations.
Sometimes we cannot look at each other.
We lose our capacity to listen deeply
and to speak loving, harmonious words.
The communication between us
meets so many difficulties and obstacles.
There seems to be no way to resolve our suffering.
Every day, understanding and love are fading.
The heavy, obstructed atmosphere
stifles all our happiness.
With all my resolve,
I touch the Earth,
determined to follow the teachings
of the Tathagata.
I shall begin to practice listening deeply
and speaking lovingly, according
to the way which benefits the practice
and my fellow practitioners,
so that communication can be quickly restored.

I shall practice diligently
to guard my body and mind
with conscious breathing
and through awareness of my steps,
so that I can recognize and embrace
the anger and irritation in my heart;
so I can sit and listen deeply
with all my compassion
and so the other person has a chance to share
all their hidden suffering.
I want to learn to listen deeply
with sincere loving kindness

So that the other person can suffer less.
I promise the Buddha
that even if the other person says
things that are not true,
even if his or her words are full of blame,
I shall continue to listen attentively.
I shall wait for the right time
to find a way to let the other person know
what really happened,
so the other person has a chance to rectify
his or her perceptions.
I want to practice using
harmonious and loving words
to help the person sitting with me
hear and understand
what I need to say.
But for as long as I still have
some irritation, I shall just practice
mindful breathing and mindful walking,
determined to avoid any discussion.
I am determined only to speak
when I am able to master my mind.

Lord Buddha,
Bodhisattva of Great Wisdom, Manjushri,
Bodhisattva of Great Action, Samantabhadra,
Bodhisattva of Great Compassion, Avalokita,
Be with me and light my way,
so that I can soon be successful
on the path of practice.
[BELL, BELL]

REPENTANCE AND TAKING REFUGE FOR LIFE

With our whole life, we go for refuge
to the ones with the highest awakening in the Ten Directions,
to the deep and wonderful Dharma which has been propounded,
and to the holy Sangha which realizes the four fruits
and practices the three vehicles of liberation.

In compassion, please stretch out your arms to protect us.
[BELL]

For a long time, we have gone against the stream of our true nature,
floundering in the ocean of sorrows and the river of confusion,
unable to see a way out or a path to our true home.
Bobbing up and down on the waves, we have not been able to turn
around.
We have laid down the conditions for the formation of afflictions.
Over so many lifetimes, we have committed actions that have hindered us.
We have not been able to distinguish the straight path from the crooked.
The fruit of our resentment and injustice has become heavy and deep.
Now we sincerely bow my heads.
As we lay open our hearts to begin anew, we rely on the Great Favor.
[BELL]

With utmost sincerity, we call on the true hero, Descendant of the Sun
to rescue us with all beings from the ocean of birth and death.
We are determined to set out with good spiritual friends
in order to leave behind the realm of our afflictions and find the shore of
liberation.
In this lifetime, may we build our life of practice
and heighten merit to solidify the foundations of practice in lives to come,
so that our highest career may be cultivated
until understanding and love spring up, fresh and lovely.
May we always be born as humans.
And may we meet the teachings and live a life of true practice.

May we be guided on the path of practice by an enlightened teacher.
Equipped with true faith, may we join an authentic Fourfold Sangha.
May the six sense faculties and the Three Actions be in balance and
harmony.
May we not run after people of the world, causing us to be caught in
bondage.
Wholeheartedly and diligently, may we practice the teachings of our
loving Root Teacher,
holding to brahmacharya and leaving behind all worldly actions.
May we practice fine manners and right conduct until they shine brightly.

With a heart of loving kindness, may we protect the life of even the
smallest beings.
May we always create sufficient wholesome causes and conditions
so that countless misfortunes can dissipate like the morning mist.
With one-pointed mind, may we make the aspiration to develop
bodhicitta so that the Lotus Throne of the true understanding
of emptiness may manifest.
With our constant practice,
may we witness the awakening to the highest truth
and become capable of transmitting the True Mind.
May we go beyond the cycle of drowning in the ocean of rebirth,
developing the practice of the Six Paramitas in order to rescue beings.
May we open practice centers in many places
so that the net of doubt is destroyed and the person and the environment
can be purified.
May we subdue all unwholesome spirits,
transmitting the lamp of the Dharma and carrying on the lineage
infinitely.
May we be happy to serve the Buddhas in the Ten Directions,
not discouraged because of weariness or toil.
However many deep and wonderful Dharma doors there are,
may we realize them all to rescue ourselves,
and then bring that merit and wisdom to rescue other beings,
so that the fruit of Buddhahood is witnessed and the Dharmakaya is
wholly realized.
May we adapt ourselves to circumstances in the ordinary world,
realizing numberless bodies to rescue, little by little, all living beings.
May the nectar of loving kindness rain on the realms of gods and men
so that the ocean of actions and vows to rescue beings becomes vast.
Everywhere, may the various regions of the world, whether near or far
away, be in harmony.
By proclaiming the wonderful Dharma doors may we rescue all beings,
may the light of understanding shine forth from the wonderful
Nirmanakaya, making wholesome the realms where animals, plants,
and minerals suffer.
May ten thousand species upon seeing our form and hearing our name
be released from bondage and pain.
May we give rise to our deepest aspiration

so that the suffering of Ten Thousand Realms will dissipate.
However many wrong actions there are, leading to unspeakable injustice,
however many sufferings there are in the animal realms,
may they all, due to the power of fine manners and spirituality,
vanish like the dew on the green mountain when dawn appears.

May we give medicines to the sick in urgent need.
May we give food and clothes to the destitute.
May so many benefits arise and prosper.
May peace and joy be realized right in the cycle of samsara.
May all beings regardless of race or belief,
whether they are friends or enemies,
have the same chance to cross over the ocean of afflictions.
May we leave behind unwholesome attachment forever,
untying the knots which bind body and mind.
May we cultivate the wholesome conditions for our highest career
so that, together with numberless other species, we turn in the direction
of the Dharmakaya.

Even though the heavens should move,
my vows will not be shaken for countless lifetimes.
We pray that all beings that ever existed
may wholly realize the career of Great Understanding
and sit solidly at the foot of the Bodhi tree.
[BELL, BELL]

HAPPINESS IN THE PRESENT MOMENT

The past has already gone,
and the future has not yet come.
Let us not drown ourselves
in regret for what has passed
or in expectations and worry for the future.
The Buddha has said that we can
be peaceful, happy, and free
in this present moment.
Let us hear the Buddha's words
and let go of our sadness and anxiety.

Let us come back to ourselves
and establish ourselves in what is present right now.
Let us learn to recognize
the conditions for happiness
that are present within us
and around us.

Can we hear the birds singing
and the wind in the pines?
Can we see the green mountains,
the white clouds, the golden moon?
The Pure Land is available
in the present moment.
Every day we can enjoy ourselves
in the Buddha Land.
Every mindful breath and step
takes us to the Pure Land,
revealing all the wonders
of the Dharma body.

I am determined to let go of
hurrying, competing,
being busy and disgruntled.
I shall not run after fame, power,
riches, and sex
because I know
that this does not lead to true happiness.
All it will bring me is
misery and misfortune.

I shall learn to know what is sufficient,
to live simply,
so that I have time to live deeply
every moment of my daily life,
giving my body and mind a chance to heal,
and to have the time to look after and protect
those I have vowed to love.

I shall practice for my mind to grow
in love and compassion,

so that I have the ability to help
beings anywhere
who are drowning in craving.

I ask the Buddhas everywhere
to protect and guide me,
to support me on my path,
so that I can live in peace, joy,
and freedom every day,
fulfilling the deepest aspiration
as your disciple
whom you trust and love.
[BELL, BELL]

WATERING SEEDS OF JOY ♪

My mother, my father,
they are in me.
And when I look,
I see myself in them.

The Buddha, the patriarchs,
they are in me.
And when I look,
I see myself in them.
I am a continuation
of my mother, my father, and my ancestors.
It is my aspiration to preserve
and continue to nourish
seeds of goodness, skill, and happiness
which I have inherited.
It is also my desire to recognize
the seeds of fear and suffering I have inherited,
and, bit by bit, to transform them.

I am a continuation
of the Buddha and my spiritual teachers.
It is my deep aspiration
to preserve, nourish, and develop

the seeds of understanding, love, and freedom
which they have transmitted to me.

I desire to continue
the career of the Buddha and my Ancestral Teachers,
and do my best to realize
all that the Buddha and my Ancestral Teachers
expect of me.

In my daily life,
I also want to sow
seeds of love and compassion
in my own consciousness
and in the heart of other people.
I am determined not to water
seeds of craving, aversion, and violence
in myself and the other.

I know that if I practice
all this in the right way,
after only seven days,
I shall already have been able
to change the situation,
establish communication,
smile and transform some suffering
and increase my happiness.

Please, Lord Buddha
be witness to what is in my heart.
With mind and body in perfect unity,
I bow my head and prostrate.
[BELL, BELL]

AWAKENING THE SOURCE OF LOVE

We bow respectfully to Avalokiteshvara,
to your great vow always to be there for all beings,
your capacity to look deeply at the world with compassionate eyes,
listen deeply to understand and to relieve suffering,

and with your holy willow branch,
to sprinkle the nectar of immortality,
cleansing my mind from all impurities.
I vow to take refuge in you with all my heart
Respectfully, I offer you my vow in thousands of words:
[BELL]

Namo Avalokiteshvara, I vow to look deeply into the Five Skandhas.
I vow to see the true nature of emptiness.
I vow soon to reach the shore of awakening.
I vow to overcome all obstacles.
I vow to take the boat of Perfect Understanding.

Namo Avalokiteshvara, I vow to be present in all three bodies.
I vow to realize the fruits of liberation.
I vow to cultivate great compassion.
I vow to penetrate deeply the Tathagata Store.
I vow to purify my mind.
[BELL]

Namo Avalokiteshvara, please help me get out of the abyss of craving.
Please help me dissolve the worries of my mind.
Please give me skillful means.
Please help me build Sangha.
Please help me transform my anger and hatred.
Please help me uproot my ignorance.
Please help me hold the high torch of right faith.
Please give me the clear eyes of understanding.
[BELL]

Namo Avalokiteshvara, please place in my hand the golden lotus.
Please allow me to see the Dharma Body.
I vow to build brotherhood and sisterhood.
I vow to show gratitude to my spiritual lineage.
I vow to practice loving speech.
I vow to look with loving eyes.
Namo Avalokiteshvara, I vow to practice deep listening
I vow to live mindfully and with clarity.
I vow to realize meditative concentration.

I vow to advance night and day on the heroic path.
I vow to abide peacefully in the ground of reality.
I vow to cultivate the five kinds of eyes, and the six miraculous powers.
[BELL]

Namo Avalokiteshvara,
Please come with me to the war zones
to stop the killing and bombing.
Please walk with me to the places of sickness and suffering,
bringing compassionate nectar and medicine.
Please walk with me to the realm of the hungry ghosts.
bringing the Dharma food of understanding and love
Please walk with me to the realm of hell
in order to cool the heat of afflictions.
Please walk with me to places of conflict
in order to remove hatred and anger
and help the source of love to flow again.

Homage to the Bodhisattva of Great Compassion
Homage to the Bodhisattva of Great Compassion
Homage to the Bodhisattva of Great Compassion
[BELL, BELL]

MASTERING ANGER

I bow my head and touch the Earth
before the highest charioteer who trains humankind.
Stretch out your arms of compassion;
bring us to the shore of peace and solidity.
For so long, confusion has inhabited us
so that we have not had the chance to learn,
and we have often acted foolishly,
allowed seeds of anger and violence
to be watered in our deep consciousness.

Whenever seeds of irritation or fury
arise and operate in my mind,
They always cause wounds and resentment
in myself and in so many others.

Listening to Avalokita's teaching,
I begin right now with a deep aspiration:
Whenever anger arises,
I shall come back to myself,
taking refuge in my mindful breathing and steps
so as to look after and embrace,
to protect and recognize
the painful mental formations in me.

I shall remember to look deeply
to see the true nature and source
of hatred and anger.
Heeding the Buddha's teachings,
I shall know how to guard my mind.
When anger arises in me
I shall not do or say anything
until I have mastered it.
I shall look deeply to see
the real nature of my pain.

The seed of ignorance
is the cause of my suffering,
and the reason why the seed of
anger in me has grown so strong.
The person who makes me angry
has so much suffering himself, herself.

Such a person has had no chance
to learn how to protect, to come home to himself or herself
to take care
and to transform
the deep-seated habit energies within.

Contemplating in this way,
I will be able to bring about understanding and acceptance,
and help the other person
to practice and to transform
the suffering within him or her.

The Blessed One has said,
When we are capable of conquering our anger,
we bring a double victory to ourself and to the other person.

I want to practice with all my heart
in order to respond to the Great Grace.
May the Three Jewels give me energy and blessing
so that we can reach promptly
the shore of peace and happiness.
[BELL, BELL]

JOYFULLY SHARING THE MERIT ♪

Blessed Ones who dwell in the world, grant to us compassion.
In this and countless lives before, from beginningless time,
our mistakes have caused much suffering to ourselves and others.
We have done wrong, encouraged others to do wrong,
and given our consent to acts of killing, stealing, deceiving,
sexual misconduct, and other harmful actions
among the Ten Unwholesome Deeds.
Whether our faults are known to others or whether they are hidden,
they have brought us to the realms of hell, hungry ghosts, and animals,
causing us to be born in places filled with pain and suffering.
We have not yet had the chance to realize our full potential.
Today we are determined, with one-pointed concentration,
to repent the obstacles of our past unwholesome actions.
[BELL]

Blessed Ones, be our witness and look upon us with compassion.
We surrender before you and make this aspiration:
If at all within this very life and countless lives before,
we have given, even if only a handful of food or simple garment;
if we have ever spoken kindly, even if only a few words;
if we have ever looked with eyes of compassion,
even if only for a moment;
if we have ever comforted or consoled, even if only once or twice;
if we have ever listened carefully to wonderful teachings,
even if only to one talk;
if we have ever offered a meal to monks and nuns, even if only once;

if we have ever saved a life, even if only that of an ant or a worm;
if we have ever recited a sutra, even if only one or two lines;
if we have ever been a monk or a nun, even if only for one life;
if we have ever supported others on the path of practice,
even if only two or three people;
if we have ever observed the Mindfulness Trainings,
even if imperfectly;
all of this merit has slowly formed wholesome seeds within us.
Today we gather them together like a fragrant flower garland
and, with great respect, we offer it to all Awakened Ones —
a contribution to the fruit of the highest path.
[BELL]

Opening our hearts wide to the Perfect Highest Awakening,
we are resolved to attain Great Understanding.
We will realize compassion and embody deep love.
We will practice diligently, transforming our suffering
and the suffering of all other species.
Please transfer the merits of body, speech, and mind
to the happiness of people and all other beings.
Apart from bodhicitta and apart from the thirst
for great understanding and the embodiment of love,
there is no other desire within us.
All Buddhas in the Three Times and the Ten Directions
have offered their merit as we are doing today.
Repenting all our faults, we joyfully contribute
to the immeasurable ocean of merit
and the towering peaks of the Highest Understanding.
The Buddhas and the Ancestral Teachers
are the light which shows us the way.
In this solemn moment, with all my life's force,
I come back to myself and bow deeply with respect.
[BELL, BELL]

BEGINNING ANEW

With great respect, we turn towards the conqueror of afflictions,
offering heartfelt words of repentance.
We have lived in forgetfulness for a long time.
As we have not had the opportunity to encounter the Dharma,

our habit energies have led us into suffering.
We have made many mistakes out of unskillfulness.
We have been blinded by our wrong perceptions
for a very long time.
Our heart's garden is sown with attachment, hatred, and pride.
In us are seeds of killing, stealing, sexual misconduct, and lies.
Our everyday deeds and words do damage.
All these wrong actions are obstacles to our peace and joy.
Let us begin anew.
[BELL]

We see that we have been thoughtless,
straying from the path of mindfulness.
We have stored up afflictions and ignorance,
which have brought about so much aversion and sorrow.
There are times we have been weary of life
because we are so full of anxiety.
Because we do not understand others,
we are angry and resentful.
First we try to reason with each other, then we blame.
Every day the suffering increases, making the rift greater.
There are days when we are unwilling to speak to each other,
unwilling to look each other in the face.
And we create internal formations, which last for a long time.
Now we turn to the Three Jewels.
Sincerely recognizing our errors, we bow our heads.
[BELL]

We know so well that in our consciousness
are buried all the wholesome seeds —
seeds of love and understanding and seeds of peace and joy.
But because we do not know how to water them,
the wholesome seeds do not sprout fresh and green.
We continue to allow sorrow to overwhelm us
until there is no light in our lives.
When we chase after a distant happiness,
life becomes but a shadow of the reality.
Our mind is occupied by the past,
or worrying about this or that in the future.
We cannot let go of our anger,

and we consider of no value the precious gifts of life
which are already in our hands,
thereby trampling on real happiness.
As month follows month, we are sunk in sorrow.
So now in the precious presence of the Buddha,
fragrant with sandalwood incense,
we recognize our errors and begin anew.
[BELL]

With all our heart we go for refuge,
turning to the Buddhas in the Ten Directions
and all the Bodhisattvas, noble disciples, and self-achieved Buddhas.
Very sincerely we recognize our errors
and the mistakes of our wrong judgments.
Please bring the balm of clear water
to pour on the roots of our afflictions.
Please bring the raft of the true teachings
to carry us over the ocean of sorrows.
We vow to live an awakened life,
to practice smiling and conscious breathing,
and to study the teachings, authentically transmitted.
Diligently, we shall live in mindfulness.
[BELL]

We come back to live in the wonderful present,
to plant our heart's garden with good seeds,
and to make strong foundations of understanding and love.
We vow to train ourselves in mindfulness and concentration,
practicing to look and understand deeply
to be able to see the nature of all that is,
and so to be free of the bonds of birth and death.
We learn to speak lovingly, to be affectionate,
to care for others whether it is early morn or late afternoon,
to bring the roots of joy to many places,
helping people to abandon sorrow,
to respond with deep gratitude
to the kindness of parents, teachers, and friends.
With deep faith we light up the incense of our heart.
We ask the Lord of Compassion to be our protector

on the wonderful path of practice.
We vow to practice diligently,
cultivating the fruits of this path.
[BELL, BELL]

MEDITATION BEFORE A SANGHA MEETING

Dear Lord Buddha and teachers over many generations:
   We vow to go through this meeting in a spirit of togetherness as we review all ideas and consolidate them to a harmonious understanding (consensus). We vow to use the methods of loving speech and deep listening in order to bring about the success of this meeting, as an offering to the Three Jewels. We vow not to hesitate to share our ideas and insights but also vow not to say anything when the feeling of irritation is present in us. We are resolutely determined not to allow tension to build up in this meeting. If anyone of us senses the start of tension, we will stop immediately and practice Beginning Anew right away, so as to re-establish the atmosphere of togetherness and harmony in the Sangha.

MEDITATION BEFORE A SHINING LIGHT SESSION

Dear Lord Buddha and teachers over many generations:
   Today we will shine light on the practice of our elder brothers (sisters) and younger brothers (sisters). We know that all of us are the various parts, the bones and flesh, of one Sangha body. Knowing this, we are very aware that in shining light on the practice of any one member of the Sangha, we are shining light on our own practice. We vow to do the practice of Shining Light with all our love and understanding. We vow that everything we say will stem from the wholesome intention of reaching as accurate an insight about our brother (sister) as possible, and of offering concrete suggestions for practice that will help our brother (sister) in the process of true transformation. We vow to avoid allowing our anger and misperceptions distort our views. We vow that every word spoken will be from a place of love within us. We know that in shining light on a member of the Sangha, we are also shining light on our own being. Thus, the practice of Shining Light will also be very beneficial for each and every one of us. We ask Lord Buddha and all our spiritual ancestors to protect and support us so that this Shining Light session will be a great success.

Ceremonies

Opening Practices

[THE FOLLOWING VERSES ARE USED TO OPEN MANY CEREMONIES, GENERALLY RE-
CITED ALONE BY THE CEREMONY LEADER. IT IS INDICATED IN THE PAGES DEDI-
CATED TO EACH CEREMONY WHEN EACH OF THESE PRACTICES IS TO BE USED.]

INCENSE OFFERING *Version One* ♪

[BELL, BELL, BELL]

In gratitude, we offer this incense
throughout space and time
to all Buddhas and Bodhisattvas.
May it be fragrant as Earth herself,
reflecting careful efforts,
wholehearted awareness,
and the fruit of understanding,
slowly ripening.
May we and all beings
be companions of Buddhas and Bodhisattvas.
May we awaken from forgetfulness
and realize our true home.
[BELL]

Incense Offering Version Two ♪

[BELL, BELL, BELL]
The fragrance of this incense
invites the awakened mind
to be truly present with us now.
The fragrance of this incense
fills our practice center,
protects and guards our mind
from all wrong thinking.
The fragrance of this incense
collects us and unites us.
Precepts, concentration, and insight
we offer for all that is.

Namo Bodhisattvebhyah
Namo Mahasattvebhyah
[BELL]

TOUCHING THE EARTH ♪

Opening Gatha
The one who bows and the one who is bowed to
are both, by nature, empty.
Therefore the communication between them
is inexpressibly perfect.
Our practice center is the Net of Indra
reflecting all Buddhas everywhere.
And with my person in front of each Buddha,
I go with my whole life for refuge.
[BELL]

Prostrations
[TOUCH THE EARTH ONE TIME AT THE SOUND OF EACH BELL.]

Offering light in the Ten Directions,
the Buddha, the Dharma, and the Sangha,
to whom we bow in gratitude.
[BELL]

Teaching and living the way of awareness
in the very midst of suffering and confusion,
Shakyamuni Buddha, the Fully Enlightened One,
to whom we bow in gratitude.
[BELL]

Cutting through ignorance, awakening our hearts and our minds,
Manjushri, the Bodhisattva of Great Understanding,
to whom we bow in gratitude.
[BELL]

Working mindfully, working joyfully for the sake of all beings,
Samantabhadra, the Bodhisattva of Great Action,
to whom we bow in gratitude.
[BELL]

Listening deeply, serving beings in countless ways,
Avalokiteshvara, the Bodhisattva of Great Compassion,
to whom we bow in gratitude.
[BELL]

Fearless and persevering through realms of suffering and darkness,
Kshitigarbha, the Bodhisattva of Great Aspiration,
to whom we bow in gratitude.
[BELL]

Seed of awakening and loving kindness
in children and all beings,
Maitreya, the Buddha to-be-born,
to whom we bow in gratitude.
[BELL]

[YOU MAY CHOOSE TO ADD ANY OF THE FOLLOWING OPTIONAL VERSES.]

Seeing the Buddha in everyone,
Sadaparibhuta, the Bodhisattva of Constant Respect,
to whom we bow in gratitude.
[BELL]

Convener of the Sangha, the teacher Mahakashyapa,
to whom we bow in gratitude.
[BELL]

Wise elder brother, the teacher Shariputra,
to whom we bow in gratitude.
[BELL]

Showing love for parents, the teacher Mahamaudgalyayana,
to whom we bow in gratitude.
[BELL]

Master of the Vinaya, the teacher Upali,
to whom we bow in gratitude.
[BELL]

Recorder of the teachings, the teacher Ananda,
to whom we bow in gratitude.
[BELL]

The first bhikshuni, Mahagotami,
to whom we bow in gratitude.
[BELL]

Showing the way fearlessly and compassionately,
the stream of all our Ancestral Teachers,
to whom we bow in gratitude.
[BELL, BELL]

Ceremonies

Ceremony to Recite the Three Refuges, Two Promises, and Five Mindfulness Trainings ♪

[DURING THE FIVE MINDFULNESS TRAININGS RECITATION CEREMONY, THE HEAD OF CEREMONY SHOULD BE SOMEONE WHO IS STABLE IN THE PRACTICE.]

1. Opening the Ceremony

Sitting Meditation [12 MINUTES]
Incense Offering [page 87]
Touching the Earth [page 88]

2. Opening Verse ♪

[BELL, BELL, BELL]

Namo Tassa Bhagavato Arahato Samma Sambuddhassa
Namo Tassa Bhagavato Arahato Samma Sambuddhassa
Namo Tassa Bhagavato Arahato Samma Sambuddhassa
[BELL]

The Dharma is deep and lovely.
We now have a chance to see, study, and practice it.
We vow to realize its true meaning.
[BELL]

3. The Heart of Perfect Understanding ♪

The Bodhisattva Avalokita,
while moving in the deep course of Perfect Understanding,
shed light on the Five Skandhas and found them equally empty.
After this penetration, he overcame ill-being.
[BELL]

Listen, Shariputra,
form is emptiness, and emptiness is form.

Form is not other than emptiness, emptiness is not other than form.
The same is true with feelings, perceptions, mental formations, and
consciousness.
[BELL]

Listen, Shariputra,
all dharmas are marked with emptiness.
They are neither produced nor destroyed,
neither defiled nor immaculate,
neither increasing nor decreasing.
Therefore in emptiness there is neither form, nor feelings, nor
perceptions,
nor mental formations, nor consciousness.
No eye, or ear, or nose, or tongue, or body, or mind.
No form, no sound, no smell, no taste, no touch, no object of mind.
No realms of elements (from eyes to mind consciousness),
no interdependent origins and no extinction of them
(from ignorance to death and decay).
No ill-being, no cause of ill-being, no end of ill-being, and no path.
No understanding and no attainment.
[BELL]

Because there is no attainment,
the Bodhisattvas, grounded in Perfect Understanding,
find no obstacles for their minds.
Having no obstacles, they overcome fear,
liberating themselves forever from illusion, realizing perfect nirvana.
All Buddhas in the past, present, and future,
thanks to this Perfect Understanding,
arrive at full, right, and universal enlightenment.
[BELL]

Therefore one should know
that Perfect Understanding is the highest mantra, the unequaled mantra,
the destroyer of ill-being, the incorruptible truth.
A mantra of Prajñaparamita should therefore be proclaimed:

Gate gate paragate parasamgate bodhi svaha
Gate gate paragate parasamgate bodhi svaha

Gate gate paragate parasamgate bodhi svaha
[BELL, BELL]

4. Introductory Words

Today the community has gathered to recite the Three Refuges, the Two
Promises, and the Five Mindfulness Trainings. First we will recite the Three
Refuges and the Two Promises. Young members of the community, please
come forward. Upon hearing the sound of the bell, please touch the Earth
three times to show your gratitude to the Buddha, the Dharma, and the
Sangha.
[BELL, BELL, BELL]
[YOUNG PEOPLE TOUCH THE EARTH THREE TIMES]

5. The Three Refuges

Young students of the Buddha, you have taken refuge in the Buddha, the
one who shows you the way in this life; in the Dharma, the way of understanding and love; and in the Sangha, the community that lives in harmony
and awareness. It is beneficial to recite the Three Refuges regularly. Will the
entire community please join the young people in reciting after me:

I take refuge in the Buddha,
the one who shows me the way in this life.
[BELL]

I take refuge in the Dharma,
the way of understanding and of love.
[BELL]

I take refuge in the Sangha,
the community that lives in harmony and awareness.
[BELL, BELL]

6. The Two Promises ♪
[FOR CHILDREN]

Young students of the Buddha, we have completed the recitation of the
Three Refuges. Now we will recite the Two Promises that you have made

with the Buddha, the Dharma, and the Sangha. Will the entire community please join the young people in reciting after me:

I vow to develop understanding, in order to live peacefully with people, animals, plants, and minerals.

This is the first promise you have made with the Buddha, our teacher. Have you tried to learn more about it and to keep your promise during the past two weeks?
[BELL]

I vow to develop my compassion, in order to protect the lives of people, animals, plants, and minerals.

This is the second promise you have made with the Buddha, our teacher. Have you tried to learn more about it and to keep your promise during the past two weeks?
[BELL]

Young students of the Enlightened One, understanding and love are the two most important teachings of the Buddha. If we do not make the effort to be open, to understand the suffering of other people, we will not be able to love them and to live in harmony with them. We should also try to understand and protect the lives of animals, plants, and minerals and live in harmony with them. If we cannot understand, we cannot love. The Buddha teaches us to look at living beings with the eyes of love and understanding. Please learn to practice this teaching.

Young people, upon hearing the sound of the bell, please stand up and touch the Earth three times to the Three Jewels.
[BELL, BELL, BELL]
[THE YOUNG PEOPLE TOUCH THE EARTH]
[THE YOUNG PEOPLE MAY NOW LEAVE THE HALL OR THEY MAY STAY TO LISTEN TO THE OTHER TRAININGS.]

7. SANGHAKARMAN PROCEDURE

Sanghakarman Master: Has the entire community assembled?
Sangha Convener: The entire community has assembled.

Sanghakarman Master: Is there harmony in the community?*
Sangha Convener: Yes, there is harmony.
Sanghakarman Master: Is there anyone not able to be present who has asked to be represented, and have they declared themselves to have done their best to study and practice the Five Mindfulness Trainings?
Sangha Convener: No, there is not.

or

Sangha Convener: Yes, [NAME], for health reasons, cannot be at the recitation today. She has asked [NAME] to represent her and she declares that she has done her best to study and practice the mindfulness trainings.
Sanghakarman Master: What is the reason for the community gathering today?
Sangha Convener: The community has gathered to practice the recitation of the Five Mindfulness Trainings.
Sanghakarman Master: Noble community, please listen. Today, [DATE], has been declared to be the Mindfulness Training Recitation Day. We have gathered at the appointed time. The noble community is ready to hear and recite the mindfulness trainings in an atmosphere of harmony, and the recitation can proceed. Is this statement clear and complete?
Everyone: Clear and complete.
[BELL]

8. Introductory Words

Brothers and Sisters, it is now time to recite the Five Mindfulness Trainings. [OPTIONAL: Please, those who have been ordained as Upasaka and Upasika kneel with joined palms in the direction of the Buddha, our teacher.]

Brothers and Sisters, please listen. The Five Mindfulness Trainings are the basis for a happy life. They have the capacity to protect life and to make it beautiful and worth living. They are also the door that opens to enlightenment and liberation. Please listen to each mindfulness training, and answer "yes" silently every time you see that you have made an effort to study, practice, and observe the mindfulness training read.

---

* The recitation of the Five Mindfulness Trainings should be done when the community is in harmony. The practice of Beginning Anew will help the community resolve conflicts.

9. RECITING THE FIVE MINDFULNESS TRAININGS

The First Mindfulness Training
Aware of the suffering caused by the destruction of life, I am committed to cultivating compassion and learning ways to protect the lives of people, animals, plants, and minerals. I am determined not to kill, not to let others kill, and not to support any act of killing in the world, in my thinking, and in my way of life.

This is the first of the Five Mindfulness Trainings. Have you made an effort to study, practice and observe it during the past two weeks?
[THREE BREATHS]
[BELL]*

The Second Mindfulness Training
Aware of the suffering caused by exploitation, social injustice, stealing, and oppression, I am committed to cultivating loving kindness and learning ways to work for the well-being of people, animals, plants, and minerals. I will practice generosity by sharing my time, energy, and material resources with those who are in real need. I am determined not to steal and not to possess anything that should belong to others. I will respect the property of others, but I will prevent others from profiting from human suffering or the suffering of other species on Earth.

This is the second of the Five Mindfulness Trainings. Have you made an effort to study, practice and observe it during the past two weeks?
[THREE BREATHS]
[BELL]

The Third Mindfulness Training
Aware of the suffering caused by sexual misconduct, I am committed to cultivating responsibility and learning ways to protect the safety and integrity of individuals, couples, families, and society. I am determined not to engage in sexual relations without love and a long-term commitment. To preserve the happiness of myself and others, I am determined to respect my commitments and the commitments of others. I will do everything in my power to

---

* After three breaths, the bell master "stops" the bell by holding the striker gently against the rim, thereby signaling the reader to continue with the next mindfulness training.

protect children from sexual abuse and to prevent couples and families from being broken by sexual misconduct.

This is the third of the Five Mindfulness Trainings. Have you made an effort to study, practice and observe it during the past two weeks?
[THREE BREATHS]
[BELL]

The Fourth Mindfulness Training

Aware of the suffering caused by unmindful speech and the inability to listen to others, I am committed to cultivating loving speech and deep listening in order to bring joy and happiness to others and relieve others of their suffering. Knowing that words can create happiness or suffering, I am determined to speak truthfully, with words that inspire self-confidence, joy, and hope. I will not spread news that I do not know to be certain and will not criticize or condemn things of which I am not sure. I will refrain from uttering words that can cause division or discord, or that can cause the family or the community to break. I am determined to make all efforts to reconcile and resolve all conflicts, however small.

This is the fourth of the Five Mindfulness Trainings. Have you made an effort to study, practice and observe it during the past two weeks?
[THREE BREATHS]
[BELL]

The Fifth Mindfulness Training

Aware of the suffering caused by unmindful consumption, I am committed to cultivating good health, both physical and mental, for myself, my family, and my society by practicing mindful eating, drinking, and consuming. I will ingest only items that preserve peace, well-being, and joy in my body, in my consciousness, and in the collective body and consciousness of my family and society. I am determined not to use alcohol or any other intoxicant or to ingest foods or other items that contain toxins, such as certain TV programs, magazines, books, films, and conversations. I am aware that to damage my body or my consciousness with these poisons is to betray my ancestors, my parents, my society, and future generations. I will work to transform violence, fear, anger, and confusion in myself and in society by practicing a diet for myself and for society. I understand that a proper diet is crucial for self-transformation and for the transformation of society.

This is the fifth of the Five Mindfulness Trainings. Have you made an effort to study, practice and observe it during the past two weeks?
[THREE BREATHS]
[BELL]

10. CONCLUDING WORDS

Brothers and Sisters, we have recited the Five Mindfulness Trainings, the foundation of happiness for the individual, the family, and society. We should recite them regularly so that our study and practice of the mindfulness trainings can deepen day by day.

Upon hearing the sound of the bell, please stand up and touch the Earth three times to show your gratitude to the Buddha, the Dharma, and the Sangha.
[BELL, BELL, BELL]

11. THE THREE REFUGES ♪

I take refuge in the Buddha,
the one who shows me the way in this life.
I take refuge in the Dharma,
the way of understanding and of love.
I take refuge in the Sangha,
the community that lives in harmony and awareness.
[BELL]

Dwelling in the refuge of Buddha,
I clearly see the path of light and beauty in the world.
Dwelling in the refuge of Dharma,
I learn to open many doors on the path of transformation.
Dwelling in the refuge of Sangha,
shining light that supports me, keeping my practice free of obstruction.
[BELL]

Taking refuge in the Buddha in myself,
I aspire to help all people recognize their own awakened nature,
realizing the Mind of Love.
Taking refuge in the Dharma in myself,
I aspire to help all people fully master the ways of practice

and walk together on the path of liberation.
Taking refuge in the Sangha in myself,
I aspire to help all people build Fourfold Communities
to embrace all beings and support their transformation.
[BELL, BELL]

12. Sharing the Merit ♪

Reciting the trainings, practicing the way of awareness
gives rise to benefits without limit.
We vow to share the fruits with all beings.
We vow to offer tribute to parents, teachers, friends, and numerous beings
who give guidance and support along the path.
[BELL, BELL, BELL]

Ceremony to Recite
the Fourteen Mindfulness Trainings ♫
[DURING THE FOURTEEN MINDFULNESS TRAININGS RECITATION CEREMONY, THE HEAD OF CEREMONY SHOULD BE SOMEONE WHO IS STABLE IN THE PRACTICE.]

1. Opening the Ceremony
Sitting Meditation [12 MINUTES]
Incense Offering [page 87]
Touching the Earth [page 88]

2. Opening Verse ♪
[BELL, BELL, BELL]

Namo Tassa Bhagavato Arahato Samma Sambuddhassa
Namo Tassa Bhagavato Arahato Samma Sambuddhassa
Namo Tassa Bhagavato Arahato Samma Sambuddhassa
[BELL]

The Dharma is deep and lovely.
We now have a chance to see, study, and practice it.
We vow to realize its true meaning.
[BELL]

3. The Heart of Perfect Understanding ♪
The Bodhisattva Avalokita,
while moving in the deep course of Perfect Understanding,
shed light on the Five Skandhas and found them equally empty.
After this penetration, he overcame ill-being.
[BELL]

Listen, Shariputra,
form is emptiness, and emptiness is form.
Form is not other than emptiness, emptiness is not other than form.
The same is true with feelings, perceptions, mental formations,
and consciousness.
[BELL]

Listen, Shariputra,
all dharmas are marked with emptiness.
They are neither produced nor destroyed,
neither defiled nor immaculate,
neither increasing nor decreasing.
Therefore in emptiness there is neither form, nor feelings,
nor perceptions,
nor mental formations, nor consciousness.
No eye, or ear, or nose, or tongue, or body, or mind.
No form, no sound, no smell, no taste, no touch, no object of mind.
No realms of elements (from eyes to mind consciousness),
no interdependent origins and no extinction of them
(from ignorance to death and decay).
No ill-being, no cause of ill-being, no end of ill-being, and no path.
No understanding and no attainment.
[BELL]

Because there is no attainment,
the Bodhisattvas, grounded in Perfect Understanding,
find no obstacles for their minds.
Having no obstacles, they overcome fear,
liberating themselves forever from illusion, realizing perfect nirvana.
All Buddhas in the past, present, and future,
thanks to this Perfect Understanding,
arrive at full, right, and universal enlightenment.
[BELL]

Therefore one should know
that Perfect Understanding is the highest mantra, the unequaled mantra,
the destroyer of ill-being, the incorruptible truth.
A mantra of Prajñaparamita should therefore be proclaimed:

Gate gate paragate parasamgate bodhi svaha
Gate gate paragate parasamgate bodhi svaha
Gate gate paragate parasamgate bodhi svaha
[BELL, BELL]

4. SANGHAKARMAN PROCEDURE

Sanghakarman Master: Has the entire community assembled?

Sangha Convener: The entire community has assembled.

Sanghakarman Master: Is there harmony in the community?*

Sangha Convener: Yes, there is harmony.

Sanghakarman Master: Is there anyone not able to be present who has asked to be represented, and have they declared themselves to have done their best to study and practice the mindfulness trainings?

Sangha Convener: No, there is not.

or

Sangha Convener: Yes, Brother (or Sister) [NAME], for health reasons, cannot be at the recitation today. He has asked Brother (or Sister) [NAME], to represent him, and he declares that he has done his best to study and practice the mindfulness trainings.

Sanghakarman Master: Why has the community assembled today?

Sangha Convener: The community has assembled to practice the recitation of the Fourteen Mindfulness Trainings of the Order of Interbeing.

Sanghakarman Master: Noble community, please listen. Today, [DATE], has been declared as the day to recite the Fourteen Mindfulness Trainings of the Order of Interbeing. The community has assembled at the appointed time and is ready to hear and to recite the Fourteen Mindfulness Trainings in an atmosphere of harmony. Thus, the recitation can proceed.

Is this statement clear and complete?

Everyone: Clear and complete.

[BELL]

5. INTRODUCTORY WORDS

Today I have been asked by the community to recite the Fourteen Mindfulness Trainings. I ask the community for spiritual support. Please, Brothers and Sisters, listen.

The Fourteen Mindfulness Trainings are the very essence of the Order of Interbeing. They are the torch lighting our path, the boat carrying us, the teacher guiding us. I ask the community to listen with a serene mind. Con-

---

* The recitation of the Fourteen Mindfulness Trainings should be done when the community is in harmony. The practice of Beginning Anew will help the community resolve conflicts.

sider the mindfulness trainings as a clear mirror in which to look at ourselves. Say yes, silently, every time you see that during the past two weeks you have made an effort to study, practice, and observe the mindfulness training read.
[BELL]

Brothers and Sisters, are you ready?
Everyone: [SILENTLY] I am ready.

These then are the Fourteen Mindfulness Trainings of the Order of Interbeing:

6. Reciting the Fourteen Mindfulness Trainings

The First Mindfulness Training: Openness
Aware of the suffering created by fanaticism and intolerance, we are determined not to be idolatrous about or bound to any doctrine, theory, or ideology, even Buddhist ones. Buddhist teachings are guiding means to help us learn to look deeply and to develop our understanding and compassion. They are not doctrines to fight, kill, or die for.

This is the First Mindfulness Training of the Order of Interbeing. Have we made an effort to study, practice, and observe it during the past two weeks?
[THREE BREATHS]
[BELL]

The Second Mindfulness Training: Nonattachment to Views
Aware of the suffering created by attachment to views and wrong perceptions, we are determined to avoid being narrow-minded and bound to present views. We shall learn and practice nonattachment from views in order to be open to others' insights and experiences. We are aware that the knowledge we presently possess is not changeless, absolute truth. Truth is found in life, and we will observe life within and around us in every moment, ready to learn throughout our lives.

This is the Second Mindfulness Training of the Order of Interbeing. Have we made an effort to study, practice, and observe it during the past two weeks?
[THREE BREATHS]

[BELL]

The Third Mindfulness Training: Freedom of Thought
Aware of the suffering brought about when we impose our views on others,
we are committed not to force others, even our children, by any means whatsoever — such as authority, threat, money, propaganda, or indoctrination —
to adopt our views. We will respect the right of others to be different and to
choose what to believe and how to decide. We will, however, help others renounce fanaticism and narrowness through compassionate dialogue.

This is the Third Mindfulness Training of the Order of Interbeing. Have we
made an effort to study, practice and observe it during the past two weeks?
[THREE BREATHS]
[BELL]

The Fourth Mindfulness Training: Awareness of Suffering
Aware that looking deeply at the nature of suffering can help us develop
compassion and find ways out of suffering, we are determined not to avoid
or close our eyes before suffering. We are committed to finding ways, including personal contact, images, and sounds, to be with those who suffer,
so we can understand their situation deeply and help them transform their
suffering into compassion, peace, and joy.

This is the Fourth Mindfulness Training of the Order of Interbeing. Have
we made an effort to study, practice and observe it during the past two
weeks?
[THREE BREATHS]
[BELL]

The Fifth Mindfulness Training: Simple, Healthy Living
Aware that true happiness is rooted in peace, solidity, freedom, and compassion, and not in wealth or fame, we are determined not to take as the aim of
our life fame, profit, wealth, or sensual pleasure, nor to accumulate wealth
while millions are hungry and dying. We are committed to living simply and
sharing our time, energy, and material resources with those in need. We will
practice mindful consuming, not using alcohol, drugs, or any other products
that bring toxins into our own and the collective body and consciousness.

This is the Fifth Mindfulness Training of the Order of Interbeing. Have we

made an effort to study, practice and observe it during the past two weeks?
[THREE BREATHS]
[BELL]

The Sixth Mindfulness Training: Dealing with Anger
Aware that anger blocks communication and creates suffering, we are determined to take care of the energy of anger when it arises and to recognize and transform the seeds of anger that lie deep in our consciousness. When anger comes up, we are determined not to do or say anything, but to practice mindful breathing or mindful walking and acknowledge, embrace, and look deeply into our anger. We will learn to look with the eyes of compassion at those we think are the cause of our anger.

This is the Sixth Mindfulness Training of the Order of Interbeing. Have we made an effort to study, practice and observe it during the past two weeks?
[THREE BREATHS]
[BELL]

The Seventh Mindfulness Training:
Dwelling Happily in the Present Moment
Aware that life is available only in the present moment and that it is possible to live happily in the here and now, we are committed to training ourselves to live deeply each moment of daily life. We will try not to lose ourselves in dispersion or be carried away by regrets about the past, worries about the future, or craving, anger, or jealousy in the present. We will practice mindful breathing to come back to what is happening in the present moment. We are determined to learn the art of mindful living by touching the wondrous, refreshing, and healing elements that are inside and around us, and by nourishing seeds of joy, peace, love, and understanding in ourselves, thus facilitating the work of transformation and healing in our consciousness.

This is the Seventh Mindfulness Training of the Order of Interbeing. Have we made an effort to study, practice and observe it during the past two weeks?
[THREE BREATHS]
[BELL]

The Eighth Mindfulness Training: Community and Communication
Aware that lack of communication always brings separation and suffering,

we are committed to training ourselves in the practice of compassionate listening and loving speech. We will learn to listen deeply without judging or reacting and refrain from uttering words that can create discord or cause the community to break. We will make every effort to keep communications open and to reconcile and resolve all conflicts, however small.

This is the Eighth Mindfulness Training of the Order of Interbeing. Have we made an effort to study, practice and observe it during the past two weeks?
[THREE BREATHS]
[BELL]

The Ninth Mindfulness Training: Truthful and Loving Speech

Aware that words can create suffering or happiness, we are committed to learning to speak truthfully and constructively, using only words that inspire hope and confidence. We are determined not to say untruthful things for the sake of personal interest or to impress people, nor to utter words that might cause division or hatred. We will not spread news that we do not know to be certain nor criticize or condemn things of which we are not sure. We will do our best to speak out about situations of injustice, even when doing so may threaten our safety.

This is the Ninth Mindfulness Training of the Order of Interbeing. Have we made an effort to study, practice and observe it during the past two weeks?
[THREE BREATHS]
[BELL]

The Tenth Mindfulness Training: Protecting the Sangha

Aware that the essence and aim of a Sangha is the practice of understanding and compassion, we are determined not to use the Buddhist community for personal gain or profit or transform our community into a political instrument. A spiritual community should, however, take a clear stand against oppression and injustice and should strive to change the situation without engaging in partisan conflicts.

This is the Tenth Mindfulness Training of the Order of Interbeing. Have we made an effort to study, practice and observe it during the past two weeks? [THREE BREATHS]
[BELL]

The Eleventh Mindfulness Training: Right Livelihood

Aware that great violence and injustice have been done to our environment and society, we are committed not to live with a vocation that is harmful to humans and nature. We will do our best to select a livelihood that helps realize our ideal of understanding and compassion. Aware of global economic, political, and social realities, we will behave responsibly as consumers and as citizens, not investing in companies that deprive others of their chance to live.

This is the Eleventh Mindfulness Training of the Order of Interbeing. Have we made an effort to study, practice and observe it during the past two weeks? [THREE BREATHS]
[BELL]

The Twelfth Mindfulness Training: Reverence for Life

Aware that much suffering is caused by war and conflict, we are determined to cultivate nonviolence, understanding, and compassion in our daily lives, to promote peace education, mindful mediation, and reconciliation within families, communities, nations, and in the world. We are determined not to kill and not to let others kill. We will diligently practice deep looking with our Sangha to discover better ways to protect life and prevent war.

This is the Twelfth Mindfulness Training of the Order of Interbeing. Have we made an effort to study, practice and observe it during the past two weeks? [THREE BREATHS]
[BELL]

The Thirteenth Mindfulness Training: Generosity

Aware of the suffering caused by exploitation, social injustice, stealing, and oppression, we are committed to cultivating loving kindness and learning ways to work for the well-being of people, animals, plants, and minerals. We will practice generosity by sharing our time, energy, and material resources with those who are in need. We are determined not to steal and not to possess anything that should belong to others. We will respect the property of others, but will try to prevent others from profiting from human suffering or the suffering of other beings.

This is the Thirteenth Mindfulness Training of the Order of Interbeing. Have we made an effort to study, practice and observe it during the past two weeks?
[THREE BREATHS]
[BELL]

The Fourteenth Mindfulness Training: Right Conduct
[FOR LAY MEMBERS]: Aware that sexual relations motivated by craving cannot dissipate the feeling of loneliness but will create more suffering, frustration, and isolation, we are determined not to engage in sexual relations without mutual understanding, love, and a long-term commitment. In sexual relations, we must be aware of future suffering that may be caused. We know that to preserve the happiness of ourselves and others, we must respect the rights and commitments of ourselves and others. We will do everything in our power to protect children from sexual abuse and to protect couples and families from being broken by sexual misconduct. We will treat our bodies with respect and preserve our vital energies (sexual, breath, spirit) for the realization of our bodhisattva ideal. We will be fully aware of the responsibility of bringing new lives into the world, and will meditate on the world into which we are bringing new beings.

[FOR MONASTIC MEMBERS]: Aware that the aspiration of a monk or a nun can only be realized when he or she wholly leaves behind the bonds of worldly love, we are committed to practicing chastity and to helping others protect themselves. We are aware that loneliness and suffering cannot be alleviated by the coming together of two bodies in a sexual relationship, but by the practice of true understanding and compassion. We know that a sexual relationship will destroy our life as a monk or a nun, will prevent us from realizing our ideal of serving living beings, and will harm others. We are determined not to suppress or mistreat our body or to look upon our body as only an instrument, but to learn to handle our body with respect. We are determined to preserve vital energies (sexual, breath, spirit) for the realization of our bodhisattva ideal.

This is the Fourteenth Mindfulness Training of the Order of Interbeing. Have we made an effort to study, practice and observe it during the past two weeks?
[THREE BREATHS]
[BELL]

7. CONCLUDING WORDS

Brothers and Sisters, I have recited the Fourteen Mindfulness Trainings of the Order of Interbeing as the community has wished. I thank all my Sisters and Brothers for helping me do it serenely.

8. THE THREE REFUGES ♪

I take refuge in the Buddha,
the one who shows me the way in this life.
I take refuge in the Dharma,
the way of understanding and of love.
I take refuge in the Sangha,
the community that lives in harmony and awareness.
[BELL]

Dwelling in the refuge of Buddha,
I clearly see the path of light and beauty in the world.
Dwelling in the refuge of Dharma,
I learn to open many doors on the path of transformation.
Dwelling in the refuge of Sangha,
shining light that supports me, keeping my practice free of obstruction.
[BELL]

Taking refuge in the Buddha in myself,
I aspire to help all people recognize their own awakened nature,
realizing the Mind of Love.
Taking refuge in the Dharma in myself,
I aspire to help all people fully master the ways of practice
and walk together on the path of liberation.
Taking refuge in the Sangha in myself,
I aspire to help all people build Fourfold Communities,
to embrace all beings and support their transformation.
[BELL, BELL]

9. SHARING THE MERIT ♪

Reciting the trainings, practicing the way of awareness
gives rise to benefits without limit.
We vow to share the fruits with all beings.
We vow to offer tribute to parents, teachers, friends,
and numerous beings
who give guidance and support along the path.
[BELL, BELL, BELL]

Ceremony to Transmit the Three Refuges, Two Promises, and Five Mindfulness Trainings ♪

[THIS CEREMONY MUST BE PRESIDED OVER BY SOMEONE WHO HAS RECEIVED THE FULL ORDINATION OF A MONK OR A NUN, OR A MEMBER OF THE ORDER OF INTERBEING WHO HAS RECEIVED THE TRANSMISSION OF THE LAMP AND IS A DHARMA TEACHER.]

1. Opening the Ceremony
Sitting Meditation [12 MINUTES]
Incense Offering [page 87]
Touching the Earth [page 88]

2. Opening Verse ♪
[BELL, BELL, BELL]

Namo Tassa Bhagavato Arahato Samma Sambuddhassa
Namo Tassa Bhagavato Arahato Samma Sambuddhassa
Namo Tassa Bhagavato Arahato Samma Sambuddhassa
[BELL]

The Dharma is deep and lovely.
We now have a chance to see, study, and practice it.
We vow to realize its true meaning.
[BELL]

3. The Heart of Perfect Understanding ♪
The Bodhisattva Avalokita,
while moving in the deep course of Perfect Understanding,
shed light on the Five Skandhas and found them equally empty.
After this penetration, he overcame ill-being.
[BELL]

Listen, Shariputra,
form is emptiness, and emptiness is form.
Form is not other than emptiness, emptiness is not other than form.

The same is true with feelings, perceptions, mental formations, and consciousness.
[BELL]

Listen, Shariputra,
all dharmas are marked with emptiness.
They are neither produced nor destroyed,
neither defiled nor immaculate,
neither increasing nor decreasing.
Therefore in emptiness there is neither form, nor feelings, nor perceptions, nor mental formations, nor consciousness.
No eye, or ear, or nose, or tongue, or body, or mind.
No form, no sound, no smell, no taste, no touch, no object of mind.
No realms of elements (from eyes to mind consciousness),
no interdependent origins and no extinction of them
(from ignorance to death and decay).
No ill-being, no cause of ill-being, no end of ill-being, and no path.
No understanding and no attainment.
[BELL]

Because there is no attainment,
the Bodhisattvas, grounded in Perfect Understanding,
find no obstacles for their minds.
Having no obstacles, they overcome fear,
liberating themselves forever from illusion, realizing perfect nirvana.
All Buddhas in the past, present, and future,
thanks to this Perfect Understanding,
arrive at full, right, and universal enlightenment.
[BELL]

Therefore one should know
that Perfect Understanding is the highest mantra, the unequaled mantra,
the destroyer of ill-being, the incorruptible truth.
A mantra of Prajñaparamita should therefore be proclaimed:

Gate gate paragate parasamgate bodhi svaha
Gate gate paragate parasamgate bodhi svaha
Gate gate paragate parasamgate bodhi svaha
[BELL, BELL]

4. Sanghakarman Procedure

Sanghakarman Master: Has the entire community assembled?

Sangha Convener: The entire community has assembled.

Sanghakarman Master: Is there harmony in the community?*

Sangha Convener: Yes, there is harmony.

Sanghakarman Master: Why has the community assembled today?

Sangha Convener: The community has assembled to perform the Sanghakarman of transmitting the Three Refuges, Two Promises, and Five Mindfulness Trainings.

Sanghakarman Master: Noble community, today, [DATE], has been chosen as the day to transmit the Three Refuges, Two Promises, and Five Mindfulness Trainings. The community has assembled at the appointed time and is ready to transmit and receive the Three Refuges, Two Promises, and Five Mindfulness Trainings in an atmosphere of harmony. Thus, the transmission can proceed.

Is this statement clear and complete?

Everyone: Clear and complete.

[REPEAT QUESTION AND ANSWER THREE TIMES]

[BELL]

5. Introductory Words

Today the community has gathered to give spiritual support to our brothers and sisters [NAMES] who will go for refuge to the Three Jewels and make the vow to practice the Two Promises and Five Mindfulness Trainings. Will the entire community please enjoy your breathing and remain mindful when you hear the three sounds of the bell. The sound of the bell is the voice of the Buddha, bringing us back to our true selves.

[BELL, BELL, BELL]

6. Touching the Earth in Gratitude

Will our brothers and sisters who are receiving the promises and the mindfulness trainings please come forward with joined palms and stand before the Three Jewels? If there is anyone whose name was not read and who

---

* The transmission of the Five Mindfulness Trainings should be done when the community is in harmony. The practice of Beginning Anew will help the community resolve conflicts.

wishes to receive the Three Refuges, Two Promises, and Five Mindfulness Trainings, please stand up now and say your name clearly, then come forward before the Three Jewels.

Ordinees, on hearing the sound of the bell, after the recitation of each line, please touch the Earth one time.

In gratitude to our parents who have given us life,
we touch the Earth before the Three Jewels.
[BELL]

In gratitude to our teachers who show us how to love,
understand, and live in the present moment,
we touch the Earth before the Three Jewels.
[BELL]

In gratitude to our friends who guide us on the path
and support us in difficult moments,
we touch the Earth before the Three Jewels.
[BELL]

In gratitude to all species in the animal, plant, and mineral worlds,
who support our life and make our world beautiful,
we touch the Earth before the Three Jewels.
[BELL, BELL]

7. THE THREE REFUGES

Today the community has gathered to give support to those who will vow to go for refuge to the Three Jewels and receive and practice the Two Promises and Five Mindfulness Trainings. You have had the chance to learn about and observe the way of understanding and love that has been handed down to us by teachers over many centuries, and today you have made the decision to go for refuge to the Three Jewels and receive the Two Promises and Five Mindfulness Trainings.

To take refuge in the Three Jewels is to turn to the Buddha, the Dharma, and the Sangha for protection. The Buddha, the Dharma, and the Sangha are Three Precious Gems. To take refuge in the Buddha is to take refuge in the Awakened One who has the ability to show us the way in this life. To take refuge in the Dharma is to take refuge in the way of understanding, love, and compassion. To take refuge in the Sangha is to take refuge in a community that practices according to the path of understanding, love, and compassion and lives in an awakened way.

The Buddha, the Dharma, and the Sangha are present in every quarter of the universe as well as in every person and all other species. To go for refuge to the Buddha, the Dharma, and the Sangha also means to have confidence in our own ability to be awakened, to develop and manifest understanding and love in ourselves, and to practice the Way for ourselves and for our family, our community, and society. Will the brothers and sisters please repeat after me the Three Great Refuge Vows:

I take refuge in the Buddha,
the one who shows me the way in this life.
[BELL]
[ORDINEES TOUCH THE EARTH ONE TIME]

I take refuge in the Dharma,
the way of understanding and love.
[BELL]
[ORDINEES TOUCH THE EARTH ONE TIME]

I take refuge in the Sangha,
the community that lives in harmony and awareness.
[BELL, BELL]
[ORDINEES TOUCH THE EARTH ONE TIME]

Brothers and Sisters, you have formally received the Three Refuges. Receiving them will enable you to see the Three Jewels in your own heart and bring them into your daily life. Today you have become students of the Awakened One and have made the vow to live an awakened life. Beginning from today you will apply your mind to learning about and practicing the way of understanding, love, and compassion, which means to nourish the ability to love and understand within yourselves. You will also go for refuge to your Sangha in order to learn and practice, and you will attend days and retreats of mindfulness and recitations of the trainings and other activities of your Sangha.

The transmitter of the Refuges to you is [NAME OF TRANSMITTER], and your Dharma name will be chosen by him (or her). You should take refuge in your teacher and your Sangha to learn and practice the path.

8. THE TWO PROMISES (FOR CHILDREN)

Young people, you have received the Three Refuges into your heart. Now you have become students of the Awakened Ones, and will live in an awakened way. Now you are going to receive the Two Promises that you will make with the Buddha-seed in yourself. These two promises will help you be aware of the suffering and the happiness of people, animals, plants, and minerals. You will be able to look after and preserve this planet Earth. Will the entire community please join the young people in repeating after me:

I vow to develop understanding
in order to life peacefully
with people, animals, plants, and minerals.

This is the first Promise. Do you promise to the Buddha-seed within you that you will do your best to practice it?
[BELL]

I vow to develop my compassion
in order to protect the lives
of people, animals, plants, and minerals.

This is the second Promise. Do you promise to the Buddha-seed within you that you will do your best to practice it?
[BELL]

Young students of the Enlightened One, understanding and love are the two most important teachings of the Buddha. If we try to be open and to understand the difficulties of other people, we will be able to love them and to live in harmony with them. The same is true for animals, plants, and minerals. If we cannot understand others then we cannot love. The Buddha teaches us to look at living beings with the eyes of love and understanding. Please learn to practice this teaching.

Young people, upon hearing the sound of the bell, please stand up and touch the Earth three times to the Three Jewels, and then, you can go back to your seat.
[BELL, BELL, BELL]
[THE YOUNG PEOPLE TOUCH THE EARTH]

9. Reading the Two Promises Certificate

[THE TRANSMITTER READS THE CERTIFICATE ON WHICH ARE WRITTEN THE TWO
PROMISES, THE DHARMA NAME OF THE CHILD, AND THE NAME OF HIS OR HER
TEACHER. THEN THE CERTIFICATE IS GIVEN TO THE YOUNG PERSON.]

Brothers and Sisters I will now read the Mindfulness Trainings Certificate.
When you hear your name, please come forward to receive your certificate.
[THE YOUNG PEOPLE MAY NOW LEAVE THE HALL OR THEY MAY STAY TO LISTEN TO
THE OTHER TRAININGS.]

10. Transmitting the Five Mindfulness Trainings

Brothers and Sisters, now is the time to transmit the Five Mindfulness
Trainings. They have the capacity to protect life and make it beautiful. The
Five Mindfulness Trainings encourage us in the direction of peace, joy, liberation, and awakening. They are the foundation for individual happiness
and the happiness of the family and society. If we practice according to the
Five Mindfulness Trainings, we are already on the path of a bodhisattva. The
Five Mindfulness Trainings protect us and help us avoid making mistakes
and creating suffering, fear, and despair. Practicing these trainings, we are
able to build peace and happiness in ourselves and our family, and joy and
peace in our society.

I will now recite the Five Mindfulness Trainings. Listen carefully with a
calm and clear mind. Say, "Yes, I do" every time you see you have the capacity to receive, learn, and practice the mindfulness training read.
[BELL]

Sisters and Brothers, are you ready?
Ordinees: Yes, I am ready.

The First Mindfulness Training
Aware of the suffering caused by the destruction of life, I am committed to
cultivating compassion and learning ways to protect the lives of people, animals, plants, and minerals. I am determined not to kill, not to let others kill,
and not to support any act of killing in the world, in my thinking, and in
my way of life.

This is the first of the Five Mindfulness Trainings. Do you make the commitment to receive, study, and practice it?

Ordinees: Yes, I do.
[BELL]
[ORDINEES TOUCH THE EARTH ONE TIME]

The Second Mindfulness Training

Aware of the suffering caused by exploitation, social injustice, stealing, and oppression, I am committed to cultivating loving kindness and learning ways to work for the well-being of people, animals, plants, and minerals. I will practice generosity by sharing my time, energy, and material resources with those who are in real need. I am determined not to steal and not to possess anything that should belong to others. I will respect the property of others, but I will prevent others from profiting from human suffering or the suffering of other species on Earth.

This is the second of the Five Mindfulness Trainings. Do you make the commitment to receive, study, and practice it?

Ordinees: Yes, I do.
[BELL]
[ORDINEES TOUCH THE EARTH ONE TIME]

The Third Mindfulness Training

Aware of the suffering caused by sexual misconduct, I am committed to cultivating responsibility and learning ways to protect the safety and integrity of individuals, couples, families, and society. I am determined not to engage in sexual relations without love and a long-term commitment. To preserve the happiness of myself and others, I am determined to respect my commitments and the commitments of others. I will do everything in my power to protect children from sexual abuse and to prevent couples and families from being broken by sexual misconduct.

This is the third of the Five Mindfulness Trainings. Do you make the commitment to receive, study, and practice it?

Ordinees: Yes, I do.
[BELL]
[ORDINEES TOUCH THE EARTH ONE TIME]

The Fourth Mindfulness Training

Aware of the suffering caused by unmindful speech and the inability to listen to others, I am committed to cultivating loving speech and deep listening in order to bring joy and happiness to others and relieve others of their suffering. Knowing that words can create happiness or suffering, I am determined to speak truthfully, with words that inspire self-confidence, joy, and hope. I will not spread news that I do not know to be certain and will not criticize or condemn things of which I am not sure. I will refrain from uttering words that can cause division or discord, or that can cause the family or the community to break. I am determined to make all efforts to reconcile and resolve all conflicts, however small.

This is the fourth of the Five Mindfulness Trainings. Do you make the commitment to receive, study, and practice it?

Ordinees: Yes, I do.
[BELL]
[ORDINEES TOUCH THE EARTH ONE TIME]

The Fifth Mindfulness Training

Aware of the suffering caused by unmindful consumption, I am committed to cultivating good health, both physical and mental, for myself, my family, and my society by practicing mindful eating, drinking, and consuming. I will ingest only items that preserve peace, well-being, and joy in my body, in my consciousness, and in the collective body and consciousness of my family and society. I am determined not to use alcohol or any other intoxicant or to ingest foods or other items that contain toxins, such as certain TV programs, magazines, books, films, and conversations. I am aware that to damage my body or my consciousness with these poisons is to betray my ancestors, my parents, my society, and future generations. I will work to transform violence, fear, anger, and confusion in myself and in society by practicing a diet for myself and for society. I understand that a proper diet is crucial for self-transformation and for the transformation of society.

This is the fifth of the Five Mindfulness Trainings. Do you make the commitment to receive, study, and practice it?

Ordinees: Yes, I do.
[BELL]
[ORDINEES TOUCH THE EARTH ONE TIME]

Brothers and Sisters, you have received the Five Mindfulness Trainings which are the foundation of happiness in the family and in society. They are the basis for the aspiration to help others. You should recite the trainings often, at least once a month, so that your understanding and practice of the Five Mindfulness Trainings can grow deeper every day.

A mindfulness trainings recitation ceremony can be organized in a practice center, with your local Sangha, or at home with friends. If you do not recite the trainings at least once in three months, you lose the transmission and today's ceremony will be nullified. Brothers and Sisters, as students of the Awakened One, you should be energetic in practicing the way the Buddha has taught to create peace and happiness for yourselves and all species. Upon hearing the sound of the bell, please stand up and bow deeply three times to show your gratitude to the Three Jewels.

[BELL, BELL, BELL]

[ORDINEES TOUCH THE EARTH THREE TIMES]

11. Reading the Mindfulness Trainings Certificate

[THE TRANSMITTER OF THE MINDFULNESS TRAININGS READS THE CERTIFICATE ON WHICH ARE WRITTEN THE DHARMA NAME OF THE ORDINEE AND THE NAME OF HIS OR HER TEACHER. EACH ORDINEE KNEELS WHILE LISTENING TO THE READING OF HIS OR HER CERTIFICATE, AFTER WHICH THE CERTIFICATE IS GIVEN TO HIM OR HER.]

Brothers and Sisters, I will now read the Mindfulness Trainings Certificate. When you hear your name, please come forward to receive your certificate.

12. Closing the Ceremony

Noble community, to lend spiritual support to our brothers and sisters who have been ordained, let us recite the closing verses in mindfulness:

13. The Three Refuges ♪

I take refuge in the Buddha,
the one who shows me the way in this life.
I take refuge in the Dharma,
the way of understanding and of love.
I take refuge in the Sangha,
the community that lives in harmony and awareness.

[BELL]

Dwelling in the refuge of Buddha,
I clearly see the path of light and beauty in the world.
Dwelling in the refuge of Dharma,
I learn to open many doors on the path of transformation.
Dwelling in the refuge of Sangha,
shining light that supports me, keeping my practice free of obstruction.
[BELL]

Taking refuge in the Buddha in myself,
I aspire to help all people recognize their own awakened nature,
realizing the Mind of Love.
Taking refuge in the Dharma in myself,
I aspire to help all people fully master the ways of practice
and walk together on the path of liberation.
Taking refuge in the Sangha in myself,
I aspire to help all people build Fourfold Communities,
to embrace all beings and support their transformation.
[BELL, BELL]

14. Sharing the Merit ♪

Transmitting the trainings, practicing the way of awareness
gives rise to benefits without limit.
We vow to share the fruits with all beings.
We vow to offer tribute to parents, teachers, friends,
and numerous beings
who give guidance and support along the path.
[BELL, BELL, BELL]

CEREMONY TO TRANSMIT
THE FOURTEEN MINDFULNESS TRAININGS ॐ

[THE FOURTEEN MINDFULNESS TRAININGS CAN ONLY BE TRANSMITTED
IN THE NAME OF VENERABLE THICH NHAT HANH BY A DHARMA TEACHER
OF FIVE YEARS' STANDING IN THE ORDER OF INTERBEING, ASSISTED
BY THREE ORDAINED MEMBERS OF THE CORE COMMUNITY; AND CAN BE
OFFERED ONLY TO THOSE WHO HAVE COMPLETED A MINIMUM ONE-YEAR
MENTORING PROGRAM PREPARING THEM TO ENTER THE CORE ORDER
OF INTERBEING. ALL MEMBERS OF THE SANGHA, WHETHER OF THE CORE
OR EXTENDED COMMUNITY, ARE INVITED TO ATTEND.]

1. OPENING THE CEREMONY

Sitting Meditation [12 MINUTES]
Incense Offering [page 87]
Touching the Earth [page 88]

2. OPENING VERSE ♪

[BELL, BELL, BELL]

Namo Tassa Bhagavato Arahato Samma Sambuddhassa
Namo Tassa Bhagavato Arahato Samma Sambuddhassa
Namo Tassa Bhagavato Arahato Samma Sambuddhassa
[BELL]

The Dharma is deep and lovely.
We now have a chance to see, study, and practice it.
We vow to realize its true meaning.
[BELL]

3. THE HEART OF PERFECT UNDERSTANDING ♪

The Bodhisattva Avalokita,
while moving in the deep course of Perfect Understanding,
shed light on the Five Skandhas and found them equally empty.
After this penetration, he overcame ill-being.
[BELL]

Listen, Shariputra,
form is emptiness, and emptiness is form.
Form is not other than emptiness, emptiness is not other than form.
The same is true with feelings, perceptions, mental formations,
and consciousness.
[BELL]

Listen, Shariputra,
all dharmas are marked with emptiness.
They are neither produced nor destroyed,
neither defiled nor immaculate,
neither increasing nor decreasing.
Therefore in emptiness there is neither form, nor feelings,
nor perceptions, nor mental formations, nor consciousness.
No eye, or ear, or nose, or tongue, or body, or mind.
No form, no sound, no smell, no taste, no touch, no object of mind.
No realms of elements (from eyes to mind consciousness),
no interdependent origins and no extinction of them
(from ignorance to death and decay).
No ill-being, no cause of ill-being, no end of ill-being, and no path.
No understanding and no attainment.
[BELL]

Because there is no attainment,
the Bodhisattvas, grounded in Perfect Understanding,
find no obstacles for their minds.
Having no obstacles, they overcome fear,
liberating themselves forever from illusion, realizing perfect nirvana.
All Buddhas in the past, present, and future,
thanks to this Perfect Understanding,
arrive at full, right, and universal enlightenment.
[BELL]

Therefore one should know
that Perfect Understanding is the highest mantra, the unequaled mantra,
the destroyer of ill-being, the incorruptible truth.
A mantra of Prajñaparamita should therefore be proclaimed:

Gate gate paragate parasamgate bodhi svaha
Gate gate paragate parasamgate bodhi svaha
Gate gate paragate parasamgate bodhi svaha
[BELL, BELL]

4. SANGHAKARMAN PROCEDURE

Sanghakarman Master: Has the entire community assembled?

Sangha Convener: The entire community has assembled.

Sanghakarman Master: Is there harmony in the community?*

Sangha Convener: Yes, there is harmony.

Sanghakarman Master: Why has the community assembled today?

Sangha Convener: The community has assembled to perform the Sanghakarman of transmitting the Fourteen Mindfulness Trainings of the Order of Interbeing.

Sanghakarman Master: Noble Order of Interbeing, please listen. Today, [DATE], has been chosen as the day to transmit the Fourteen Mindfulness Trainings of the Order of Interbeing. The community has assembled at the appointed time and is ready to transmit and receive the Fourteen Mindfulness Trainings in an atmosphere of harmony. Thus, the transmission can proceed.

Is this statement clear and complete?

Everyone: Clear and complete.

Sanghakarman Master: This is the proposal. If you agree with the proposal, please remain silent. If you do not agree, please speak out.

[THREE BREATHS]

This is the first time of asking.

If you agree with the proposal, please remain silent. If you do not agree, please speak out.

[THREE BREATHS]

This is the second time of asking.

If you agree with the proposal, please remain silent. If you do not agree, please speak out.

[THREE BREATHS]

This is the third time of asking.

[BELL]

---

* The transmission of the Fourteen Mindfulness Trainings should be done when the community is in harmony. The practice of Beginning Anew will help the community resolve conflicts.

5. Touching the Earth in Gratitude

Will the Ordinees with the following names please come forward with joined palms and stand before the Three Jewels.
[NAMES OF THE ORDINEES ARE READ]

On hearing the sound of the bell, after the recitation of each line, touch the Earth one time.

In gratitude to our father and mother, who have given us life,
we bow deeply before the Three Jewels in the Ten Directions.
[BELL]

In gratitude to our teachers, who have shown us how to understand, love, and live deeply the present moment, we bow deeply before the Three Jewels in the Ten Directions.
[BELL]

In gratitude to our friends, who guide us and support us in difficult moments,
we bow deeply before the Three Jewels in the Ten Directions.
[BELL]

In gratitude to all beings in the animal, plant, and mineral worlds,
we bow deeply before the Three Jewels in the Ten Directions.
[BELL, BELL]

6. Introductory Words

Today the community has gathered to give spiritual support to our brothers and sisters [NAMES] at the solemn moment when they will undertake to receive and observe the Fourteen Mindfulness Trainings of the Order of Interbeing and enter the core community of the Order of Interbeing.

Ordinees, please listen. Following in the steps of the Bodhisattvas as your teachers and companions on the path, you have made the aspiration to receive and observe the mindfulness trainings of the Order of Interbeing. You have given rise to the seed of bodhicitta, the Mind of Love. You have made it your aspiration to develop this seed. Your own awakening and liberation, as well as the liberation and awakening of all other species, have now become your highest career. Brothers and Sisters in the community, please establish your mindfulness by enjoying your breathing, so that you may be truly present and give support to the seed of bodhicitta, the Mind of Love in the Ordinees. With your support, they will develop this seed solidly and courageously so that it will become indestructible.

Ordinees, this is the solemn moment for receiving the Fourteen Mindfulness Trainings of the Order of Interbeing. Listen carefully, with a clear and concentrated mind, to each mindfulness training as it is read, and answer, "Yes, I do," clearly every time you see that you have the intention and capacity to receive, study, and practice the mindfulness training that has been read.

[BELL]

Brothers and Sisters, are you ready?
Ordinees: Yes, I am ready.
These then are the Fourteen Mindfulness Trainings of the Order of Interbeing:

7. Transmitting the Fourteen Mindfulness Trainings

The First Mindfulness Training: Openness
Aware of the suffering created by fanaticism and intolerance, we are determined not to be idolatrous about or bound to any doctrine, theory, or ideology, even Buddhist ones. Buddhist teachings are guiding means to help us learn to look deeply and to develop our understanding and compassion. They are not doctrines to fight, kill, or die for.

This is the First Mindfulness Training of the Order of Interbeing. Do you make the commitment to receive, study, and practice it?
Ordinees: Yes, I do.
[BELL] *
[ORDINEES TOUCH THE EARTH ONE TIME]

The Second Mindfulness Training: Nonattachment to Views
Aware of the suffering created by attachment to views and wrong percep-

---

* After three breaths, the bell master "stops" the bell by holding the striker gently against the rim, thereby signaling the reader to continue with the next training.

tions, we are determined to avoid being narrow-minded and bound to present views. We shall learn and practice nonattachment from views in order to be open to others' insights and experiences. We are aware that the knowledge we presently possess is not changeless, absolute truth. Truth is found in life, and we will observe life within and around us in every moment, ready to learn throughout our lives.

This is the Second Mindfulness Training of the Order of Interbeing. Do you make the commitment to receive, study, and practice it?
Ordinees: Yes, I do.
[BELL]
[ORDINEES TOUCH THE EARTH ONE TIME]

The Third Mindfulness Training: Freedom of Thought
Aware of the suffering brought about when we impose our views on others, we are committed not to force others, even our children, by any means whatsoever — such as authority, threat, money, propaganda, or indoctrination — to adopt our views. We will respect the right of others to be different and to choose what to believe and how to decide. We will, however, help others renounce fanaticism and narrowness through compassionate dialogue.

This is the Third Mindfulness Training of the Order of Interbeing. Do you make the commitment to receive, study, and practice it?
Ordinees: Yes, I do.
[BELL]
[ORDINEES TOUCH THE EARTH ONE TIME]

The Fourth Mindfulness Training: Awareness of Suffering
Aware that looking deeply at the nature of suffering can help us develop compassion and find ways out of suffering, we are determined not to avoid or close our eyes before suffering. We are committed to finding ways, including personal contact, images, and sounds, to be with those who suffer, so we can understand their situation deeply and help them transform their suffering into compassion, peace, and joy.

This is the Fourth Mindfulness Training of the Order of Interbeing. Do you make the commitment to receive, study, and practice it?

Ordinees: Yes, I do.

[BELL]

[ORDINEES TOUCH THE EARTH ONE TIME]

The Fifth Mindfulness Training: Simple, Healthy Living
Aware that true happiness is rooted in peace, solidity, freedom, and compassion, and not in wealth or fame, we are determined not to take as the aim of our life fame, profit, wealth, or sensual pleasure, nor to accumulate wealth while millions are hungry and dying. We are committed to living simply and sharing our time, energy, and material resources with those in need. We will practice mindful consuming, not using alcohol, drugs, or any other products that bring toxins into our own and the collective body and consciousness.

This is the Fifth Mindfulness Training of the Order of Interbeing. Do you make the commitment to receive, study, and practice it?

Ordinees: Yes, I do.

[BELL]

[ORDINEES TOUCH THE EARTH ONE TIME]

The Sixth Mindfulness Training: Dealing with Anger
Aware that anger blocks communication and creates suffering, we are determined to take care of the energy of anger when it arises and to recognize and transform the seeds of anger that lie deep in our consciousness. When anger comes up, we are determined not to do or say anything, but to practice mindful breathing or mindful walking and acknowledge, embrace, and look deeply into our anger. We will learn to look with the eyes of compassion at those we think are the cause of our anger.

This is the Sixth Mindfulness Training of the Order of Interbeing. Do you make the commitment to receive, study, and practice it?

Ordinees: Yes, I do.

[BELL]

[ORDINEES TOUCH THE EARTH ONE TIME]

The Seventh Mindfulness Training:
Dwelling Happily in the Present Moment
Aware that life is available only in the present moment and that it is possible to live happily in the here and now, we are committed to training ourselves to live deeply each moment of daily life. We will try not to lose ourselves in dispersion or be carried away by regrets about the past, worries about the future, or craving, anger, or jealousy in the present. We will practice mindful breathing to come back to what is happening in the present moment. We are determined to learn the art of mindful living by touching the wondrous, refreshing, and healing elements that are inside and around us, and by nourishing seeds of joy, peace, love, and understanding in ourselves, thus facilitating the work of transformation and healing in our consciousness.

This is the Seventh Mindfulness Training of the Order of Interbeing. Do you make the commitment to receive, study, and practice it?

Ordinees: Yes, I do.
[BELL]
[ORDINEES TOUCH THE EARTH ONE TIME]

The Eighth Mindfulness Training: Community and Communication
Aware that lack of communication always brings separation and suffering, we are committed to training ourselves in the practice of compassionate listening and loving speech. We will learn to listen deeply without judging or reacting and refrain from uttering words that can create discord or cause the community to break. We will make every effort to keep communications open and to reconcile and resolve all conflicts, however small.

This is the Eighth Mindfulness Training of the Order of Interbeing. Do you make the commitment to receive, study, and practice it?

Ordinees: Yes, I do.
[BELL]
[ORDINEES TOUCH THE EARTH ONE TIME]

The Ninth Mindfulness Training: Truthful and Loving Speech
Aware that words can create suffering or happiness, we are committed to learning to speak truthfully and constructively, using only words that in-

spire hope and confidence. We are determined not to say untruthful things for the sake of personal interest or to impress people, nor to utter words that might cause division or hatred. We will not spread news that we do not know to be certain nor criticize or condemn things of which we are not sure. We will do our best to speak out about situations of injustice, even when doing so may threaten our safety.

This is the Ninth Mindfulness Training of the Order of Interbeing. Do you make the commitment to receive, study, and practice it?

Ordinees: Yes, I do.
[BELL]
[ORDINEES TOUCH THE EARTH ONE TIME]

The Tenth Mindfulness Training: Protecting the Sangha
Aware that the essence and aim of a Sangha is the practice of understanding and compassion, we are determined not to use the Buddhist community for personal gain or profit or transform our community into a political instrument. A spiritual community should, however, take a clear stand against oppression and injustice and should strive to change the situation without engaging in partisan conflicts.

This is the Tenth Mindfulness Training of the Order of Interbeing. Do you make the commitment to receive, study, and practice it?

Ordinees: Yes, I do.
[BELL]
[ORDINEES TOUCH THE EARTH ONE TIME]

The Eleventh Mindfulness Training: Right Livelihood
Aware that great violence and injustice have been done to our environment and society, we are committed not to live with a vocation that is harmful to humans and nature. We will do our best to select a livelihood that helps realize our ideal of understanding and compassion. Aware of global economic, political, and social realities, we will behave responsibly as consumers and as citizens, not investing in companies that deprive others of their chance to live.

This is the Eleventh Mindfulness Training of the Order of Interbeing. Do you make the commitment to receive, study, and practice it?

Ordinees: Yes, I do.
[BELL]
[ORDINEES TOUCH THE EARTH ONE TIME]

The Twelfth Mindfulness Training: Reverence for Life

Aware that much suffering is caused by war and conflict, we are determined to cultivate nonviolence, understanding, and compassion in our daily lives, to promote peace education, mindful mediation, and reconciliation within families, communities, nations, and in the world. We are determined not to kill and not to let others kill. We will diligently practice deep looking with our Sangha to discover better ways to protect life and prevent war.

This is the Twelfth Mindfulness Training of the Order of Interbeing. Do you make the commitment to receive, study, and practice it?

Ordinees: Yes, I do.
[BELL]
[ORDINEES TOUCH THE EARTH ONE TIME]

The Thirteenth Mindfulness Training: Generosity

Aware of the suffering caused by exploitation, social injustice, stealing, and oppression, we are committed to cultivating loving kindness and learning ways to work for the well-being of people, animals, plants, and minerals. We will practice generosity by sharing our time, energy, and material resources with those who are in need. We are determined not to steal and not to possess anything that should belong to others. We will respect the property of others, but will try to prevent others from profiting from human suffering or the suffering of other beings.

This is the Thirteenth Mindfulness Training of the Order of Interbeing. Do you make the commitment to receive, study, and practice it?

Ordinees: Yes, I do.
[BELL]
[ORDINEES TOUCH THE EARTH ONE TIME]

The Fourteenth Mindfulness Training: Right Conduct

[FOR LAY MEMBERS]: Aware that sexual relations motivated by craving cannot dissipate the feeling of loneliness but will create more suffering, frustration, and isolation, we are determined not to engage in sexual relations without mutual understanding, love, and a long-term commitment. In sexual relations, we must be aware of future suffering that may be caused. We know that to preserve the happiness of ourselves and others, we must respect the rights and commitments of ourselves and others. We will do everything in our power to protect children from sexual abuse and to protect couples and families from being broken by sexual misconduct. We will treat our bodies with respect and preserve our vital energies (sexual, breath, spirit) for the realization of our bodhisattva ideal. We will be fully aware of the responsibility of bringing new lives into the world, and will meditate on the world into which we are bringing new beings.

[FOR MONASTIC MEMBERS]: Aware that the aspiration of a monk or a nun can only be realized when he or she wholly leaves behind the bonds of worldly love, we are committed to practicing chastity and to helping others protect themselves. We are aware that loneliness and suffering cannot be alleviated by the coming together of two bodies in a sexual relationship, but by the practice of true understanding and compassion. We know that a sexual relationship will destroy our life as a monk or a nun, will prevent us from realizing our ideal of serving living beings, and will harm others. We are determined not to suppress or mistreat our body or to look upon our body as only an instrument, but to learn to handle our body with respect. We are determined to preserve vital energies (sexual, breath, spirit) for the realization of our bodhisattva ideal.

This is the Fourteenth Mindfulness Training of the Order of Interbeing. Do you make the commitment to receive, study, and practice it?

Ordinees: Yes, I do.
[BELL]
[ORDINEES TOUCH THE EARTH ONE TIME]

8. Concluding Words

Ordinees, you have received the Fourteen Mindfulness Trainings of the Order of Interbeing. You have taken the first step on the path of the Bodhisattvas: the path of great understanding of Bodhisattva Manjushri that puts an end to countless wrong perceptions, prejudice, and discrimination; the path of great compassion of Bodhisattva Avalokiteshvara, who loves, values, and protects the life of all species and listens deeply to the cries of all species far and near in order to help them; the path of great action of Bodhisattva Samantabhadra, who takes every opportunity to create love, understanding, and harmony in the world.

Brothers and Sisters in the community, with one heart please give your spiritual support to the Ordinees in this present moment to help them now and in the future. Brothers and Sisters, the Buddhas and Bodhisattvas will be with you on your path of practice. When you hear the sound of the bell, please stand up and bow deeply three times to show your gratitude to the Three Jewels. Noble community, please concentrate your mind in order to recite the name of the Buddha so that the mindfulness trainings body of the Ordinees may be courageous, strong, and may endure.

9. Invocation of the Buddhas and Bodhisattvas ♪
[ORDINEES TOUCH THE EARTH THREE TIMES AS THE COMMUNITY RECITES EACH NAME THREE TIMES.]

Namo Shakyamunaye Buddhaya
[Homage to Shakyamuni Buddha, the Fully Awakened One]
[BELL]

Namo Amitabhaya Buddhaya
[Homage to the Buddha of Infinite Light]
[BELL]

Namo Manjushriye Bodhisattvaya
[Homage to Manjushri, Bodhisattva of Great Understanding]
[BELL]

Namo Samantabhadraya Bodhisattvaya
[Homage to Samantabhadra, Bodhisattva of Great Action]
[BELL]

Namo Avalokiteshvaraya Bodhisattvaya
[Homage to Avalokiteshvara, Bodhisattva of Great Compassion]
[BELL]

Namo Kshitigarbhaya Bodhisattvaya
[Homage to Kshitigarbha, Bodhisattva of Great Aspiration]
[BELL, BELL]

10. TRANSMISSION OF CERTIFICATE OF ORDINATION AND BROWN JACKET
[IF AVAILABLE]

11. CLOSING THE CEREMONY

Noble community, to lend spiritual support to our brothers and sisters who have been ordained, please recite the closing verses in mindfulness:

12. THE THREE REFUGES ♪

I take refuge in the Buddha,
the one who shows me the way in this life.
I take refuge in the Dharma,
the way of understanding and of love.
I take refuge in the Sangha,
the community that lives in harmony and awareness.
[BELL]

Dwelling in the refuge of Buddha,
I clearly see the path of light and beauty in the world.
Dwelling in the refuge of Dharma,
I learn to open many doors on the path of transformation.
Dwelling in the refuge of Sangha,
shining light that supports me, keeping my practice free
of obstruction.
[BELL]

Taking refuge in the Buddha in myself,
I aspire to help all people recognize their own awakened nature,
realizing the Mind of Love.
Taking refuge in the Dharma in myself,
I aspire to help all people fully master the ways of practice
and walk together on the path of liberation.
Taking refuge in the Sangha in myself,

I aspire to help all people build Fourfold Communities,
to embrace all beings and support their transformation.
[BELL, BELL]

13. Sharing the Merit ♪

Transmitting the trainings, practicing the way of awareness
gives rise to benefits without limit.
We vow to share the fruits with all beings.
We vow to offer tribute to parents, teachers, friends,
and numerous beings
who give guidance and support along the path.
[BELL, BELL, BELL]

Beginning Anew Ceremony* ॐ

1. Opening the Ceremony

Sitting Meditation [12 minutes]
Incense Offering [page 87]
Touching the Earth [page 88]

2. Opening Verse ♪

[BELL, BELL, BELL]

Namo Tassa Bhagavato Arahato Samma Sambuddhassa
Namo Tassa Bhagavato Arahato Samma Sambuddhassa
Namo Tassa Bhagavato Arahato Samma Sambuddhassa
[BELL]

The Dharma is deep and lovely.
We now have a chance to see, study, and practice it.
We vow to realize its true meaning.
[BELL]

3. The Heart of Perfect Understanding ♪

The Bodhisattva Avalokita,
while moving in the deep course of Perfect Understanding,
shed light on the Five Skandhas and found them equally empty.
After this penetration, he overcame ill-being.
[BELL]

Listen, Shariputra,
form is emptiness, and emptiness is form.
Form is not other than emptiness, emptiness is not other than form.
The same is true with feelings, perceptions, mental formations, and consciousness.
[BELL]

---

*For more on the Beginning Anew practice, see Thich Nhat Hanh, *Teachings on Love* (Berkeley, CA: Parallax Press, 1997), and Thich Nhat Hanh, *Touching Peace* (Berkeley, CA: Parallax Press, 1992), pp. 55–57.

Listen, Shariputra,
all dharmas are marked with emptiness.
They are neither produced nor destroyed,
neither defiled nor immaculate,
neither increasing nor decreasing.
Therefore in emptiness there is neither form, nor feelings, nor
perceptions, nor mental formations, nor consciousness.
No eye, or ear, or nose, or tongue, or body, or mind.
No form, no sound, no smell, no taste, no touch, no object of mind.
No realms of elements (from eyes to mind consciousness),
no interdependent origins and no extinction of them
(from ignorance to death and decay).
No ill-being, no cause of ill-being, no end of ill-being, and no path.
No understanding and no attainment.
[BELL]

Because there is no attainment,
the Bodhisattvas, grounded in Perfect Understanding,
find no obstacles for their minds.
Having no obstacles, they overcome fear,
liberating themselves forever from illusion, realizing perfect nirvana.
All Buddhas in the past, present, and future,
thanks to this Perfect Understanding,
arrive at full, right, and universal enlightenment.
[BELL]

Therefore one should know
that Perfect Understanding is the highest mantra, the unequaled
mantra,
the destroyer of ill-being, the incorruptible truth.
A mantra of Prajñaparamita should therefore be proclaimed:

Gate gate paragate parasamgate bodhi svaha
Gate gate paragate parasamgate bodhi svaha
Gate gate paragate parasamgate bodhi svaha
[BELL, BELL]

4. BEGINNING ANEW

With great respect, we turn towards the conqueror of afflictions,
offering heartfelt words of repentance.
We have lived in forgetfulness for a long time.
As we have not had the opportunity to encounter the Dharma,
our habit energies have led us into suffering.
We have made many mistakes out of unskillfulness.
We have been blinded by our wrong perceptions
for a very long time.
Our heart's garden is sown with attachment, hatred, and pride.
In us are seeds of killing, stealing, sexual misconduct, and lies.
Our everyday deeds and words do damage.
All these wrong actions are obstacles to our peace and joy.
Let us begin anew.
[BELL]

We see that we have been thoughtless,
straying from the path of mindfulness.
We have stored up afflictions and ignorance,
which have brought about so much aversion and sorrow.
There are times we have been weary of life
because we are so full of anxiety.
Because we do not understand others,
we are angry and resentful.
First we try to reason with each other, then we blame.
Every day the suffering increases, making the rift greater.
There are days when we are unwilling to speak to each other,
unwilling to look each other in the face.
And we create internal formations, which last for a long time.
Now we turn to the Three Jewels.
Sincerely recognizing our errors, we bow our heads.
[BELL]

We know so well that in our consciousness
are buried all the wholesome seeds —
seeds of love and understanding and seeds of peace and joy.
But because we do not know how to water them,
the wholesome seeds do not sprout fresh and green.

We continue to allow sorrow to overwhelm us
until there is no light in our lives.
When we chase after a distant happiness,
life becomes but a shadow of the reality.
Our mind is occupied by the past,
or worrying about this or that in the future.
We cannot let go of our anger,
and we consider of no value the precious gifts of life
which are already in our hands,
thereby trampling on real happiness.
As month follows month, we are sunk in sorrow.
So now in the precious presence of the Buddha,
fragrant with sandalwood incense,
we recognize our errors and begin anew.
[BELL]

With all our heart we go for refuge,
turning to the Buddhas in the Ten Directions
and all the Bodhisattvas, noble disciples, and self
achieved Buddhas.
Very sincerely we recognize our errors
and the mistakes of our wrong judgments.
Please bring the balm of clear water
to pour on the roots of our afflictions.
Please bring the raft of the true teachings
to carry us over the ocean of sorrows.
We vow to live an awakened life,
to practice smiling and conscious breathing,
and to study the teachings, authentically transmitted.
Diligently, we shall live in mindfulness.
[BELL]

We come back to live in the wonderful present,
to plant our heart's garden with good seeds,
and to make strong foundations of understanding and love.
We vow to train ourselves in mindfulness and concentration,
practicing to look and understand deeply
to be able to see the nature of all that is,
and so to be free of the bonds of birth and death.

We learn to speak lovingly, to be affectionate,
to care for others whether it is early morn or late afternoon,
to bring the roots of joy to many places,
helping people to abandon sorrow,
to respond with deep gratitude
to the kindness of parents, teachers, and friends.
With deep faith we light up the incense of our heart.
We ask the Lord of Compassion to be our protector
on the wonderful path of practice.
We vow to practice diligently,
cultivating the fruits of this path.
[BELL, BELL, BELL]

5. Touching the Earth in Gratitude
[ALL TOUCH THE EARTH ONE TIME AT THE SOUND OF EACH BELL]

The Buddha Vipashyin, to whom we bow in gratitude.
[BELL]
The Buddha Shikhin, to whom we bow in gratitude.
[BELL]
The Buddha Vishvabhu, to whom we bow in gratitude.
[BELL]
The Buddha Krakkucchandha, to whom we bow in gratitude.
[BELL]
The Buddha Konagamana, to whom we bow in gratitude.
[BELL]
The Buddha Kashyapa, to whom we bow in gratitude.
[BELL]
The Buddha Shakyamuni, to whom we bow in gratitude.
[BELL]
The Bodhisattva of Great Understanding, Manjushri,
to whom we bow in gratitude.
[BELL]
The Bodhisattva of Great Action, Samantabhadra,
to whom we bow in gratitude.
[BELL]
The Bodhisattva of Great Compassion, Avalokiteshvara,
to whom we bow in gratitude.
[BELL]

The Bodhisattva of the Great Vow, Kshitigarbha,
to whom we bow in gratitude.
[BELL]
The Venerable Kashyapa, to whom we bow in gratitude.
[BELL]
The Venerable Shariputra, to whom we bow in gratitude.
[BELL]
The Venerable Maudgalyayana, to whom we bow in gratitude.
[BELL]
The Venerable Upali, to whom we bow in gratitude.
[BELL]
The Venerable Ananda, to whom we bow in gratitude.
[BELL]
The Venerable Mahagotami, to whom we bow in gratitude.
[BELL, BELL]

6. Repentance Gatha

All wrongdoing arises from the mind.
When the mind is purified, what trace of wrong is left?
After repentance, my heart is light like the white clouds
that have always floated over the ancient forest in freedom.
[BELL, BELL]

7. The Refuge Chant ♪

Incense perfumes the atmosphere.
A lotus blooms and the Buddha appears.
The world of suffering and discrimination
is filled with the light of the rising sun.
As the dust of fear and anxiety settles,
with open heart, one-pointed mind,
I turn to the Three Jewels.
[BELL]

The Fully Enlightened One, beautifully seated, peaceful and smiling,
a living source of understanding and compassion,
to the Buddha I go for refuge.
[BELL]

The path of mindful living,
leading to healing, joy, and enlightenment, the way of peace,
to the Dharma I go for refuge.
[BELL]

The loving and supportive community of practice,
realizing harmony, awareness, and liberation,
to the Sangha I go for refuge.
[BELL]

I am aware that the Three Gems are within my heart.
I vow to realize them,
practicing mindful breathing and smiling,
looking deeply into things.
I vow to understand living beings and their suffering,
to cultivate compassion and loving kindness,
to practice joy and equanimity.
[BELL]

I vow to offer joy to one person in the morning,
to help relieve the grief of one person in the afternoon,
living simply and sanely with few possessions,
keeping my body healthy.
I vow to let go of all worries and anxiety
in order to be light and free.
[BELL]

I am aware that I owe so much
to my parents, teachers, friends, and all beings.
I vow to be worthy of their trust, to practice wholeheartedly
so that understanding and compassion will flower,
helping living beings be free from their suffering.
May the Buddha, the Dharma, and the Sangha
support my efforts.
[BELL, BELL]

8. The Three Refuges ♪

I take refuge in the Buddha,
the one who shows me the way in this life.
I take refuge in the Dharma,
the way of understanding and of love.
I take refuge in the Sangha,
the community that lives in harmony and awareness.
[BELL]

I clearly see the path of light and beauty in the world.
Dwelling in the refuge of Dharma,
I learn to open many doors on the path of transformation.
Dwelling in the refuge of Sangha,
shining light that supports me, keeping my practice free of obstruction.
[BELL]

Taking refuge in the Buddha in myself,
I aspire to help all people recognize their own awakened nature,
realizing the Mind of Love.
Taking refuge in the Dharma in myself,
I aspire to help all people fully master the ways of practice
and walk together on the path of liberation.
Taking refuge in the Sangha in myself,
I aspire to help all people build Fourfold Communities,
to embrace all beings and support their transformation.
[BELL, BELL]

9. Sharing the Merit ♪
Beginning anew, practicing the way of awareness
gives rise to benefits without limit.
We vow to share the fruits with all beings.
We vow to offer tribute to parents, teachers, friends,
and numerous beings
who give guidance and support along the path.
[BELL, BELL, BELL]

Buddha's Birthday Ceremony ♪

[THE BUDDHA'S BIRTHDAY IS CELEBRATED IN THE SPRING. THE EXACT DATE VARIES AMONG TRADITIONS, BUT MOST CEREMONIES INCLUDE BATHING THE BABY BUDDHA. THIS CEREMONY CAN BE ORGANIZED BY THE CHILDREN WITH THE HELP OF A FEW ADULTS.

A SMALL HOUSE OF BAMBOO OR WOOD CAN BE MADE FOR THE STATUE OF THE BABY BUDDHA. THE STATUE SHOULD BE SET ON A STONE IN THE MIDDLE OF WATER. THE ROOF OF THE HOUSE AND THE SUPPORTING PILLARS CAN BE DECORATED WITH FLOWERS AND LEAVES. THE CHILDREN CAN FIND FLOWERS TO DECORATE THE HOUSE. THE WATER THAT IS USED TO BATHE THE BUDDHA CAN BE PERFUMED WITH FLOWERS AND HERBS. AT THE EDGE OF THE WATER IS A LADLE (PREFERABLY OF WOOD OR COCONUT SHELL) TO POUR WATER OVER THE STATUE DURING THE CEREMONY. THERE SHOULD BE ENOUGH ROOM FOR THE PARTICIPANTS TO LEAVE CANDLES AND FLOWERS. ALL THE PARTICIPANTS COME UP IN TURN TO OFFER A FLOWER AND A CANDLE TO THE BUDDHA BEFORE BATHING THE STATUE.]

1. Opening the Ceremony
Walking Meditation [30 MINUTES]
Sitting Meditation [12 MINUTES]
Incense Offering [page 87]
Touching the Earth [page 88]

2. Introductory Words

Today the community has gathered to celebrate the birth of the Buddha and to bathe the baby Buddha. Please, will the community listen. Two thousand six hundred years ago in the town of Kapilavastu, a Buddha known as Shakyamuni was born. He was a human being just as we are, but in him understanding and love were developed to a very high degree, and he became a fully awakened being. He was a beautiful and precious flower in the garden of humanity, an udumbara flower that blooms only once every three thousand years.

3. The Three Refuges Song ♪

I take refuge in the Buddha,
the one who shows me the way in this life.

Namo Buddhaya, Namo Buddhaya, Namo Buddhaya.
I take refuge in the Dharma,
the way of understanding and love.
Namo Dharmaya, Namo Dharmaya, Namo Dharmaya.
I take refuge in the Sangha,
the community of mindful harmony.
Namo Sanghaya, Namo Sanghaya, Namo Sanghaya.
Namo Buddhaya, Namo Dharmaya, Namo Sanghaya.

4. Dharma Words
[CHANTED BY HEAD OF CEREMONY]

The Buddha is a flower of humanity
who practiced the Way for countless lives.
He appeared on this Earth as a prince who left his royal palace
to practice at the foot of the Bodhi tree.
He conquered illusion.
When the morning star arose,
he realized the great path of awakening
and turned the wheel of the Dharma.
[BELL]

With single-mindedness, all species aspire to experience
the path free from birth.
With single-mindedness, all species will experience
a path free from birth.
[BELL]

Namo Tassa Bhagavato Arahato Samma Sambuddhassa
[BELL, BELL]

5. Praising the Buddha

The Buddha is like the fresh, full moon
that soars across the immense sky.
When the river of mind is truly calm,
the moon is reflected perfectly
upon the surface of the deep waters.
The countenance of the World-Honored One,

like the full moon or like the orb of the sun,
shines with the light of clarity,
a halo of wisdom spreading in every direction,
enveloping all with love, compassion, joy, and equanimity.
The inexhaustible virtues of the World-Honored One
cannot be adequately praised.
We in the [NAME] practice center, on this day
gather as a Fourfold Sangha, come to the altar, meditate and chant,
praise the virtuous actions of the Buddha, and offer this prayer:
May the path of the Buddha grow brighter.
May the Dharma become clearer.
May wind and rain be favorable.
May this country be at peace in the cities and rural areas.
May all follow the way of right practice.
May nature be safe. May people in society be free and equal.
May the refreshing breeze of compassion enter into this world of heat,
allowing the sun of wisdom to shine clearly in the cloudy sky
so that the path of liberation is appreciated everywhere
and the Dharma rain falls, benefiting all species.
May the Sangha that is present here practice diligently,
showing concern and love for each other
as they would for their own family,
transforming their consciousness.
We aspire to follow the example
of the Bodhisattvas Samantabhadra and Avalokiteshvara
and all other Bodhisattva Mahasattvas,
and the Great Perfection of Wisdom.
[BELL]

6. Opening Verse ♪

[BELL, BELL, BELL]

Namo Tassa Bhagavato Arahato Samma Sambuddhassa
Namo Tassa Bhagavato Arahato Samma Sambuddhassa
Namo Tassa Bhagavato Arahato Samma Sambuddhassa
[BELL]

The Dharma is deep and lovely.
We now have a chance to see, study, and practice it.

We vow to realize its true meaning.
[BELL]

7. The Heart of Perfect Understanding ♪

The Bodhisattva Avalokita,
while moving in the deep course of Perfect Understanding,
shed light on the Five Skandhas and found them equally empty.
After this penetration, he overcame ill-being.
[BELL]

Listen, Shariputra,
form is emptiness, and emptiness is form.
Form is not other than emptiness, emptiness is not other than form.
The same is true with feelings, perceptions, mental formations, and consciousness.
[BELL]

Listen, Shariputra,
all dharmas are marked with emptiness.
They are neither produced nor destroyed,
neither defiled nor immaculate,
neither increasing nor decreasing.
Therefore in emptiness there is neither form, nor feelings, nor perceptions,
nor mental formations, nor consciousness.
No eye, or ear, or nose, or tongue, or body, or mind.
No form, no sound, no smell, no taste, no touch, no object of mind.
No realms of elements (from eyes to mind consciousness),
no interdependent origins and no extinction of them
(from ignorance to death and decay).
No ill-being, no cause of ill-being, no end of ill-being, and no path.
No understanding and no attainment.
[BELL]

Because there is no attainment,
the Bodhisattvas, grounded in Perfect Understanding,
find no obstacles for their minds.
Having no obstacles, they overcome fear,
liberating themselves forever from illusion, realizing perfect nirvana.

All Buddhas in the past, present, and future,
thanks to this Perfect Understanding,
arrive at full, right, and universal enlightenment.
[BELL]

Therefore one should know
that Perfect Understanding is the highest mantra, the unequaled mantra,
the destroyer of ill-being, the incorruptible truth.
A mantra of Prajñaparamita should therefore be proclaimed:

Gate gate paragate parasamgate bodhi svaha
Gate gate paragate parasamgate bodhi svaha
Gate gate paragate parasamgate bodhi svaha
[BELL, BELL]

8. BATHING THE BABY BUDDHA

Opening Verse
Today we bathe the Tathagata.
Deep wisdom and clarity bring great happiness.
May all living beings who are overwhelmed by suffering
see the Dharmakaya in this very world.

Recitation ♪
[CHANT THIS VERSE, INTERSPERSED WITH "THE THREE REFUGES SONG"
(SEE PAGE 412) WHILE EVERYONE COMES FORWARD TO OFFER A FLOWER
AND A CANDLE TO THE BABY BUDDHA. THE HEAD OF CEREMONY IS THE
FIRST PERSON TO OFFER A CANDLE AND A FLOWER AND TO LADLE FRAGRANT
WATER OVER THE STATUE OF THE BUDDHA. THE CHILDREN THEN FOLLOW,
AND AFTER THEM THE ADULTS COME FORWARD.]

Namo Budh Shakyamuni

9. THE REFUGE CHANT ♪

Incense perfumes the atmosphere.
A lotus blooms and the Buddha appears.
The world of suffering and discrimination
is filled with the light of the rising sun.

As the dust of fear and anxiety settles,
with open heart, one-pointed mind,
I turn to the Three Jewels.
[BELL]

The Fully Enlightened One, beautifully seated, peaceful and smiling,
a living source of understanding and compassion,
to the Buddha I go for refuge.
[BELL]

The path of mindful living,
leading to healing, joy, and enlightenment, the way of peace,
to the Dharma I go for refuge.
[BELL]

The loving and supportive community of practice,
realizing harmony, awareness, and liberation,
to the Sangha I go for refuge.
[BELL]

I am aware that the Three Gems are within my heart.
I vow to realize them,
practicing mindful breathing and smiling,
looking deeply into things.
I vow to understand living beings and their suffering,
to cultivate compassion and loving kindness,
to practice joy and equanimity.
[BELL]

I vow to offer joy to one person in the morning,
to help relieve the grief of one person in the afternoon,
living simply and sanely with few possessions,
keeping my body healthy.
I vow to let go of all worries and anxiety
in order to be light and free.
[BELL]

I am aware that I owe so much
to my parents, teachers, friends, and all beings.

I vow to be worthy of their trust, to practice wholeheartedly
so that understanding and compassion will flower,
helping living beings be free from their suffering.
May the Buddha, the Dharma, and the Sangha
support my efforts.
[BELL, BELL]

10. THE THREE REFUGES ♪

I take refuge in the Buddha,
the one who shows me the way in this life.
I take refuge in the Dharma,
the way of understanding and of love.
I take refuge in the Sangha,
the community that lives in harmony and awareness.
[BELL]

Dwelling in the refuge of Buddha,
I clearly see the path of light and beauty in the world.
Dwelling in the refuge of Dharma,
I learn to open many doors on the path of transformation.
Dwelling in the refuge of Sangha,
shining light that supports me, keeping my practice free of obstruction.
[BELL]

Taking refuge in the Buddha in myself,
I aspire to help all people recognize their own awakened nature,
realizing the Mind of Love.
Taking refuge in the Dharma in myself,
I aspire to help all people fully master the ways of practice
and walk together on the path of liberation.
Taking refuge in the Sangha in myself,
I aspire to help all people build Fourfold Communities,
to embrace all beings and support their transformation.
[BELL, BELL]

11. Sharing the Merit ♪

Reciting the sutras, practicing the way of awareness
gives rise to benefits without limit.
We vow to share the fruits with all beings.
We vow to offer tribute to parents, teachers, friends,
and numerous beings
who give guidance and support along the path.
[BELL, BELL, BELL]

Rose Ceremony ॐ

1. Opening the Ceremony

Sitting Meditation [12 MINUTES]
Incense Offering [page 87]
Touching the Earth [page 88]

2. Opening Verse ♪

[BELL, BELL, BELL]

Namo Tassa Bhagavato Arahato Samma Sambuddhassa
Namo Tassa Bhagavato Arahato Samma Sambuddhassa
Namo Tassa Bhagavato Arahato Samma Sambuddhassa
[BELL]

The Dharma is deep and lovely.
We now have a chance to see, study, and practice it.
We vow to realize its true meaning.
[BELL]

3. The Heart of Perfect Understanding ♪

The Bodhisattva Avalokita,
while moving in the deep course of Perfect Understanding,
shed light on the Five Skandhas and found them equally empty.
After this penetration, he overcame ill-being.
[BELL]

Listen, Shariputra,
form is emptiness, and emptiness is form.

Form is not other than emptiness, emptiness is not other than form.
The same is true with feelings, perceptions, mental formations,
and consciousness.
[BELL]

Listen, Shariputra,
all dharmas are marked with emptiness.
They are neither produced nor destroyed,
neither defiled nor immaculate,
neither increasing nor decreasing.
Therefore in emptiness there is neither form, nor feelings, nor
perceptions, nor mental formations, nor consciousness.
No eye, or ear, or nose, or tongue, or body, or mind.
No form, no sound, no smell, no taste, no touch, no object of mind.
No realms of elements (from eyes to mind consciousness),
no interdependent origins and no extinction of them
(from ignorance to death and decay).
No ill-being, no cause of ill-being, no end of ill-being, and no path.
No understanding and no attainment.
[BELL]

Because there is no attainment,
the Bodhisattvas, grounded in Perfect Understanding,
find no obstacles for their minds.
Having no obstacles, they overcome fear,
liberating themselves forever from illusion, realizing perfect nirvana.
All Buddhas in the past, present, and future,
thanks to this Perfect Understanding,
arrive at full, right, and universal enlightenment.
[BELL]

Therefore one should know
that Perfect Understanding is the highest mantra,
the unequaled mantra,
the destroyer of ill-being, the incorruptible truth.
A mantra of Prajñaparamita should therefore be proclaimed:

Gate gate paragate parasamgate bodhi svaha
Gate gate paragate parasamgate bodhi svaha

Gate gate paragate parasamgate bodhi svaha
[BELL, BELL]

4. First Musical Offering

[SONG, PREFERABLY WITH WORDS CONNECTED WITH MEDITATION PRACTICE, WITH INSTRUMENTAL ACCOMPANIMENT.]

5. Introductory Words

Today the community has gathered to celebrate the Rose Ceremony. Please listen with a serene mind. The work of a father is like a great mountain. The loyalty and love of a mother are like clear spring water. We come together today to remember our parents who have given us birth. Keep your father and mother in mind before the Buddha, Dharma, and Sangha, and light up your awareness of love, gratitude, and happiness.

6. Reading of *A Rose for Your Pocket*

The thought "mother" cannot be separated from that of "love." Love is sweet, tender, and delicious. Without love, a child cannot flower, an adult cannot mature. Without love, we weaken, wither. The day my mother died, I made this entry in my journal: "The greatest misfortune of my life has come!" Even an old person, when he loses his mother, doesn't feel ready. He too has the impression that he is not yet ripe, that he is suddenly alone. He feels as abandoned and unhappy as a young orphan.

All songs and poems praising motherhood are beautiful, effortlessly beautiful. Even songwriters and poets without much talent seem to pour their hearts into these works, and when they are recited or sung, the performers also seem deeply moved, unless they have lost their mothers too early even to know what love for mother is. Writings extolling the virtues of motherhood have existed since the beginning of time throughout the world.

When I was a child I heard a simple poem about losing your mother, and it is still very important for me. If your mother is still alive, you may feel tenderness for her each time you read this, fearing this distant yet inevitable event.

That year, although I was still very young,
my mother left me,

and I realized that I was an orphan.
Everyone around me was crying.
I suffered in silence. . .
allowing the tears to flow.
I felt my pain soften.
Evening enveloped Mother's tomb.
The pagoda bell rang sweetly.
I realized that to lose your mother
is to lose the whole universe.

We swim in a world of tender love for many years, and, without even knowing it, we are quite happy there. Only after it is too late do we become aware of it.

People in the countryside do not understand the complicated language of city people. When people from the city say that mother is "a treasure of love," that is already too complex for them. Country people in Vietnam compare their mothers to the finest varieties of bananas or to honey, sweet rice, or sugarcane. They express their love in these simple and direct ways. For me, a mother is like a *ba huong* banana of the highest quality, like the best *nep mot* sweet rice, the most delicious *mia lau* sugarcane!

There are moments after a fever when you have a bitter, flat taste in your mouth, and nothing tastes good. Only when your mother comes and tucks you in, gently pulls the covers over your chin, puts her hand on your burning forehead — is it really a hand, or is it the silk of heaven? — and gently whispers, "My poor darling!" do you feel restored, surrounded with the sweetness of maternal love. Her love is so fragrant, like a banana, like sweet rice, like sugarcane.

Father's work is enormous, as huge as a mountain. Mother's devotion is overflowing, like water from a mountain spring. Maternal love is our first taste of love, the origin of all feelings of love. Our mother is the teacher who first teaches us love, the most important subject in life. Without my mother I could never have known how to love. Thanks to her I can love my neighbors. Thanks to her I can love all living beings. Through her I acquired my first notions of understanding and compassion. Mother is the foundation of all love, and many religious traditions recognize this and pay deep honor to a maternal figure, the Virgin Mary, the goddess Kuan Yin. Hardly an infant has opened her mouth to cry without her mother already running to the cradle. Mother is a gentle and sweet spirit who makes unhappiness and worries disappear. When the word "mother" is uttered, already we feel our hearts overflowing with love. From love, the distance to belief and action is very short.

In the West, we celebrate Mother's Day in May. I am from the countryside of Vietnam, and I had never heard of this tradition. One day, I was visiting the Ginza district of Tokyo with the monk Thien An, and we were met outside a bookstore by several Japanese students who were friends of his. One discreetly asked him a question, and then took a white carnation from her bag and pinned it on my robe. I was surprised and a little embarrassed. I had no idea what this gesture meant, and I didn't dare ask. I tried to act natural, thinking this must be some local custom.

When they were finished talking (I don't speak Japanese), Thien An and I went into the bookstore, and he told me that today was what is called Mother's Day. In Japan, if your mother is still alive, you wear a red flower on your pocket or your lapel, proud that you still have your mother. If she is no longer alive, you wear a white flower. I looked at the white flower on my robe and suddenly I felt so unhappy. I was as much an orphan as any other unhappy orphan; we orphans could no longer proudly wear red flowers in our buttonholes. Those who wear white flowers suffer, and their thoughts cannot avoid returning to their mothers. They cannot forget that she is no longer there. Those who wear red flowers are so happy, knowing their mothers are still alive. They can try to please her before she is gone and it is too late. I find this a beautiful custom. I propose that we do the same thing in Vietnam, and in the West as well.

Mother is a boundless source of love, an inexhaustible treasure. But unfortunately, we sometimes forget. A mother is the most beautiful gift life offers us. Those of you who still have your mother near, please don't wait for her death to say, "My God, I have lived beside my mother all these years without ever looking closely at her. Just brief glances, a few words exchanged — asking for a little pocket money or one thing or another." You cuddle up to her to get warm, you sulk, you get angry with her. You only complicate her life, causing her to worry, undermining her health, making her go to sleep late and get up early. Many mothers die young because of their children. Throughout her life we expect her to cook, wash, and clean up after us, while we think only about our grades and our careers. Our mothers no longer have time to look deeply at us, and we are too busy to look closely at them. Only when she is no longer there do we realize that we have never been conscious of having a mother.

This evening, when you return from school or work or, if you live far away, the next time you visit your mother, you may wish to go into her room and, with a calm and silent smile, sit down beside her. Without saying anything, make her stop working. Then, look at her for a long time, look at her deeply. Do this in order to see her, to realize that she is there, she is alive, beside you. Take her hand and ask her one short question to capture her attention, "Mother, do you know something?" She will be a little surprised and will probably smile when she asks you, "What, dear?" Keep looking into her eyes, smiling serenely, and say, "Do you know that I love you?" Ask this question without waiting for an answer. Even if you are thirty or forty years old, or older, ask her as the child of your mother. Your mother and you will be happy, conscious of living in eternal love. Then tomorrow, when she leaves you, you will have no regrets.

In Vietnam, on the holiday of Ullambana, we listen to stories and legends about the Bodhisattva Maudgalyayana, and about filial love, the work of the father, the devotion of the mother, and the duty of the child. Everyone prays for the longevity of his or her parents, or if they are dead, for their rebirth in the heavenly Pure Land. We believe that a child without filial love is without worth. But filial devotion also arises from love itself. Without love, filial devotion is just artificial. When love is present, that is enough, and there is no need to talk of obligation. To love your mother is enough. It is not a duty, it is completely natural, like drinking when you are thirsty. Every child must have a mother, and it is totally natural to love her. The mother loves her child, and the child loves his mother. The child needs his mother, and the mother needs her child. If the mother doesn't need her child, nor the child his mother, then this is not a mother, and this is not a child. It is a misuse of the words "mother" and "child."

When I was young, one of my teachers asked me, "What do you have to do when you love your mother?" I told him, "I must obey her, help her, take care of her when she is old, and pray for her, keeping the ancestral altar when she has disappeared forever behind the mountain." Now I know that his question was superfluous. If you love your mother, you don't have to do anything. You love her; that is enough. To love your mother is not a question of morality or virtue.

Please do not think I have written this to give a lesson in morality. Loving your mother is to your own benefit. A mother is like a spring of pure water, like the very finest sugarcane or honey, the best quality sweet rice. If you do not know how to profit from this, it is unfortunate for you. I simply want to bring this to your attention, to help you avoid one day complaining that there is nothing left in life for you. If a gift such as the presence of your own mother doesn't satisfy you, even if you are president of a large corporation or king of the universe, you probably will not be satisfied. I know that the Creator is not happy, for the Creator arises spontaneously and does not have the good fortune to have a mother.

I would like to tell a story. Please don't think that I am thoughtless. It could have been that my sister didn't marry, and I didn't become a monk. In any case, we both left our mother — one to lead a new life beside the man she loved, and the other to follow an ideal of life that he adored. The night my sister married, my mother worried about a thousand and one things, and didn't even seem sad. But when we sat down at the table for some light refreshments, while waiting for our in-laws to come for my sister, I saw that my mother hadn't eaten a bite. She said, "For eighteen years she has eaten with us and today is her last meal here before going to another family's home to take her meals." My sister cried, her head bowing barely above her plate, and she said, "Mama, I won't get married." But she married nonetheless. As for me, I left my mother to become a monk. To congratulate those who are firmly resolved to leave their families to become monks, one says that they are following the way of understanding, but I am not proud of it. I love my mother, but I also have an ideal, and to serve it I had to leave her — so much the worse for me.

In life, it is often necessary to make difficult choices. We cannot catch two fish at the same time, one in each hand. It is difficult, because if we accept growing up, we must accept suffering. I don't regret leaving my mother to become a monk, but I am sorry I had to make such a choice. I didn't have the chance to profit fully from this precious treasure. Each night I pray for my mother, but it is no longer possible for me to savor the excellent ba huong banana, the best quality nep mot sweet rice, and the delicious mia lau sugarcane. Please don't think that I am suggesting that you not follow your career and remain home at your mother's side. I have already said I do not want to give advice or lessons in morality. I only want to remind you that a mother is like a banana, like good rice, like honey, like sugar. She is tenderness, she is love; so you, my brothers and sisters, please do not forget her. Forgetting creates an immense loss, and I hope you do not, either through ignorance or through lack of attention, have to endure such a loss. I gladly put a red flower, a rose, on your lapel so that you will be happy. That is all.

If I were to have any advice, it would be this: Tonight, when you return from school or work, or the next time you visit your mother, go into her room calmly, silently, with a smile, and sit down beside her. Without saying anything, make her stop working, and look at her for a long time. Look at her well, in order to see her well, in order to realize she is there, alive, sitting beside you. Then take her hand and ask her this short question, "Mother, do you know something?" She will be a little surprised, and will ask you, smiling, "What, dear?" Continuing to look into her eyes with a serene smile, tell her, "Do you know that I love you?" Ask her without waiting for an answer. Even if you are thirty, forty years old, or older, ask her simply because you are the child of your mother. Your mother and you will both be happy, conscious of living in eternal love. And tomorrow when she leaves you, you will not have any regrets.

This is the refrain I give you to sing today. Brothers and Sisters, please chant it, please sing it, so you will not live in indifference or forgetfulness. This red rose, I have already placed it on your lapel. Please be happy.

[BELL]

7. Second Musical Offering
[INSTRUMENTAL PIECE WITHOUT WORDS, IN THE SPIRIT OF OPENNESS AND ACCEPTANCE.]

8. A Father's Love
[PERSONAL STATEMENT ON A FATHER'S LOVE READ BY SOMEONE.]

9. A Mother's Love
[PERSONAL STATEMENT ON A MOTHER'S LOVE READ BY SOMEONE.]

10. Third Musical Offering
[YOUNG PEOPLE ARE INVITED TO SING ABOUT THE LOVE THEY HAVE BEEN SHOWN BY THEIR PARENTS. WITH OR WITHOUT MUSICAL ACCOMPANIMENT.]

11. PINNING THE ROSES

[SEVERAL YOUNG PEOPLE, BEAUTIFULLY DRESSED, COME FORWARD AND KNEEL
BEFORE THE ALTAR WITH THEIR PALMS JOINED. THE HEAD OF CEREMONY
COMES FORWARD AND KNEELS BEFORE THE YOUNG PEOPLE, JOINS HIS OR HER
PALMS AND BOWS TO EACH PERSON. HE OR SHE ASKS THE YOUNG PEOPLE
WHAT COLOR ROSES THEY NEED. A RED ROSE REPRESENTS A PARENT STILL
ALIVE, AND A WHITE ROSE REPRESENTS A PARENT WHO IS DECEASED.
THEN THE HEAD OF CEREMONY TAKES THE TWO ROSES FROM A TRAY THAT
CONTAINS WHITE AND RED ROSES. THE TWO ROSES ARE PINNED TO EACH
YOUNG PERSON ON THEIR LEFT LAPEL.

WHEN THE YOUNG PEOPLE HAVE EACH RECEIVED TWO ROSES, THE HEAD
OF CEREMONY INVITES THE BELL TO SOUND, AND THE YOUNG PEOPLE TOUCH
THE EARTH THREE TIMES TO EXPRESS GRATITUDE, BEARING THEIR FATHER
AND MOTHER IN MIND AND WISHING THAT THEY MAY BE SAFE, WELL,
AND HAPPY WHETHER THEY ARE ALIVE OR HAVE PASSED AWAY.

AFTER THE DEEP BOWING, THE YOUNG PEOPLE STAND UP AND TURN TO FACE
THE COMMUNITY IN ORDER TO PIN ROSES ON OTHER COMMUNITY MEMBERS.
FOR EXAMPLE, IF THERE ARE SIX YOUNG PEOPLE, THEN SIX PEOPLE COME UP AT
A TIME WITH THEIR PALMS JOINED AND KNEEL DOWN FOR THE YOUNG PEOPLE
TO PIN ON THE ROSES. THEY TELL THE YOUNG PEOPLE WHAT COLOR ROSES
THEY NEED. THE YOUNG PEOPLE SELECT TWO ROSES FROM TRAYS NEXT TO
THEM AND PIN THE ROSES ON THE LEFT LAPELS OF THE COMMUNITY MEMBERS.

WHEN THESE SIX COMMUNITY MEMBERS HAVE RECEIVED TWO ROSES,
THEY STAND UP, WALK TOWARDS THE ALTAR, AND BOW DEEPLY THREE TIMES
BEFORE THE THREE JEWELS TO EXPRESS THEIR GRATITUDE TO THEIR PARENTS.
THEIR BOWS ARE ACCOMPANIED BY SOUNDS OF THE BELL. THEN THEY
RETURN TO THEIR SEATS.

WHILE THEY ARE BOWING, SIX MORE PEOPLE FROM THE COMMUNITY COME
UP AND KNEEL BEFORE THE SIX YOUNG PEOPLE TO RECEIVE THEIR ROSES.
THIS CONTINUES UNTIL EVERYONE HAS RECEIVED TWO ROSES AND HAD
THE OPPORTUNITY TO BOW.]

12. THE REFUGE CHANT ♪

Incense perfumes the atmosphere.
A lotus blooms and the Buddha appears.
The world of suffering and discrimination
is filled with the light of the rising sun.
As the dust of fear and anxiety settles,

with open heart, one-pointed mind,
I turn to the Three Jewels.
[BELL]

The Fully Enlightened One, beautifully seated, peaceful and smiling,
a living source of understanding and compassion,
to the Buddha I go for refuge.
[BELL]

The path of mindful living,
leading to healing, joy, and enlightenment, the way of peace,
to the Dharma I go for refuge.
[BELL]

The loving and supportive community of practice,
realizing harmony, awareness, and liberation,
to the Sangha I go for refuge.
[BELL]

I am aware that the Three Gems are within my heart.
I vow to realize them,
practicing mindful breathing and smiling,
looking deeply into things.
I vow to understand living beings and their suffering,
to cultivate compassion and loving kindness,
to practice joy and equanimity.
[BELL]

I vow to offer joy to one person in the morning,
to help relieve the grief of one person in the afternoon,
living simply and sanely with few possessions,
keeping my body healthy.
I vow to let go of all worries and anxiety
in order to be light and free.
[BELL]

I am aware that I owe so much
to my parents, teachers, friends, and all beings.
I vow to be worthy of their trust, to practice wholeheartedly

so that understanding and compassion will flower,
helping living beings be free from their suffering.
May the Buddha, the Dharma, and the Sangha
support my efforts.
[BELL, BELL]

13. THE THREE REFUGES ♪

I take refuge in the Buddha,
the one who shows me the way in this life.
I take refuge in the Dharma,
the way of understanding and of love.
I take refuge in the Sangha,
the community that lives in harmony and awareness.
[BELL]

Dwelling in the refuge of Buddha,
I clearly see the path of light and beauty in the world.
Dwelling in the refuge of Dharma,
I learn to open many doors on the path of transformation.
Dwelling in the refuge of Sangha,
shining light that supports me, keeping my practice free of obstruction.
[BELL]

Taking refuge in the Buddha in myself,
I aspire to help all people recognize their own awakened nature,
realizing the Mind of Love.
Taking refuge in the Dharma in myself,
I aspire to help all people fully master the ways of practice
and walk together on the path of liberation.
Taking refuge in the Sangha in myself,
I aspire to help all people build Fourfold Communities,
to embrace all beings and support their transformation.
[BELL, BELL]

14. SHARING THE MERIT ♪

Showing our gratitude, practicing the way of awareness
gives rise to benefits without limit.

We vow to share the fruits with all beings.
We vow to offer tribute to parents, teachers, friends,
and numerous beings
who give guidance and support along the path.
[BELL, BELL, BELL]

New Year's Ceremony ॐ

[THE OCCASION OF THE NEW YEAR IS A WONDERFUL TIME TO PRACTICE BEGINNING ANEW WITHIN OURSELVES, WITH FAMILY AND FRIENDS, AND AS A COMMUNITY. IN PLUM VILLAGE, THE WHOLE COMMUNITY GATHERS ON NEW YEAR'S EVE TO ENJOY TRADITIONAL FOODS, ARTISTIC PERFORMANCES, AND THE NEW YEAR'S CEREMONY. THE SITTING MEDITATION PERIOD IS TIMED TO END AS THE FIRST FEW SECONDS OF THE NEW YEAR BEGIN. THUS, THE FIRST ACTIVITY OF THE COMMUNITY FOR THE NEW YEAR IS THIS CEREMONY TO PAY RESPECT TO OUR TEACHERS AND OUR ANCESTORS. ALONG WITH ALL THE PREPARATIONS FOR THE EVENING MEAL AND PERFORMANCES, AN OFFERING OF FRUIT, FLOWERS, AND TEA SHOULD BE PLACED ON THE ANCESTRAL ALTAR IN THE MEDITATION HALL. INCENSE STICKS SHOULD ALSO BE AVAILABLE FOR EVERYONE WHO IS ATTENDING THE CEREMONY.]

1. Opening the Ceremony
Sitting Meditation [12 MINUTES]
Incense Offering [page 87]
Touching the Earth [page 88]
[AT THIS POINT, ONE SUTRA IS USUALLY CHANTED: EITHER THE PRAJÑAPARAMITA, THE DISCOURSE ON LOVE, THE DISCOURSE ON HAPPINESS, OR A SHORTENED VERSION OF THE ASPIRATION AND PRAISE CEREMONY.]

2. Address to Our Ancestors at the New Year
[AT THIS TIME, THE ENTIRE COMMUNITY IS INVITED TO GATHER AROUND THE ANCESTRAL ALTAR. MANY STICKS OF INCENSE ARE LIT BY SEVERAL YOUNG PARTICIPANTS AND MINDFULLY PASSED TO VARIOUS OTHERS, REPRESENTING THE FOURFOLD SANGHA. THEN A SENIOR PRACTITIONER REPRESENTING THE COMMUNITY COMES BEFORE THE ANCESTRAL ALTAR, KNEELS DOWN, AND READS THIS ADDRESS.]

We your descendants who are practicing in the [NAME] practice center at the occasion of the New Year, come with sincere respect before your altar. We go back to our source and ask you, our ancestors, to be our witness.

Trees have their roots and water has its source. We know that you, our ancestors, are our roots and we are your continuation. We are determined to receive your cultural and spiritual heritage, to conserve and to develop what is good, beautiful, and true in it. We are also determined to realize the aspirations which you have handed on to us, transforming your suffering and opening up for future generations the way to a peaceful, unburdened and meaningful life. We are determined to help build a society in which people are not always busy, where little is consumed, and there is plenty of time to live with nature, look after nature, and bring happiness to, care for, and smile to each other.

This is the moment when the New Year begins. We promise to let go of all our anger, sadness, and resentment, and to forgive, love, and accept each other. We know that only by doing this do we really express our feelings of gratitude and loyalty towards you.

Please be witness to our sincerity as we offer incense, flowers, fruit, and tea. All these things are offered with our heartfelt sincerity and our loyalty. Please be our protectors and the protectors of our children and grandchildren so that we have enough health, faith, and joy to be able to continue your work.

[AFTER THE ADDRESS HAS BEEN READ, ALL THE INCENSE STICKS ARE COLLECTED AND OFFERED TO THE ALTAR BY THE YOUNG PARTICIPANTS. THEN, AS THE BELL IS INVITED, THE WHOLE COMMUNITY TOUCHES THE EARTH FOUR TIMES TO REMEMBER THE FOUR GRATITUDES — TO PARENTS, TEACHERS, FRIENDS, AND ALL BEINGS IN THE ANIMAL, PLANT, AND MINERAL WORLDS.]
[BELL]

3. Opening Verse ♪

[BELL, BELL, BELL]

Namo Tassa Bhagavato Arahato Samma Sambuddhassa
Namo Tassa Bhagavato Arahato Samma Sambuddhassa
Namo Tassa Bhagavato Arahato Samma Sambuddhassa
[BELL]

The Dharma is deep and lovely.
We now have a chance to see, study, and practice it.
We vow to realize its true meaning.
[BELL]

4. Sutra Reading

[ANY SUITABLE SUTRA MAY BE CHOSEN FROM AMONG THOSE ON PAGES
269–348. THE DISCOURSE ON HAPPINESS IS PARTICULARLY RECOMMENDED.]

5. Sharing the Merit ♪

Reciting the sutras, practicing the way of awareness
gives rise to benefits without limit.
We vow to share the fruits with all beings.
We vow to offer tribute to parents, teachers, friends,
and numerous beings
who give guidance and support along the path.
[BELL, BELL, BELL]

6. Hugging Meditation*

[PARTICIPANTS ARE INVITED TO TURN TO EACH OTHER AND PRACTICE
HUGGING MEDITATION AS A FORM OF "BEGINNING ANEW" IN ORDER
TO CLOSE THE CEREMONY AND ENTER INTO THE NEW YEAR WITH OPEN
HEARTS AND HARMONY BETWEEN EACH OTHER.]

---

* For instruction on Hugging Meditation practice, please see page 21.

Wedding Ceremony ॐ

[ADAPT WORDING AS APPROPRIATE FOR COUPLES OF THE SAME GENDER.]

1. Opening the Ceremony
Walking Meditation [30 MINUTES]
Sitting Meditation [12 MINUTES]
Incense Offering [page 87]
Touching the Earth [page 88]

2. Opening Verse ♪
[BELL, BELL, BELL]

Namo Tassa Bhagavato Arahato Samma Sambuddhassa
Namo Tassa Bhagavato Arahato Samma Sambuddhassa
Namo Tassa Bhagavato Arahato Samma Sambuddhassa
[BELL]

The Dharma is deep and lovely.
We now have a chance to see, study, and practice it.
We vow to realize its true meaning.
[BELL]

3. The Heart of Perfect Understanding ♪

The Bodhisattva Avalokita,
while moving in the deep course of Perfect Understanding,
shed light on the Five Skandhas and found them equally empty.
After this penetration, he overcame ill-being.
[BELL]

Listen, Shariputra,
form is emptiness, and emptiness is form.
Form is not other than emptiness, emptiness is not other than form.
The same is true with feelings, perceptions, mental formations, and consciousness.
[BELL]

Listen, Shariputra,
all dharmas are marked with emptiness.
They are neither produced nor destroyed,
neither defiled nor immaculate,
neither increasing nor decreasing.
Therefore in emptiness there is neither form, nor feelings, nor perceptions,
nor mental formations, nor consciousness.
No eye, or ear, or nose, or tongue, or body, or mind.
No form, no sound, no smell, no taste, no touch, no object of mind.
No realms of elements (from eyes to mind consciousness),
no interdependent origins and no extinction of them
(from ignorance to death and decay).
No ill-being, no cause of ill-being, no end of ill-being, and no path.
No understanding and no attainment.
[BELL]

Because there is no attainment,
the Bodhisattvas, grounded in Perfect Understanding,
find no obstacles for their minds.
Having no obstacles, they overcome fear,
liberating themselves forever from illusion, realizing perfect nirvana.
All Buddhas in the past, present, and future,
thanks to this Perfect Understanding,
arrive at full, right, and universal enlightenment.
[BELL]

Therefore one should know
that Perfect Understanding is the highest mantra, the unequaled mantra,
the destroyer of ill-being, the incorruptible truth.
A mantra of Prajñaparamita should therefore be proclaimed:

Gate gate paragate parasamgate bodhi svaha
Gate gate paragate parasamgate bodhi svaha
Gate gate paragate parasamgate bodhi svaha
[BELL, BELL]

4. INTRODUCTORY WORDS

Today the community gathers to lend spiritual support to our brother

[NAME] and our sister [NAME], in their taking the vow to practice the Five Awarenesses. Please, everyone, follow your breathing in mindfulness when you hear the sound of the bell.

[BELL, BELL, BELL]

Brother [NAME] and Sister [NAME], please come forward in front of the altar of the Three Jewels, forming a lotus bud with your palms.

5. Touching the Earth in Gratitude

On hearing the sound of each bell, after the recitation of each line, please touch the Earth one time.

In gratitude to your father and mother, who have brought you to life, Brother and Sister, bow deeply before the Three Jewels in the Ten Directions.

[BELL]

In gratitude to your teachers, who have shown you the way to understand and love, Brother and Sister, bow deeply before the Three Jewels in the Ten Directions.

[BELL]

In gratitude to your friends, who give you guidance and support on the path, Brother and Sister, bow deeply before the Three Jewels in the Ten Directions.

[BELL]

In gratitude to all beings in the animal, plant, and mineral worlds, Brother and Sister, bow deeply before the Three Jewels in the Ten Directions.

[BELL, BELL]

6. The Five Awarenesses

Brother [NAME] and Sister [NAME], please kneel down.

Noble community, please listen. This is the moment when our brother [NAME] and sister [NAME] will make the vow to practice the Five Awarenesses and thus become husband and wife. Students of the Buddha are aware that life is one and that happiness is not an individual matter. By living and practicing awareness, we bring peace and joy to our lives and the lives of those related to us. Brother and Sister, please repeat the Five Awarenesses after me, and say "Yes, I do" firmly if you intend to make the vow to practice them. After each Awareness, when you hear the sound of the bell, touch the Earth before the Three Jewels.

The First Awareness
We are aware that all generations of our ancestors and all future generations are present in us.

This is the first of the Five Awarenesses. Do you make the vow to receive, study, and practice it?

Bride and Groom together: Yes, I do.
[BELL]
[BRIDE AND GROOM TOUCH THE EARTH ONE TIME]

The Second Awareness
We are aware of the expectations that our ancestors, our children, and their children have of us.

This is the second of the Five Awarenesses. Do you make the vow to receive, study, and practice it?

Bride and Groom together: Yes, I do.
[BELL]
[BRIDE AND GROOM TOUCH THE EARTH ONE TIME]

The Third Awareness
We are aware that our joy, peace, freedom, and harmony are the joy, peace, freedom, and harmony of our ancestors, our children, and their children.

This is the third of the Five Awarenesses. Do you make the vow to receive, study, and practice it?

Bride and Groom together: Yes, I do.
[BELL]
[BRIDE AND GROOM TOUCH THE EARTH ONE TIME]

The Fourth Awareness
We are aware that understanding is the very foundation of love.

This is the fourth of the Five Awarenesses. Do you make the vow to receive, study, and practice it?

Bride and Groom together: Yes, I do.
[BELL]
[BRIDE AND GROOM TOUCH THE EARTH ONE TIME]

The Fifth Awareness
We are aware that blaming and arguing can never help us and only create a wider gap between us; that only understanding, trust, and love can help us change and grow.

This is the fifth of the Five Awarenesses. Do you make the vow to receive, study, and practice it?

Bride and Groom together: Yes, I do.
[BELL, BELL]
[BRIDE AND GROOM TOUCH THE EARTH ONE TIME]

7. STATEMENT OF SUPPORT

Brother [NAME] and Sister [NAME], you have made the solemn vow to study and practice the Five Awarenesses. You have become husband and wife with the support of the Three Gems. As long as you continue this practice, you continue to have the spiritual support of the Buddha, the Dharma, and the Sangha, and your happiness will be the happiness of many others. Each full-moon day, you should recite together these Five Awarenesses. This community will continue to support you in this practice. Hearing the sound of the bell, please stand up and touch the Earth three times before the Buddha, the Dharma, and the Sangha.
[THREE BELLS AS BRIDE AND GROOM TOUCH THE EARTH]

8. Bowing to Each Other

Brother and Sister, now is the time for you to face each other and bow deeply to each other to show your mutual respect. Your love and commitment will continue to grow based on this ground of mutual respect.
[TWO BELLS AS BRIDE AND GROOM TOUCH THE EARTH]

9. Offering of Rings [optional] and Promises*

Brother and Sister, please kneel down in front of each other. It is the time for you to exchange rings and promises.

10. Invocation of the Buddhas and Bodhisattvas ♪

Please, will the whole community invoke the names of the Buddhas and the Bodhisattvas in support of the newly-wedded couple.

[CHANT EACH NAME THREE TIMES]
Namo Shakyamunaye Buddhaya
[Homage to Shakyamuni Buddha, the Fully Awakened One]
[BELL]

Namo Amitabhaya Buddhaya
[Homage to the Buddha of Infinite Light]
[BELL]

Namo Manjushriye Bodhisattvaya
[Homage to Manjushri, Bodhisattva of Great Understanding]
[BELL]

Namo Samantabhadraya Bodhisattvaya
[Homage to Samantabhadra, Bodhisattva of Great Action]
[BELL]

Namo Avalokiteshvaraya Bodhisattvaya
[Homage to Avalokiteshvara, Bodhisattva of Great Compassion]
[BELL]

* The promises are written by the bride and groom and read to each other.

Namo Kshitigarbhaya Bodhisattvaya
[Homage to Kshitigarbha, Bodhisattva of Great Aspiration]
[BELL, BELL]

11. The Three Refuges ♪

I take refuge in the Buddha,
the one who shows me the way in this life.
I take refuge in the Dharma,
the way of understanding and of love.
I take refuge in the Sangha,
the community that lives in harmony and awareness.
[BELL]

Dwelling in the refuge of Buddha,
I clearly see the path of light and beauty in the world.
Dwelling in the refuge of Dharma,
I learn to open many doors on the path of transformation.
Dwelling in the refuge of Sangha,
shining light that supports me, keeping my practice free of obstruction.
[BELL]

Taking refuge in the Buddha in myself,
I aspire to help all people recognize their own awakened nature,
realizing the Mind of Love.
Taking refuge in the Dharma in myself,
I aspire to help all people fully master the ways of practice
and walk together on the path of liberation.
Taking refuge in the Sangha in myself,
I aspire to help all people build Fourfold Communities,
to embrace all beings and support their transformation.
[BELL, BELL]

12. Sharing the Merit ♪

Reciting the sutras, practicing the way of awareness
gives rise to benefits without limit.
We vow to share the fruits with all beings.
We vow to offer tribute to parents, teachers, friends,

and numerous beings
who give guidance and support along the path.
[BELL, BELL, BELL]

BLESSING CEREMONY ᧡

1. OPENING VERSE ♪

[BELL, BELL, BELL]
Namo Tassa Bhagavato Arahato Samma Sambuddhassa
Namo Tassa Bhagavato Arahato Samma Sambuddhassa
Namo Tassa Bhagavato Arahato Samma Sambuddhassa
[BELL]

The Dharma is deep and lovely.
We now have a chance to see, study, and practice it.
We vow to realize its true meaning.
[BELL]

2. INTRODUCTORY VERSE

On the tip of the willow branch is the supreme nectar.
When one drop falls, it fills the Ten Directions
and puts an end to countless afflictions.
It has the power to purify.
Homage to the Bodhisattva Who Refreshes the Earth.
[BELL]

3. PRAISING THE BODHISATTVA OF COMPASSION ♪

The nectar of compassion is seen on the willow branch
held by the Bodhisattva.

A single drop of this nectar is enough to bring life
to the Ten Directions of the Cosmos.
May all afflictions of this world disappear totally and
may this place of practice be completely purified
by the Bodhisattva's nectar of compassion.

Homage to the Bodhisattva Who Refreshes the Earth.

From the depths of understanding, a flower of great eloquence blooms:
The Bodhisattva stands majestically
upon the waves of birth and death, free from all afflictions.
Her great compassion eliminates all sickness,
even that once thought of as incurable.
Her wondrous light sweeps away all obstacles and dangers.
Her willow branch, once waved,
reveals countless Buddha Lands.
Her lotus flower blossoms a multitude of practice centers.
We bow to her. We see her true presence in the here and the now.
We offer her the incense of our hearts.
May the Bodhisattva of Deep Listening embrace us all
with Great Compassion.

Namo'valokiteshvaraya
[Homage to Bodhisattva Avalokiteshvara]

On the willow branch, the clear water of compassion
falls on all three chiliocosms.
Its empty nature and its Eight Virtues
are the salvation of gods and men.
They make the Dharma realms brighter and more expansive.
They put an end to animosity and anger,
changing a blazing fire into a cool lotus lake.

Homage to the Bodhisattva Who Refreshes the Earth.
[BELL, BELL]

4. Opening Verse

[THE HEAD OF CEREMONY RAISES UP THE BOWL OF CLEAR WATER WITH
THE LEFT HAND AND FORMS THE MUDRA OF PEACE WITH THE RIGHT HAND
AT THE LEVEL OF THE FOREHEAD, AND THEN CHANTS ALOUD TO CONSECRATE
THE WATER. THE ASSEMBLED COMMUNITY FOLLOWS THEIR BREATHING,
LISTENING WITH EASE AND CONCENTRATION.]
[CHANTED BY HEAD OF CEREMONY]

Holding the willow branch, sprinkling the nectar of compassion,
destroying heat, cooling and refreshing the world of humans
by listening deeply and coming to help beings,
and by teaching the Dharma,
the Bodhisattva ends the suffering of all species.
The Bodhisattva's love and compassion are unshakable.
Her appearance manifests freedom and uprightness.
She responds wherever there is a need.
No appeal for her help fails to succeed.
Now we, your disciples, with right faith and a calm mind,
recite the gatha for consecrating clear water.
[BELL]

5. Verses of Consecration

[CHANTED BY HEAD OF CEREMONY]

This water's shape is round or square
according to the container that holds it.
In the spring warmth, it is liquid; in the winter cold, it is solid.
When its path is open, it flows.
When its path is obstructed, it stands still.
How vast it is, yet its source is so small it is difficult to find.
How wonderful it is in its streams which flow endlessly.
In the jade rivulets, the footprints of dragons remain.
In the deep pond, water holds the bright halo
of the autumn moon.
On the tip of the king's pen,
water becomes the compassion of clemency.
On the willow branch,
it becomes the clear fresh balm of compassion.

Only one drop of the water of compassion is needed,
and the Ten Directions are all purified.
[BELL]

6. RECITATION OF BODHISATTVA AVALOKITESHVARA'S NAME ♪

[DURING THE RECITATION OF THE BODHISATTVA'S NAME, THE PURIFIED
WATER IS SPRINKLED WITH THE WILLOW BRANCH OR FLOWER OVER THE
HEAD OF THE ORDINEE, OR AROUND THE PERIMETER OF THE HALL OR
BUILDING TO BE BLESSED.]

Brothers and Sisters, with one-pointed concentration please recite the name
of Avalokiteshvara:

Namo Avalokiteshvaraya
[REPEAT TWENTY-ONE TIMES]
[BELL]

7. THE THREE REFUGES ♪

I take refuge in the Buddha,
the one who shows me the way in this life.
I take refuge in the Dharma,
the way of understanding and of love.
I take refuge in the Sangha,
the community that lives in harmony and awareness.
[BELL]

Dwelling in the refuge of Buddha,
I clearly see the path of light and beauty in the world.
Dwelling in the refuge of Dharma,
I learn to open many doors on the path of transformation.
Dwelling in the refuge of Sangha,
shining light that supports me, keeping my practice free of obstruction.
[BELL]

Taking refuge in the Buddha in myself,
I aspire to help all people recognize their own awakened nature,
realizing the Mind of Love.

Taking refuge in the Dharma in myself,
I aspire to help all people fully master the ways of practice
and walk together on the path of liberation.
Taking refuge in the Sangha in myself,
I aspire to help all people build Fourfold Communities,
to embrace all beings and support their transformation.
[BELL, BELL]

8. Sharing the Merit ♪

Reciting the sutras, practicing the way of awareness
gives rise to benefits without limit.
We vow to share the fruits with all beings.
We vow to offer tribute to parents, teachers, friends,
and numerous beings
who give guidance and support along the path.
[BELL, BELL, BELL]

9. Words of Gratitude by Host or Householder
[AT THIS TIME, THE HOST OR HOUSEHOLDER IS INVITED TO COME
MINDFULLY BEFORE THE COMMUNITY TO OFFER A FEW WORDS OF
GRATITUDE TO EVERYONE WHO PARTICIPATED IN THE CEREMONY.]

Midday Offering ॐ

1. Incense Offering

As wonderful as the lotus flower,
as bright as the northern star,
let us come back and take refuge
in the teacher of gods and men.
[BELL]

As the incense is lit, sandalwood perfumes the air,
making an auspicious rainbow cloud.
I, your disciple, with all my respect
offer it to the Buddhas of the Ten Directions.
May we practice the precepts seriously at all times,
may we practice concentration diligently,
may we offer the precious fruit of insight
as our offering of incense of the heart.

Respectfully we offer incense to Buddhas and Bodhisattvas.
[BELL]

2. Offering Chant

Homage to the Buddha abiding in the Ten Directions
Homage to the Dharma abiding in the Ten Directions
Homage to the Sangha abiding in the Ten Directions
Namo Sakyamunaye Buddhaya
Namo Amitabhaya Buddhaya
Homage to all Buddhas in the Ten Directions and the Three Times
Namo Manjusraye
Namo Samantabhadraya
Namo Mahasthamapraptaya
Namo Avalokiteshvaraya
Namo Kshitigarbhaya
Homage to the Bodhisattvas of the Holy Sangha present in this
place of practice,

Homage to the Bodhisattvas our Ancestral Teachers
of all generations,
Homage to the Bodhisattva who oversees the kitchen
Homage to the ten Bodhisattvas who are judges of the dead
Homage to all Buddhas and Bodhisattvas present in this practice center

3. Mantra Recitation
[EACH MANTRA TO BE RECITED THREE TIMES]

Mantra to make food universally available
Namo sarvatathagata'valokite.
Om sambhara sambhara hung.
[BELL]

Mantra to make water universally available
Namah surupaya tathagataya Tadyatha,
Om surupaya surupaya surupaya svaha.
[BELL, BELL]

4. Offering Gatha

The color, fragrance and taste of this food
is offered first to all Buddhas,
then to all the holy ones
and to the people of the six continents.
The offering is made so that all, without distinction,
may have enough to eat.
May those who have given this food
cross over to the other shore.
Everything that is in the Dharma realms
is also offering the Three Virtues and the Six Tastes
to the Buddha and the Sangha.
[BELL]

5. Gatha

In concentration we make this offering of Dharma nectar
In quantity as great as Mount Sumeru.
Its form, fragrance, beauty and taste fill the whole of space.

Please be compassionate to us and accept it.

Homage to the Bodhisattva of Universal Offering.
[REPEAT THREE TIMES]
[BELL]

6. Sharing the Merit ♪

Making this offering, practicing the way of awareness
gives rise to benefits without limit.
We vow to share the fruits with all beings.
We vow to offer tribute to parents, teachers, friends
and numerous beings who give guidance and support along the path.
[BELL, BELL]

With this offering to the Buddha
we vow that all beings
may fully realize
their career of great awakening.
[BELL, BELL, BELL]

Formal Meal Ceremony

1. Taking the Lid Off the Bowl
[RECITED IN SILENCE BY THE INDIVIDUAL]

The bowl of the Tathagata
is in my two hands.
Giver, receiver, and gift
held in perfect oneness.

2. Seeing the Empty Bowl
[RECITED IN SILENCE BY THE INDIVIDUAL]

This bowl, empty now,
will soon be filled with precious food.
I realize how fortunate I am
to have enough to eat to continue the practice.

3. Holding the Bowl Which Is Full
[RECITED IN SILENCE BY THE INDIVIDUAL]

In this food,
I clearly see the entire universe
supporting my existence.

4. Making the Offering
[THE FOLLOWING CHANT IS RECITED BY EVERYONE TOGETHER. EACH
PERSON MAKES THE MUDRA OF PEACE WITH THE RIGHT HAND AND
HOLDS IT BEFORE THE MIDDLE OF THEIR FOREHEAD. THE LEFT HAND
HOLDS UP THE BOWL IN FRONT OF THE RIGHT HAND.]

We offer this food to:
The Buddha Vairocana, the pure Dharma body,
The Buddha Locana, perfected retribution body,
The Buddha Shakyamuni, the transformation body,
which is always and everywhere,
The Buddha Maitreya yet to be born,
The Buddha Amitabha of the land of Great Happiness,
All the Buddhas in the Ten Directions and the Three Times,

Bodhisattva Manjushri of Great Wisdom,
Bodhisattva Samantabhadra of Great Action,
Bodhisattva Avalokita of Great Compassion,
Bodhisattva Mahasthamaprapta of Great Strength,
All Bodhisattva Mahasattvas.

All beings in all the Dharma realms
want to make this offering
of the Three Virtues and the Six Tastes
to the Buddha, Dharma and Sangha.
As we eat this food we want all beings
to realize perfectly
the wisdom of awakening.
[BELL]

5. OFFERING TO THE HUNGRY
[THE MASTER OF CEREMONIES MAKES THE MUDRA OF PEACE OVER
THE BOWL WHICH CONTAINS WATER AND SEVEN GRAINS OF RICE
AND RECITES THIS GATHA]

The way of the Buddhas is extraordinary.
Seven grains of rice fill the Ten Directions.
It is offered everywhere in the Dharma realms
as the nectar of compassion which has no limit.

6. MANTRA TO MAKE FOOD UNIVERSALLY AVAILABLE
[CHANTED BY THE WHOLE COMMUNITY]

Namo sarvatathagata'valokite.
Om sambhara sambhara hung.
[REPEAT THREE TIMES]

[THE ATTENDANT PLACES THE BOWL WITH SEVEN GRAINS AND WATER OUTSIDE
AND RECITES THIS GATHA]

Great Garuda bird,
hungry spirits in the great desert,
yaksa mother who ceases to eat children's flesh,
may all be satisfied by the Bodhisattva's nectar.

7. Introducing the Five Contemplations
[READ BY THE MASTER OF CEREMONIES]

The Buddha advises us to eat in mindfulness,
establishing ourselves in the present moment
so that we can be aware of the food in front of us and the community
surrounding us.
We eat in a way that makes peace, joy, brotherhood and sisterhood possible
during the whole time of eating.

Dear Sangha, at the next sound of the bell,
please practice the Five Contemplations.
[BELL]

8. The Five Contemplations
[READ BY ONE MEMBER OF THE COMMUNITY]

This food is a gift of the Earth, the sky, numerous living beings, and
much hard and loving work.
May we eat with mindfulness and gratitude so as to worthy to receive
this food.
May we recognize and transform unwholesome mental formations,
especially our greed.
May we take only foods that nourish us and keep us healthy.
We accept this food so that we may nurture our sisterhood and brother-
hood, build our Sangha, and nourish our ideal of serving living beings.
[BELL]

9. Looking Deeply
[RECITED IN SILENCE BY THE INDIVIDUAL]

There are countless beings
struggling to live on this planet.
May they all have enough to eat.

10. The First Four Mouthfuls
[RECITED IN SILENCE BY THE INDIVIDUAL]

With the first mouthful I practice the love which brings joy.
With the second mouthful I practice the love which relieves pain.
With the third mouthful I practice the happiness of being alive.
With the fourth mouthful I practice equal love for all beings.

11. Rinsing the Bowl with Clean Water
[RECITED IN SILENCE BY THE INDIVIDUAL]

The water which rinses this bowl
is the nectar of the gods.
I offer it to hungry ghosts,
that they all may drink their fill.

12. When the Meal Is Finished
[RECITED IN SILENCE BY THE INDIVIDUAL]

The meal is finished
and I am satisfied.
The four gratitudes: to parents,
teachers, friends, and all dharmas
I bear deeply in my mind.

13. The Great Chunda Mantra
[RECITED BY EVERYONE TOGETHER]

Namo Saptanam Samyak Sambuddha
Kuthinam Tadyatha
Om cale cule Cunde svaha
[REPEAT THREE TIMES]
[BELL]

14. Offering the Merit
[RECITED BY EVERYONE TOGETHER]

To practice generosity
gives rise to much happiness.

The one who offers joy
also experiences joy.
[BELL]

By the merit of this mindful meal
we aspire that all beings
may wholly realize complete awakening.
[BELL, BELL, BELL]

Offering to the Hungry Ghosts Ceremony ᴐᴎ

[THIS CEREMONY IS USED FOR OFFERING FOOD TO THE HUNGRY GHOSTS. IT IS
PRACTICED EVERY DAY IN TEMPLES IN VIETNAM AS PART OF THE AFTERNOON
LITURGY. IT CAN ALSO BE USED AT HOME ON THE AFTERNOON OF THE FULL-
MOON DAY IN THE SEVENTH LUNAR MONTH (AUGUST/SEPTEMBER). WE NEED
GREAT CONCENTRATION, AND WE SHOULD CHANT CLEARLY AND DECISIVELY
FOR THE OFFERING TO BE SUCCESSFUL.

AN ALTAR TO THE HUNGRY GHOSTS IS PLACED OUTSIDE, AND ON IT ARE PLACED
TWO CANDLES, ONE STICK OF INCENSE, RICE GRUEL, UNCOOKED RICE GRAINS,
SALT, AND DRINKING WATER. OFFERINGS OF FOOD SUITABLE TO EACH CULTURE
CAN BE USED, SUCH AS BREAD, FRUIT, SOYMILK, PEANUT BUTTER, AND SO ON.]

1. Opening the Ceremony
Incense Offering, [page 87]

2. Recollection

Homage to Buddhas and Bodhisattvas in the Avatamsaka Assembly.
Homage to Buddhas and Bodhisattvas in the Avatamsaka Assembly.
Homage to Buddhas and Bodhisattvas in the Avatamsaka Assembly.
[BELL, BELL]

3. Opening Verse

As if a fire is raging on all four sides,
a hungry ghost ceaselessly suffers from heat.
Hungry ghosts, now to be born in a Pure Land,
hear this gatha transmitted by Buddha:

Those who aspire to see and understand
the Buddhas who are present in the Three Times
must always observe that, in the nature of the Dharmadhatu,
all that is arises from the mind.
[BELL]

4. Recollection

Homage to the Avatamsaka Sutra proclaimed by the Buddhas in all quarters.
[BELL]

Homage to the Buddha who is present in the Ten Directions.
[BELL]

Homage to the Dharma that is present in the Ten Directions.
[BELL]

Homage to the Sangha that is present in the Ten Directions.
[BELL]

Homage to Shakyamuni Buddha, the Fully Enlightened One.
[BELL]

Homage to Avalokiteshvara, the Bodhisattva of Great Compassion.
[BELL]

Homage to Kshitigarbha, rescuing beings from the greatest suffering.
[BELL]

Homage to the Venerable Ananda who recorded the teachings.
[BELL, BELL]

5. Repentance and Aspiration

Practitioners of the Way have acted unskillfully
with craving, hatred, and ignorance
manifested in actions of body, speech, and mind.
All practitioners repent of this.
[BELL]

Beings of all species have acted unskillfully
with craving, hatred, and ignorance
manifested in actions of body, speech, and mind.
All beings of all species repent of this.
[BELL]

Hungry ghosts have acted unskillfully
with craving, hatred, and ignorance
manifested in actions of body, speech, and mind.
All hungry ghosts repent of this.
[BELL]

Countless beings, I vow to save.
Ceaseless afflictions, I vow to end.
Limitless Dharma Doors, I vow to open.
I vow to realize the highest path of Awakening.
[BELL]

The true nature of beings, I vow to save.
The true nature of afflictions, I vow to end.
The true nature of Dharma Doors, I vow to open.
I vow to realize the true nature of the highest path of Awakening.
[BELL, BELL]

6. Verses of Offering

Homage to the Tathagata Multiple Jewel.
[BELL]

Homage to the Tathagata Jewel Victory.
[BELL]

Homage to the Tathagata Wonderful Form Body.
[BELL]

Homage to the Tathagata Extensive Body.
[BELL]

Homage to the Tathagata Far from Fear.
[BELL]

Homage to the Tathagata of the nectar of compassion.
[BELL]

Homage to the Tathagata of Infinite Light.
[BELL]

Maintaining our concentration, consciousness is calmed.
So too in practitioners throughout the Ten Directions.
May they all be satisfied, letting go of craving,
moving out of darkness to be born into a Pure Land.

May they truly take refuge in the Three Jewels,
give rise to Awakened Mind, and realize the highest path.
For the benefit of practitioners, may the merit of the practice
form the ground on which the future Buddha stands.
[BELL]

Maintaining our concentration, consciousness is calmed.
So too in all species throughout the Ten Directions.
May they all be satisfied, letting go of craving,
moving out of darkness to be born into a Pure Land.
May they truly take refuge in the Three Jewels,
give rise to Awakened Mind, and realize the highest path.
For the benefit of all species, may the merit of the practice
form the ground on which the future Buddha stands.
[BELL]

Maintaining our concentration, consciousness is calmed.
So too in hungry ghosts throughout the Ten Directions.
May they all be satisfied, letting go of craving,
moving out of darkness to be born into a Pure Land.
May they truly take refuge in the Three Jewels,
give rise to Awakened Mind, and realize the highest path.
For the benefit of hungry ghosts, may the merit of the practice
form the ground on which the future Buddha stands.
[BELL]

O practitioners of the Way,
we make offerings of food
multiplied in Ten Directions
so that you can all receive them.
By the merit of this offering,
may we and all practitioners
be successful in the realization of the path.
[BELL]

O beings of all species,
we make offerings of food
multiplied in Ten Directions
so that you can all receive them.

By the merit of this offering,
may we and all species
be successful in the realization of the path.
[BELL]

O hungry ghosts,
we make offerings of food
multiplied in Ten Directions
so that you can all receive them.
By the merit of this offering,
may we and all hungry ghosts
be successful in the realization of the path.
[BELL]

7. CONCLUDING VERSE

We offer up this fragrant nectar
in quantity as vast as space.
May all species arrive at their deepest aspirations,
returning to the shade of Great Loving Kindness.
[BELL]

8. THE THREE REFUGES ♪

I take refuge in the Buddha,
the one who shows me the way in this life.
I take refuge in the Dharma,
the way of understanding and of love.
I take refuge in the Sangha,
the community that lives in harmony and awareness.
[BELL]

Dwelling in the refuge of Buddha,
I clearly see the path of light and beauty in the world.
Dwelling in the refuge of Dharma,
I learn to open many doors on the path of transformation.
Dwelling in the refuge of Sangha,
shining light that supports me, keeping my practice free of obstruction.
[BELL]

Taking refuge in the Buddha in myself,
I aspire to help all people recognize their own awakened nature,
realizing the Mind of Love.
Taking refuge in the Dharma in myself,
I aspire to help all people fully master the ways of practice
and walk together on the path of liberation.
Taking refuge in the Sangha in myself,
I aspire to help all people build Fourfold Communities,
to embrace all beings and support their transformation.
[BELL, BELL]

9. SHARING THE MERIT *Pure Land Version* ♪

Reciting the sutras, practicing the way of awareness
gives rise to benefits without limit.
We vow to share the fruits with all beings.
We vow to offer tribute to parents, teachers, friends,
and numerous beings
who give guidance and support along the path.
[BELL]

May we be born now in the Pure Land
within the heart of a lotus flower.
In the moment when the lotus blooms,
we touch the reality of no-birth and no-death.
May Buddhas and Bodhisattvas be our companions
on the wonderful path of practice.
[BELL]

May we end all afflictions
so that understanding can arise,
the obstacles of unwholesome acts be dissolved,
and the fruit of awakening be fully realized.
[BELL, BELL, BELL]

Ceremony of Invitation ᠊᠊

[THIS CEREMONY IS USED, IN COMBINATION WITH THE CEREMONY OF OFFER-
ING TO HUNGRY GHOSTS, FOR THE GREAT REQUIEM CEREMONY.]

1.   Light radiates out into the realms of darkness.
     We know the Buddha is present at this Requiem Ceremony:
     We pray to the Enlightened One to help all the deceased come to the
     Pure Land,
     arriving in the Land of Great Bliss,
     sitting on the lotus flowers.
     Homage to the Bodhisattva of Rebirth in the Pure Land.

2.   With flowers and incense, we invite with all our heart
     The great Bodhisattva Ksitigarbha,
     who in the past made the vow
     that until the last living being is brought to the other shore
     and until all of hell is emptied,
     he will not rest and enjoy the fruit of Buddhahood.

Please do not forget your vow, and be present today, participating in this
Requiem Ceremony.

3.   With flowers and incense, we invite with all our heart:
     The great Bodhisattva Avalokiteshvara,
     the One who practices deep compassionate listening,
     the One who is always ready to come to where he is needed,
     the One who brings the boat of compassion
     to rescue living beings drowning in the Ocean of Suffering.

Please do not forget your vow, and be present today, participating in this Requiem Ceremony.

4.   With flowers and incense, we invite with all our heart.
     In the immense Ocean of Suffering,
     each living being carries his or her own karma.
     Those of you who have not had a chance to wake up from your
     long dream,
     begin to practice calling the name of the Buddha
     in order to leave behind the shore of Delusion
     and come to the land of Bliss.

This is the first incense offering.
This is the initial invitation:

> Relying on the spiritual power of the Buddhas, the Dharma,
> and the Sangha, and of the powerful dharanis,
> our ancestors of the past seven generations, all deceased
> members of our great family, and every wandering ghost
> are summoned here tonight to participate in the Offering
> and Requiem Ceremony, to listen to the Dharma and enjoy
> the food, the drink, and the nourishing, transforming,
> and healing nectar of compassion offered tonight.

5. With flowers and incense, we invite with all our heart.
The sun has just set,
the moon is beginning to rise.
Although we do not see you in the forms we used to see,
we know you are there in new forms.

This is the second incense offering.
This is the second invitation:

> Relying on the spiritual power of the Buddhas, the Dharma,
> and the Sangha, and of the powerful dharanis, our ancestors
> of the past seven generations, all deceased members of our
> great family, and every wandering ghost are summoned here
> tonight to participate in the Offering and Requiem Ceremony,
> to listen to the Dharma and enjoy the food, the drink, and the
> nourishing, transforming, and healing nectar of compassion
> offered tonight.

6. With flowers and incense, we invite with all our heart.
All formations are like dreams,
no one escapes impermanence,
but thanks to the power of the Three Jewels,
we always have a way out of birth and death.

This is the third incense offering.
This is the third invitation:

Relying on the spiritual power of the Buddhas, the Dharma,
and the Sangha, and of the powerful dharanis,
our ancestors of the past seven generations, all deceased
members of our great family, and every wandering ghost
are summoned here tonight to participate in the Offering and
Requiem Ceremony, to listen to the Dharma and enjoy the
food, the drink, and the nourishing, transforming, and healing
nectar of compassion offered tonight.

7.   After reciting the mantras and dharanis we invite
     everyone who has awakened and has heard.
     May the energy of the Three Jewels protect everyone.
     Everyone who is able to come to the ceremony,
     please come when you have heard us.

8.   You have heard our invitation and have come.
     Everyone is invited to be served with the nectar of immortality.
     Everyone is invited to sit down peacefully to listen to the holy
     scriptures.
     May the Dharma transform all afflictions and bring back joy and
     freedom.

Please listen to the wonderful teaching on Emptiness.

Opening Verse ♪

[BELL, BELL, BELL]

Namo Tassa Bhagavato Arahato Samma Sambuddhassa
Namo Tassa Bhagavato Arahato Samma Sambuddhassa
Namo Tassa Bhagavato Arahato Samma Sambuddhassa
[BELL]

The Dharma is deep and lovely.
We now have a chance to see, study, and practice it.
We vow to realize its true meaning.
[BELL]

The Heart of Perfect Understanding ♪

The Bodhisattva Avalokita,
while moving in the deep course of Perfect Understanding,
shed light on the Five Skandhas and found them equally empty.
After this penetration, he overcame ill-being.
[BELL]

Listen, Shariputra,
form is emptiness, and emptiness is form.
Form is not other than emptiness, emptiness is not other than form.
The same is true with feelings, perceptions, mental formations, and
consciousness.
[BELL]

Listen, Shariputra,
all dharmas are marked with emptiness.
They are neither produced nor destroyed,
neither defiled nor immaculate,
neither increasing nor decreasing.
Therefore in emptiness there is neither form, nor feelings,
nor perceptions, nor mental formations, nor consciousness.
No eye, or ear, or nose, or tongue, or body, or mind.
No form, no sound, no smell, no taste, no touch, no object of mind.
No realms of elements (from eyes to mind consciousness),
no interdependent origins and no extinction of them
(from ignorance to death and decay).
No ill-being, no cause of ill-being, no end of ill-being, and no path.
No understanding and no attainment.
[BELL]

Because there is no attainment,
the Bodhisattvas, grounded in Perfect Understanding,
find no obstacles for their minds.
Having no obstacles, they overcome fear,
liberating themselves forever from illusion, realizing perfect nirvana.
All Buddhas in the past, present, and future,

thanks to this Perfect Understanding,
arrive at full, right, and universal enlightenment.
[BELL]

Therefore one should know
that Perfect Understanding is the highest mantra, the unequaled mantra,
the destroyer of ill-being, the incorruptible truth.
A mantra of Prajñaparamita should therefore be proclaimed:

Gate gate paragate parasamgate bodhi svaha
Gate gate paragate parasamgate bodhi svaha
Gate gate paragate parasamgate bodhi svaha
[BELL, BELL]

ASPIRATION AND PRAISE

[THIS CEREMONY IS JOYFUL AND WATERS SEEDS OF GRATITUDE AND
LOVE IN US. IT CAN BE PRACTICED TWICE A MONTH ON THE FULL
AND NEW-MOON DAYS DURING THE MORNING SERVICE.]

1. OPENING THE CEREMONY

Incense Offering [page 87]

2. PRAISING THE BUDDHA

[THE HEAD OF CEREMONY KNEELS BEFORE THE THREE JEWELS TO CHANT
THESE VERSES AS REPRESENTATIVE OF THE SANGHA.]

The Buddha is like the fresh, full moon
that soars across the immense sky.
When the river of mind is truly calm,
the moon is reflected perfectly
upon the surface of the deep waters.
The countenance of the World-Honored One,
like the full moon or like the orb of the sun,
shines with the light of clarity,
a halo of wisdom spreading in every direction,
enveloping all with love, compassion, joy, and equanimity.

The inexhaustible virtues of the World-Honored One
cannot be adequately praised.
We in the [NAME] practice center, on this day
gather as a Fourfold Sangha, come to the altar, meditate and chant,
praise the virtuous actions of the Buddha, and offer this prayer:
May the path of the Buddha grow brighter.
May the Dharma become clearer.
May wind and rain be favorable.
May this country be at peace in the cities and rural areas.
May all follow the way of right practice.
May nature be safe. May people in society be free and equal.
May the refreshing breeze of compassion enter into this world of heat,
allowing the sun of wisdom to shine clearly in the cloudy sky
so that the path of liberation is appreciated everywhere
and the Dharma rain falls, benefiting all species.

May the Sangha that is present here practice diligently,
showing concern and love for each other
as they would for their own family,
transforming their consciousness.
We aspire to follow the example
of the Bodhisattvas Samantabhadra and Avalokiteshvara
and all other Bodhisattva Mahasattvas,
and the Great Perfection of Wisdom.
[BELL]

3. OPENING VERSE ♪

[BELL, BELL, BELL]

Namo Tassa Bhagavato Arahato Samma Sambuddhassa
Namo Tassa Bhagavato Arahato Samma Sambuddhassa
Namo Tassa Bhagavato Arahato Samma Sambuddhassa
[BELL]

The Dharma is deep and lovely.
We now have a chance to see, study, and practice it.
We vow to realize its true meaning.
[BELL]

4. THE HEART OF PERFECT UNDERSTANDING ♪

The Bodhisattva Avalokita,
while moving in the deep course of Perfect Understanding,
shed light on the Five Skandhas and found them equally empty.
After this penetration, he overcame ill-being.
[BELL]

Listen, Shariputra,
form is emptiness, and emptiness is form.
Form is not other than emptiness, emptiness is not other than form.
The same is true with feelings, perceptions, mental formations, and con-
sciousness.
[BELL]

Listen, Shariputra,
all dharmas are marked with emptiness.
They are neither produced nor destroyed,
neither defiled nor immaculate,
neither increasing nor decreasing.
Therefore in emptiness there is neither form, nor feelings, nor perceptions,
nor mental formations, nor consciousness.
No eye, or ear, or nose, or tongue, or body, or mind.
No form, no sound, no smell, no taste, no touch, no object of mind.
No realms of elements (from eyes to mind consciousness),
no interdependent origins and no extinction of them
(from ignorance to death and decay).
No ill-being, no cause of ill-being, no end of ill-being, and no path.
No understanding and no attainment.
[BELL]

Because there is no attainment,
the Bodhisattvas, grounded in Perfect Understanding,
find no obstacles for their minds.
Having no obstacles, they overcome fear,
liberating themselves forever from illusion, realizing perfect nirvana.
All Buddhas in the past, present, and future,
thanks to this Perfect Understanding,
arrive at full, right, and universal enlightenment.
[BELL]

Therefore one should know
that Perfect Understanding is the highest mantra, the unequaled mantra,
the destroyer of ill-being, the incorruptible truth.
A mantra of Prajñaparamita should therefore be proclaimed:

Gate gate paragate parasamgate bodhi svaha
Gate gate paragate parasamgate bodhi svaha
Gate gate paragate parasamgate bodhi svaha
[BELL, BELL]

5. The Refuge Chant ♪

Incense perfumes the atmosphere.
A lotus blooms and the Buddha appears.
The world of suffering and discrimination
is filled with the light of the rising sun.
As the dust of fear and anxiety settles,
with open heart, one-pointed mind,
I turn to the Three Jewels.
[BELL]

The Fully Enlightened One, beautifully seated, peaceful and smiling,
a living source of understanding and compassion,
to the Buddha I go for refuge.
[BELL]

The path of mindful living,
leading to healing, joy, and enlightenment, the way of peace,
to the Dharma I go for refuge.
[BELL]

The loving and supportive community of practice,
realizing harmony, awareness, and liberation,
to the Sangha I go for refuge.
[BELL]

I am aware that the Three Gems are within my heart.
I vow to realize them,
practicing mindful breathing and smiling,
looking deeply into things.
I vow to understand living beings and their suffering,
to cultivate compassion and loving kindness,
to practice joy and equanimity.
[BELL]

I vow to offer joy to one person in the morning,
to help relieve the grief of one person in the afternoon,
living simply and sanely with few possessions,
keeping my body healthy.   .

I vow to let go of all worries and anxiety
in order to be light and free.
[BELL]

I am aware that I owe so much
to my parents, teachers, friends, and all beings.
I vow to be worthy of their trust, to practice wholeheartedly
so that understanding and compassion will flower,
helping living beings be free from their suffering.
May the Buddha, the Dharma, and the Sangha
support my efforts.
[BELL, BELL]

6. INVOKING THE BODHISATTVAS' NAMES

We invoke your name, Avalokiteshvara. We aspire to learn your way of listening in order to help relieve the suffering in the world. You know how to listen in order to understand. We invoke your name in order to practice listening with all our attention and openheartedness. We will sit and listen without any prejudice. We will sit and listen without judging or reacting. We will sit and listen in order to understand. We will sit and listen so attentively that we will be able to hear what the other person is saying and also what is being left unsaid. We know that just by listening deeply we already alleviate a great deal of pain and suffering in the other person.
[BELL]

We invoke your name, Manjushri. We aspire to learn your way, which is to be still and to look deeply into the heart of things and into the hearts of people. We will look with all our attention and openheartedness. We will look with unprejudiced eyes. We will look without judging or reacting. We will look deeply so that we will be able to see and understand the roots of suffering and the impermanent and selfless nature of all that is. We will practice your way of using the sword of understanding to cut through the bonds of suffering, thus freeing ourselves and other species.
[BELL]

We invoke your name, Samantabhadra. We aspire to practice your vow to act with the eyes and heart of compassion, to bring joy to one person in the morning and to ease the pain of one person in the afternoon. We know that the happiness of others is our own happiness, and we aspire to practice joy on the path of service. We know that every word, every look, every action, and every smile can bring happiness to others. We know that if we practice wholeheartedly, we ourselves may become an inexhaustible source of peace and joy for our loved ones and for all species.

[BELL]

We invoke your name, Kshitigarbha. We aspire to learn your way of being present where there is darkness, suffering, oppression, and despair, so we can bring light, hope, relief, and liberation to those places. We are determined not to forget about or abandon those in desperate situations. We will do our best to establish contact with those who cannot find a way out of their suffering, those whose cries for help, justice, equality, and human rights are not being heard. We know that hell can be found in many places on Earth. We will do our best not to contribute to creating more hells on Earth, and we will help transform the hells that already exist. We will practice in order to realize the qualities of perseverance and stability, so that, like the Earth, we can always be supportive and faithful to those in need.

[BELL]

We invoke your name, Sadaparibhuta. We aspire to learn your way of never disparaging or underestimating any living being. With great respect, you say to all you meet, "You are someone of great value, you have Buddha nature, I see this potential in you." We will look with a wise, compassionate gaze, so we are able to hold up a mirror where others can see their ultimate nature reflected. We will remind people who feel worthless that they too are a precious wonder of life. We vow to water only the positive seeds in ourselves and in others, so that our thoughts, words, and actions can encourage confidence and self-acceptance in ourselves, our children, our loved ones, and in everyone we meet. Inspired by the great faith and insight that everyone is Buddha, we will practice your way of patience and inclusiveness so we can liberate ourselves from ignorance and misunderstanding, and offer freedom, peace, and joy to ourselves, to others and to our society.

[BELL, BELL]

7. Touching the Earth

[AFTER INVOKING THE BODHISATTVAS' NAMES, EVERYONE STANDS UP
TO BOW IN GRATITUDE. THIS IS A SPECIAL PART OF THE CEREMONY.
WE TOUCH THE EARTH IN ORDER TO EXPRESS OUR GRATITUDE TO THE
BUDDHA, ANCESTRAL TEACHERS, PARENTS, TEACHERS, FRIENDS, AND ALL
SPECIES IN THE ANIMAL, PLANT, AND MINERAL WORLDS.]

[THE FOLLOWING IS CHANTED BY THE HEAD OF THE CEREMONY. THE COMMU-
NITY TOUCHES THE EARTH AS EACH BELL SOUNDS.]
Offering light in the Ten Directions,
the Buddha, the Dharma, and the Sangha,
to whom we bow in gratitude.
[BELL]

Teaching and living the way of awareness
in the very midst of suffering and confusion,
Shakyamuni Buddha, the Fully Enlightened One,
to whom we bow in gratitude.
[BELL]

Cutting through ignorance, awakening our hearts and our minds,
Manjushri, the Bodhisattva of Great Understanding,
to whom we bow in gratitude.
[BELL]

Working mindfully, working joyfully for the sake of all beings,
Samantabhadra, the Bodhisattva of Great Action,
to whom we bow in gratitude.
[BELL]

Listening deeply, serving beings in countless ways,
Avalokiteshvara, the Bodhisattva of Great Compassion,
to whom we bow in gratitude.
[BELL]

Fearless and persevering through realms of suffering and darkness,
Kshitigarbha, the Bodhisattva of Great Aspiration,
To whom we bow in gratitude.
[BELL]

Seed of awakening and loving kindness
in children and all beings,
Maitreya, the Buddha to-be-born,
to whom we bow in gratitude.
[BELL]

Convener of the Sangha, the teacher Mahakashyapa,
to whom we bow in gratitude.
[BELL]

Wise elder brother, the teacher Shariputra,
to whom we bow in gratitude.
[BELL]

Showing love for parents, the teacher Mahamaudgalyayana,
to whom we bow in gratitude.
[BELL]

Master of the Vinaya, the teacher Upali,
to whom we bow in gratitude.
[BELL]

Recorder of the teachings, the teacher Ananda,
to whom we bow in gratitude.
[BELL]

The first bhikshuni, Mahagotami,
to whom we bow in gratitude.
[BELL]

Showing the way fearlessly and compassionately,
the stream of all our Ancestral Teachers,
to whom we bow in gratitude.
[BELL]

The first Dhyana patriarch in Vietnam,
Dhyana Master Tang Hôi,
to whom we bow in gratitude.
[BELL]

The Patriarch Dharmadeva,
to whom we bow in gratitude.
[BELL]

The Patriarch Vinitaruci,
to whom we bow in gratitude.
[BELL]

The Patriarch Wu Yen Tung,
to whom we bow in gratitude.*
[BELL]

The Patriarch Cao Dong,
to whom we bow in gratitude.†
[BELL]

The Patriarch Truc Lam Dai Si,
the Great Bamboo Forest Master,
to whom we bow in gratitude.
[BELL]

The Patriarch Lin Chi, Wonderful Meaning
to whom we bow in gratitude.
[BELL]

The Patriarch Lieu Quan, True Wonder,
to whom we bow in gratitude.
[BELL]

In gratitude to our parents who bring us into the world,
we touch the Earth before the Three Jewels.
[BELL]

In gratitude to our teachers who show us how to love,
understand, and live in the present moment,
we touch the Earth before the Three Jewels.
[BELL]

---

* This patriarch's name in Vietnamese is Vo Ngon Thong.
† This patriarch's name in Vietnamese is Thao Duong.

In gratitude to our friends who guide us on the path
and support us in difficult moments,
we touch the Earth before the Three Jewels.
[BELL]

In gratitude to all species in the animal, plant, and mineral worlds,
who support our life and make our world beautiful,
we touch the Earth before the Three Jewels.
[BELL, BELL]

8. The Three Refuges ♪

I take refuge in the Buddha,
the one who shows me the way in this life.
I take refuge in the Dharma,
the way of understanding and of love.
I take refuge in the Sangha,
the community that lives in harmony and awareness.
[BELL]

Dwelling in the refuge of Buddha,
I clearly see the path of light and beauty in the world.
Dwelling in the refuge of Dharma,
I learn to open many doors on the path of transformation.
Dwelling in the refuge of Sangha,
shining light that supports me, keeping my practice free of obstruction.
[BELL]

Taking refuge in the Buddha in myself,
I aspire to help all people recognize their own awakened nature,
realizing the Mind of Love.
Taking refuge in the Dharma in myself,
I aspire to help all people fully master the ways of practice
and walk together on the path of liberation.
Taking refuge in the Sangha in myself,
I aspire to help all people build Fourfold Communities,
to embrace all beings and support their transformation.
[BELL, BELL]

9. Sharing the Merit ♪

Reciting the sutras, practicing the way of awareness
gives rise to benefits without limit.
We vow to share the fruits with all beings.
We vow to offer tribute to parents, teachers, friends,
and numerous beings
who give guidance and support along the path.
[BELL, BELL, BELL]

Praising Ancestral Teachers ᴦ

1. Offering Incense

In the precious censer burns the honored incense,
the fragrance of sandalwood and eucalyptus pervades the Ten Directions.
The bodhicitta is exceptionally courageous and strong.
Once touched, wherever it is, it gives out a halo of light.
Everywhere solidity is clearly restored.
With sincere respect we offer this incense in a high place to the
World-Honored Lord.
Respectfully we offer this incense to Buddha and the Bodhisattvas.
[BELL]

2. Chant of Praise and Aspiration

A flower held up speaks wonderfully.
Its five petals have a special fragrance.
The Dharma Treasure is transmitted from India
and continued in the Mind-Seal school in China.
May all generations of Ancestral Teachers,
residing in the nirvana of the Wonderful Mind,
seated high on the precious Dharma Throne,
with the Awakened Understanding which transcends the world,
please look down on all your descendants.
With love please be witness to our aspiration:
all generations of Ancestral Teachers have developed widely the
path of stability and freedom.
They are the example and source for all future generations.

We, your descendants, are [NAME OF SANGHA AND PLACE WHERE YOU ARE].
Today on the Memorial Day of our Ancestral Teacher whose first name is
Nhat and whose second name is Dinh [OR NAME OF OTHER TEACHER BEING
REMEMBERED], have gathered as a Fourfold Sangha.
We have come into the precious shrine before the ancestral altar,
to practice meditation, the daily liturgy
and reciting the words of the sutra,
to praise the actions and virtues of our respected Ancestral Teacher.

With whole-hearted respect and aspiration
we want to express our deep gratitude.

We respectfully prostrate before the Bodhisattvas,
our Ancestral Teachers from India and the Far East,
the Root Teacher who founded our Root Temple,
all the generations of teachers who preceded him
and who have opened up the way of practice for us, your descendants.
We are determined to practice steadfastly
to transform the afflictions,
to nourish our bodhicitta,
so that the lineage school may always grow and renew itself,
the seal of the Ancestral Teacher every day be clearer and brighter,
so that the flower of awakening may open everywhere in the forest
of meditation,
and the rain of the wonderful teachings penetrate the place of learning.
We, your disciples, being mindful of our gratitude to the teachings
of our Ancestral Teacher,
vow to accept each other, forgive each other,
and love each other as children of the same family,
so that the Sanghakaya can grow up strong,
so that happiness can be assured
and we can be a place of refuge for the ocean of beings in the Ten Directions.
May we follow in the footsteps of Mahakashyapa, Ananda,
Asangha and Vasubandhu, Masters Lin Chi and Lieu Quan,
as well as all the dragons and elephants of the meditation school,
and all those whose mind is directed to Great Action,
all the Bodhisattva Mahasattvas
and the Great Transcendental Understanding which takes us
to the other shore.
[BELL, BELL]

3. OPENING VERSE
[BELL, BELL, BELL]

Namo Tassa Bhagavato Arahato Samma Sambuddhassa
Namo Tassa Bhagavato Arahato Samma Sambuddhassa
Namo Tassa Bhagavato Arahato Samma Sambuddhassa
[BELL]

The Dharma is deep and lovely.
We now have a chance to see, study, and practice it.
We vow to realize its true meaning.
[BELL]

4. THE HEART OF PERFECT UNDERSTANDING ♪

The Bodhisattva Avalokita,
while moving in the deep course of Perfect Understanding,
shed light on the Five Skandhas and found them equally empty.
After this penetration, he overcame ill-being.
[BELL]

Listen, Shariputra,
form is emptiness, and emptiness is form.
Form is not other than emptiness, emptiness is not other than form.
The same is true with feelings, perceptions, mental formations, and consciousness.
[BELL]

Listen, Shariputra,
all dharmas are marked with emptiness.
They are neither produced nor destroyed,
neither defiled nor immaculate,
neither increasing nor decreasing.
Therefore in emptiness there is neither form, nor feelings, nor perceptions,
nor mental formations, nor consciousness.
No eye, or ear, or nose, or tongue, or body, or mind.
No form, no sound, no smell, no taste, no touch, no object of mind.
No realms of elements (from eyes to mind consciousness),
no interdependent origins and no extinction of them
(from ignorance to death and decay).
No ill-being, no cause of ill-being, no end of ill-being, and no path.
No understanding and no attainment.
[BELL]

Because there is no attainment,
the Bodhisattvas, grounded in Perfect Understanding,
find no obstacles for their minds.

Having no obstacles, they overcome fear,
liberating themselves forever from illusion, realizing perfect nirvana.
All Buddhas in the past, present, and future,
thanks to this Perfect Understanding,
arrive at full, right, and universal enlightenment.
[BELL]

Therefore one should know
that Perfect Understanding is the highest mantra, the unequaled mantra,
the destroyer of ill-being, the incorruptible truth.
A mantra of Prajñaparamita should therefore be proclaimed:

Gate gate paragate parasamgate bodhi svaha
Gate gate paragate parasamgate bodhi svaha
Gate gate paragate parasamgate bodhi svaha
[BELL, BELL]

5. The Refuge Chant ♪

Incense perfumes the atmosphere.
A lotus blooms and the Buddha appears.
The world of suffering and discrimination
is filled with the light of the rising sun.
As the dust of fear and anxiety settles,
with open heart, one-pointed mind,
I turn to the Three Jewels.
[BELL]

The Fully Enlightened One, beautifully seated, peaceful and smiling,
a living source of understanding and compassion,
to the Buddha I go for refuge.
[BELL]

The path of mindful living,
leading to healing, joy, and enlightenment, the way of peace,
to the Dharma I go for refuge.
[BELL]

The loving and supportive community of practice,
realizing harmony, awareness, and liberation,
to the Sangha I go for refuge.
[BELL]

I am aware that the Three Gems are within my heart.
I vow to realize them,
practicing mindful breathing and smiling,
looking deeply into things.
I vow to understand living beings and their suffering,
to cultivate compassion and loving kindness,
to practice joy and equanimity.
[BELL]

I vow to offer joy to one person in the morning,
to help relieve the grief of one person in the afternoon,
living simply and sanely with few possessions,
keeping my body healthy.
I vow to let go of all worries and anxiety
in order to be light and free.
[BELL]

I am aware that I owe so much
to my parents, teachers, friends, and all beings.
I vow to be worthy of their trust, to practice wholeheartedly
so that understanding and compassion will flower,
helping living beings be free from their suffering.
May the Buddha, the Dharma, and the Sangha
support my efforts.
[BELL, BELL]

6. Invocation of the Buddhas and Bodhisattvas ♪
[CHANT EACH NAME THREE TIMES]

Namo Shakyamunaye Buddhaya
[Homage to Shakyamuni Buddha, the Fully Awakened One]
[BELL]

Namo Amitabhaya Buddhaya
[Homage to the Buddha of Infinite Light]
[BELL]

Namo Manjushriye Bodhisattvaya
[Homage to Manjushri, Bodhisattva of Great Understanding]
[BELL]

Namo Samantabhadraya Bodhisattvaya
[Homage to Samantabhadra, Bodhisattva of Great Action]
[BELL]

Namo Avalokiteshvaraya Bodhisattvaya
[Homage to Avalokiteshvara, Bodhisattva of Great Compassion]
[BELL]

Namo Kshitigarbhaya Bodhisattvaya
[Homage to Kshitigarbha, Bodhisattva of Great Aspiration]
[BELL]

7. Invoking the Bodhisattvas' Names

We invoke your name, Avalokiteshvara. We aspire to learn your way of listening in order to help relieve the suffering in the world. You know how to listen in order to understand. We invoke your name in order to practice listening with all our attention and openheartedness. We will sit and listen without any prejudice. We will sit and listen without judging or reacting. We will sit and listen in order to understand. We will sit and listen so attentively that we will be able to hear what the other person is saying and also what is being left unsaid. We know that just by listening deeply we already alleviate a great deal of pain and suffering in the other person.
[BELL]

We invoke your name, Manjushri. We aspire to learn your way, which is to be still and to look deeply into the heart of things and into the hearts of people. We will look with all our attention and openheartedness. We will look with unprejudiced eyes. We will look without judging or reacting. We will look deeply so that we will be able to see and understand the roots of suffering, the impermanent and selfless nature of all that is. We will practice

your way of using the sword of understanding to cut through the bonds of suffering, thus freeing ourselves and other species.
[BELL]

We invoke your name, Samantabhadra. We aspire to practice your vow to act with the eyes and heart of compassion, to bring joy to one person in the morning and to ease the pain of one person in the afternoon. We know that the happiness of others is our own happiness, and we aspire to practice joy on the path of service. We know that every word, every look, every action, and every smile can bring happiness to others. We know that if we practice wholeheartedly, we ourselves may become an inexhaustible source of peace and joy for our loved ones and for all species.
[BELL]

We invoke your name, Kshitigarbha. We aspire to learn your way of being present where there is darkness, suffering, oppression, and despair, so we can bring light, hope, relief, and liberation to those places. We are determined not to forget about or abandon those in desperate situations. We will do our best to establish contact with those who cannot find a way out of their suffering, those whose cries for help, justice, equality, and human rights are not being heard. We know that hell can be found in many places on Earth. We will do our best not to contribute to creating more hells on Earth, and to help transform the hells that already exist. We will practice in order to realize the qualities of perseverance and stability, so that, like the Earth, we can always be supportive and faithful to those in need.
[BELL]

We invoke your name, Sadaparibhuta. We aspire to learn your way of never disparaging or underestimating any living being. With great respect, you say to all you meet, "You are someone of great value, you have Buddha nature, I see this potential in you." We will look with a wise, compassionate gaze, so we are able to hold up a mirror where others can see their ultimate nature reflected. We will remind people who feel worthless that they too are a precious wonder of life. We vow to water only the positive seeds in ourselves and in others, so that our thoughts, words, and actions can encourage confidence and self-acceptance in ourselves, our children, our loved ones, and in everyone we meet. Inspired by the great faith and insight that everyone is Buddha, we will practice your way of patience and inclusiveness so ness so we can liberate ourselves from ignorance and misunderstanding, and offer freedom, peace, and joy to ourselves, to others and to our society. [BELL, BELL]

8. Touching the Earth in Gratitude
[THE LEADER OF THE CEREMONY CHANTS EACH NAME AND THEN THERE IS A SOUND OF THE BELL FOR THE COMMUNITY TO TOUCH THE EARTH.]

Offering light in the Ten Directions, the Buddha, the Dharma and the Sangha, to whom we bow in gratitude.
[BELL]

Teaching and living the way of awareness in the very midst of suffering and confusion, Shakyamuni Buddha the Fully Enlightened One, to whom we bow in gratitude.
[BELL]

Cutting through ignorance, awakening our hearts and our minds, Manjushri the Bodhisattva of Great Understanding, to whom we bow in gratitude.
[BELL]

Working mindfully, working joyfully for the sake of all beings, Samantabhadra the Bodhisattva of Great Action, to whom we bow in gratitude.
[BELL]

Listening deeply, serving beings in countless ways, Avalokiteshvara the Bodhisattva of Great Compassion, to whom we bow in gratitude.
[BELL]

Fearless and persevering through realms of suffering and darkness, Kshitigarbha, the Bodhisattva of Great Aspiration, to whom we bow in gratitude.
[BELL]

Seed of awakening and loving kindness in children and all beings,
Maitreya, the Buddha to-be-born,
to whom we bow in gratitude.
[BELL]

Convener of the Sangha, the patriarch Mahakashyapa,
to whom we bow in gratitude.
[BELL]

Wise elder brother, the teacher Shariputra,
to whom we bow in gratitude.
[BELL]

Showing love for parents, Mahamaudgalyayana,
to whom we bow in gratitude.
[BELL]

Master of the Vinaya, the teacher Upali,
to whom we bow in gratitude.
[BELL]

Recorder of the teachings, the teacher Ananda,
to whom we bow in gratitude.
[BELL]

The first bhikshuni, Mahagotami,
to whom we bow in gratitude.
[BELL]

Showing the way fearlessly and compassionately,
the stream of all our Ancestral Teachers,
to whom we bow in gratitude.
[BELL]

The first dhyana patriarch in Vietnam,
Dhyana Master Tang Hoi,
to whom we bow in gratitude.
[BELL]

The Patriarch Dharmadeva,
to whom we bow in gratitude.
[BELL]

The Patriarch Vinitaruci,
to whom we bow in gratitude.
[BELL]

The Patriarch Wu Yen Tung,
to whom we bow in gratitude.*
[BELL]

The Patriarch Cao Dong,
to whom we bow in gratitude.†
[BELL]

The Patriarch Truc Lam Dai Si,
the Great Bamboo Forest Master,
to whom we bow in gratitude.
[BELL]

The Patriarch Lin Chi, Wonderful Meaning,
to whom we bow in gratitude.
[BELL]

The Patriarch Lieu Quan, True Wonder,
to whom we bow in gratitude.
[BELL]

The Ancestral Teacher Nhat Dinh,
to whom we bow in gratitude.
[BELL]

The Ancestral Teacher Chan That,
to whom we bow in gratitude.
[BELL]

* This patriarch's name in Vietnamese is Vo Ngon Thong.
† This patriarch's name in Vietnamese is Thao Duong.

The Precept Transmission Teachers,
to whom we bow in gratitude.
[BELL]

In gratitude to our parents who bring us into the world,
we touch the Earth before the Three Jewels.
[BELL]

In gratitude to our teachers who show us how to love,
understand, and live the present moment,
we touch the Earth before the Three Jewels.
[BELL]

In gratitude to our friends who guide us on the path
and support us in difficult moments,
we touch the Earth before the Three Jewels.
[BELL]

In gratitude to all species in the animal, plant, and mineral worlds,
who support our life and make our world beautiful,
we touch the Earth before the Three Jewels.
[BELL]

9. OUR ASPIRATION

We, your disciples, on the memorial day of our Ancestral Teacher whose first name is Nhat and whose second name is Dinh, have gathered in [NAME OF SANGHA AND PLACE] respectfully presenting ourselves before your ancestral altar. With whole-hearted aspiration we bow our heads and request all generations of Ancestral Teachers to bear compassionate witness to our words:

We are aware that trees have their roots and water has its source. Buddha and all generations of our Ancestral Teachers are our source and we are the continuation of you, our ancestors. We are determined to receive the awakened understanding, compassion, peace and joy which the Buddha and the Ancestral Teachers have transmitted. We are determined to maintain these and help them grow, never allowing this precious spiritual inheritance to come to an end. We are determined to continue to realize your aspiration to help all beings. We are determined to transform our own suffering and help people of our time to transform their suffering. We are determined to open up for future generations Dharma doors which are appropriate and can help them apply the teachings of Buddhism in all fields of life. We vow to practice to live happily and peacefully in the present moment, to nourish solidity and freedom in ourselves in order to help those around us.

We vow to recognize each other as brothers and sisters of one spiritual family, because we know that we are all your descendants. We vow to take care of each other, be aware of each other's difficulties and suffering so as to be able to understand each other, to love and to help each other in the process of transformation. We promise to use loving speech and deep listening to nourish brotherly and sisterly affection within the Sanghakaya. We vow to accept the guidance offered by the Sangha in order to recognize our abilities and our weaknesses, to strengthen our abilities and transform our weaknesses. We vow to erase all resentment and hatred so that we can rely on each other while on the path of realizing our highest career. We know that when we can do this we are truly worthy to be the descendants of the Buddha and you, our Spiritual Ancestor.

We bow our heads and ask our Ancestral Teacher, the founder of the Tu Hieu Temple, and all other Ancestral Teachers to bear compassionate witness to our deep respect and loyalty to our spiritual ancestors, which is the most precious offering we can offer up on the memorial day.

10. Gatha of Praise

Holding up the flower, showing the way to awakening,
following in the footsteps of revered teachers,
for a long time may the teachings be transported by the True Vehicle,
the practice of meditation strengthen and hold our practice
and the True Teachings shine more clearly than ever.

Namo gurobhyah
[Homage to the Ancestral Teachers of all ages]
[BELL]

11. Taking Refuge ♪

I take refuge in the Buddha,
the one who shows me the way in this life.
I take refuge in the Dharma,

the way of understanding and of love.
I take refuge in the Sangha,
the community that lives in harmony and awareness.
[BELL]

Dwelling in the refuge of Buddha,
I clearly see the path of light and beauty in the world.
Dwelling in the refuge of Dharma,
I learn to open many doors on the path of transformation.
Dwelling in the refuge of Sangha,
shining light that supports me, keeping my practice free of obstruction.
[BELL]

Taking refuge in the Buddha in myself,
I aspire to help all people recognize their own awakened nature,
realizing the Mind of Love.
Taking refuge in the Dharma in myself,
I aspire to help all people fully master the ways of practice
and walk together on the path of liberation.
Taking refuge in the Sangha in myself,
I aspire to help all people build Fourfold Communities,
to embrace all beings and support their transformation.
[BELL, BELL]

12. Sharing the Merit ♪

Reciting the trainings, practicing the way of awareness
gives rise to benefits without limit.
We vow to share the fruits with all beings.
We vow to offer tribute to parents, teachers, friends, and numerous beings
who give guidance and support along the path.
[BELL, BELL, BELL]

Ceremony to Support the Sick ༘

[THIS CEREMONY IS TO OFFER PEACE OF MIND AND COURAGE
TO THE SICK AND TO THOSE WHO HAVE BEEN VICTIMS OF DISASTERS
AS WELL AS TO THEIR RELATIVES AND FRIENDS.]

1. Opening the Ceremony

Sitting Meditation [12 MINUTES]
Incense Offering [page 87]
Touching the Earth [page 88]

2. Opening Verse ♪

[BELL, BELL, BELL]

Namo Tassa Bhagavato Arahato Samma Sambuddhassa
Namo Tassa Bhagavato Arahato Samma Sambuddhassa
Namo Tassa Bhagavato Arahato Samma Sambuddhassa
[BELL]

The Dharma is deep and lovely.
We now have a chance to see, study, and practice it.
We vow to realize its true meaning.
[BELL]

3. Mindfulness of Loved Ones

Brothers and Sisters, it is time to bring our loved ones to mind: those to
whom we wish to send the healing energy of love and compassion. Let us
sit and enjoy our breathing for a few moments, allowing our beloved ones
to be present with us now.
[TEN BREATHS IN SILENCE]

4. The Lotus of the Wonderful Dharma: Universal Door Chapter

Brothers and Sisters, please listen. The peace and joy of the entire world, including the worlds of the living and the dead, depend on our own peace and
joy in this moment. With all our heart and one-pointed mind, let us chant
the Lotus of the Wonderful Dharma [see page 327].

5. INTRODUCTORY WORDS

[ADAPT AS APPROPRIATE.]

Today the community has gathered to recite the sutra, practice mindfulness of the Buddha, and give spiritual support and offer peace to [NAME]. There are relatives and friends of [NAME] present with us to join in giving spiritual support. Brothers and Sisters, listen carefully. Once one person is able to give rise to a deep sense of peace and happiness, the whole world benefits. We have gathered today to light the lamp of peace and happiness in our hearts by practicing sitting meditation, walking meditation, reciting the Lotus Sutra, and being mindful of the Buddha in order to be in communion with the essence of great love, compassion, joy, equanimity, and fearlessness. These are motivating forces that can transform situations of fear and danger and restore peace and happiness where they have been lost. The peace and joy of the world depend on our peace and joy at this moment. With all our concentration and a one-pointed mind, let us recite the name of Avalokiteshvara:

Namo'valokiteshvaraya ♪
[REPEAT TWENTY-ONE TIMES]
[BELL, BELL]

6. PRAISING THE BODHISATTVA OF COMPASSION ♪

The nectar of compassion is seen on the willow branch
held by the Bodhisattva.
A single drop of this nectar is enough to bring life
to the Ten Directions of the Cosmos.
May all afflictions of this world disappear totally and
may this place of practice be completely purified
by the Bodhisattva's nectar of compassion.

Homage to the Bodhisattva Who Refreshes the Earth.

From the depths of understanding, a flower of great eloquence blooms:
The Bodhisattva stands majestically
upon the waves of birth and death, free from all afflictions.
Her great compassion eliminates all sickness,
even that once thought of as incurable.

Her wondrous light sweeps away all obstacles and dangers.
Her willow branch, once waved,
reveals countless Buddha Lands.
Her lotus flower blossoms a multitude of practice centers.
We bow to her. We see her true presence in the here and the now.
We offer her the incense of our hearts.
May the Bodhisattva of Deep Listening embrace us all
with Great Compassion.

Namo'valokiteshvaraya
[Homage to Bodhisattva Avalokiteshvara]
[BELL, BELL]

7. MAY THE DAY BE WELL ♪

May the day be well and the night be well.
May the midday hour bring happiness too.
In every minute and every second,
may the day and night be well.
By the blessing of the Triple Gem,
may all things be protected and safe.
May all beings born in each of the four ways
live in a land of purity.
May all in the Three Realms be born upon Lotus Thrones.
May countless wandering souls
realize the three virtuous positions of the Bodhisattva Path.
May all living beings, with grace and ease,
fulfill the Bodhisattva Stages.
The countenance of the World-Honored One, like the full moon
or like the orb of the sun, shines with the light of clarity.
A halo of wisdom spreads in every direction,
enveloping all with love and compassion,
joy and equanimity.

Namo Shakyamunaye Buddhaya
Namo Shakyamunaye Buddhaya
Namo Shakyamunaye Buddhaya
[BELL, BELL]

8. PROTECTING AND TRANSFORMING

We, your disciples, who from beginningless time
have made ourselves unhappy out of confusion and ignorance,
being born and dying with no direction,
have now found confidence in the highest awakening.
However much we may have drifted on the ocean of suffering,
today we see clearly that there is a beautiful path.
We turn toward the light of loving kindness to direct us.
We bow deeply to the Awakened One and to our spiritual ancestors
who light up the path before us, guiding every step.
[BELL]

The wrongdoings and sufferings that imprison us
are brought about by craving, hatred, ignorance, and pride.
Today we begin anew to purify and free our hearts.
With awakened wisdom, bright as the sun and the full moon,
and immeasurable compassion to help humankind,
we resolve to live beautifully.
With all of our heart, we go for refuge to the Three Precious Jewels.
With the boat of loving kindness,
we cross over the ocean of suffering.
With the light of wisdom, we leave behind the forest of confusion.
With determination, we learn, reflect, and practice.
Right View is the ground of our actions in body, speech, and mind.
Right Mindfulness embraces us,
walking, standing, lying down, and sitting,
speaking, smiling, coming in, and going out.
Whenever anger or anxiety enter our heart,
we are determined to breathe mindfully and come back to ourselves.
With every step, we will walk within the Pure Land.
With every look, the Dharmakaya is revealed.
We are careful and attentive as sense organs touch sense objects
so all habit energies can be observed and easily transformed.
May our heart's garden of awakening
bloom with hundreds of flowers.
May we bring the feelings of peace and joy into every household.
May we plant wholesome seeds on the ten thousand paths.
May we never have the need to leave the Sangha body.

May we never attempt to escape the suffering of the world,
always being present wherever beings need our help.
May mountains and rivers be our witness in this moment
as we bow our heads and request the Lord of Compassion
to embrace us all.
[BELL, BELL]

9. THE THREE REFUGES ♪

I take refuge in the Buddha,
the one who shows me the way in this life.
I take refuge in the Dharma,
the way of understanding and of love.
I take refuge in the Sangha,
the community that lives in harmony and awareness.
[BELL]

Dwelling in the refuge of Buddha,
I clearly see the path of light and beauty in the world.
Dwelling in the refuge of Dharma,
I learn to open many doors on the path of transformation.
Dwelling in the refuge of Sangha,
shining light that supports me, keeping my practice free of obstruction.
[BELL]

Taking refuge in the Buddha in myself,
I aspire to help all people recognize their own awakened nature,
realizing the Mind of Love.
Taking refuge in the Dharma in myself,
I aspire to help all people fully master the ways of practice
and walk together on the path of liberation.
Taking refuge in the Sangha in myself,
I aspire to help all people build Fourfold Communities,
to embrace all beings and support their transformation.
[BELL, BELL]

10. SHARING THE MERIT ♪

Reciting the sutras, practicing the way of awareness
gives rise to benefits without limit.
We vow to share the fruits with all beings.
We vow to offer tribute to parents, teachers, friends,
and numerous beings
who give guidance and support along the path.
[BELL, BELL, BELL]

11. WORDS OF GRATITUDE

[AT THIS TIME, A RELATIVE OR FRIEND OF THE SICK PERSON IS INVITED
TO COME MINDFULLY BEFORE THE COMMUNITY TO OFFER A FEW WORDS
OF GRATITUDE TO EVERYONE WHO PARTICIPATED IN THE CEREMONY.]

Ceremony for Closing the Coffin ✑

[THIS CEREMONY HAS SEVERAL POSSIBLE FUNCTIONS. IT CAN BE USED FOR PAYING LAST RESPECTS TO THE DECEASED AND CLOSING THE COFFIN IN A HOME, CHURCH OR TEMPLE, PRACTICE CENTER, OR FUNERAL HOME BEFORE A PROCESSION AND BURIAL CEREMONY; OR IT CAN BE USED IN THE CREMATORIUM FOR PAYING LAST RESPECTS TO THE DECEASED AND CLOSING THE COFFIN BEFORE A CEREMONY OF CREMATION. THIS CEREMONY CAN ALSO BE USED TO CLEANSE, PURIFY, AND DRESS THE BODY OF THE DECEASED AND TO PLACE IT INTO THE COFFIN, IF LOCAL CUSTOMS AND LAWS ALLOW SUCH A CEREMONY TO BE CONDUCTED BY CLERGY AND FAMILY.

DURING THIS CEREMONY, THE WATER OF THE NECTAR OF COMPASSION IS SPRINKLED ON THE BODY OF THE ONE WHO HAS PASSED AWAY AND ON THE COFFIN IN ORDER TO RESTORE FRESHNESS AND PURITY. A BOWL OF CLEAN, CLEAR WATER AND A BRANCH OF WILLOW OR A SMALL FLOWER WITH MANY PETALS ARE NEEDED TO PERFORM THE CEREMONY. THE CLEAR WATER SYMBOLIZES THE POWER OF CONCENTRATION, AND THE BRANCH OF GREEN WILLOW OR FLOWER SYMBOLIZES DEEP UNDERSTANDING. IF THIS CEREMONY IS USED TO CLEANSE, PURIFY, AND DRESS THE BODY OF THE DECEASED, THEN CLEAN CLOTHS FOR THE WASHING AND CLEAN, COMFORTABLE GARMENTS FOR DRESSING SHOULD BE PREPARED.

ONE OR MORE RELATIVES, FRIENDS, OR REPRESENTATIVES OF THE FAMILY ARE INVITED TO PREPARE AND SHARE OFFERINGS OF WORDS, SONG, AND POETRY TO REMEMBER THE VIRTUES AND ACHIEVEMENTS OF THE DECEASED.]

1. Opening the Ceremony
Incense Offering [page 87]
Touching the Earth [page 88]

2. Opening Verse ♪
[BELL, BELL, BELL]

Namo Tassa Bhagavato Arahato Samma Sambuddhassa
Namo Tassa Bhagavato Arahato Samma Sambuddhassa
Namo Tassa Bhagavato Arahato Samma Sambuddhassa
[BELL]

The Dharma is deep and lovely.
We now have a chance to see, study, and practice it.
We vow to realize its true meaning.
[BELL]

3. Introductory Words
[ADAPT AS APPROPRIATE.]

Today the community has gathered to consecrate the body of [NAME OF DE-
CEASED] with purified water, the nectar of compassion, and to pay our last
respects while invoking the names of the Buddhas and Bodhisattvas. The
children, relatives, and friends of [NAME OF DECEASED] are here to take part
in the ceremony. We ask the community to listen with a quiet mind. Please
let us be aware of our breathing and the good fortune we have to be together
today, offering all our love and support to [NAME OF DECEASED] and to each
other during these profound moments of transformation.

4. Contemplation on No-Coming and No-Going ♪

This body is not me.
I am not limited by this body.
I am life without boundaries.
I have never been born,
and I have never died.

Look at the ocean and the sky filled with stars,
manifestations from my wondrous True Mind.

Since before time, I have been free.
Birth and death are only doors through which we pass,
sacred thresholds on our journey.
Birth and death are a game of hide-and-seek.

So laugh with me,
hold my hand,
let us say good-bye,
say good-bye, to meet again soon.
We meet today.
We will meet again tomorrow.
We will meet at the source every moment.
We meet each other in all forms of life.
[BELL]

5. SHARING OF RELATIVES OR FRIENDS
[AT THIS TIME ONE OR MORE RELATIVES, FRIENDS, OR REPRESENTATIVES OF THE
FAMILY SHARE SOME WORDS OR A SONG TO REMEMBER THE VIRTUES AND
ACHIEVEMENTS OF THE DECEASED.]

6. VERSES OF CONSECRATION
[THE HEAD OF CEREMONY RAISES UP THE BOWL OF CLEAR WATER WITH HIS
LEFT HAND AND FORMS THE MUDRA OF PEACE WITH HIS RIGHT HAND AT THE
LEVEL OF THE FOREHEAD, AND THEN CHANTS ALOUD TO CONSECRATE THE
WATER. MEMBERS OF THE COMMUNITY FOLLOW THEIR BREATHING, LISTENING
WITH EASE AND CONCENTRATION.]

[CHANTED BY HEAD OF CEREMONY]
This water's shape is round or square
according to the container that holds it.
In the spring warmth, it is liquid; in the winter cold, it is solid.
When its path is open, it flows.
When its path is obstructed, it stands still.
How vast it is, yet its source is so small it is difficult to find.
How wonderful it is in its streams which flow endlessly.
In the jade rivulets, the footprints of dragons remain.
In the deep pond, water holds the bright halo
of the autumn moon.
On the tip of the king's pen, water becomes
the compassion of clemency.
On the willow branch, it becomes
the clear fresh balm of compassion.
Only one drop of the water of compassion is needed,
and the Ten Directions are all purified.
[BELL]

7. DHARMA WORDS
[THE HEAD OF CEREMONY HOLDS THE BOWL OF CONSECRATED
WATER IN HIS LEFT HAND AND A WILLOW SPRIG IN HIS RIGHT.]

[CHANTED BY HEAD OF CEREMONY]
This water has eight special qualities.
It washes away the dust and impurities of all living beings,
leading them all into the wonderful Avatamsaka World.

May all beings without exception overcome their suffering.
Water does not need to be washed by water,
that is the wonderful Dharmakaya.
Dust does not cling to dust,
that is how our mind opens naturally.
When we sprinkle the water which is the nectar of compassion,
our place of enlightenment is purified.
The wilting plant grows fresh and green again,
the world of defilement changes into a world of purity,
and all beings are refreshed and can live in peace and joy.

Homage to the Bodhisattva Who Refreshes the Earth.
[BELL, BELL, BELL]

8. Verses of Praise

The nectar of compassion is seen on the willow branch
held by the Bodhisattva.
A single drop of this nectar is enough to bring life
to the Ten Directions of the Cosmos.
May all afflictions of this world disappear totally,
and may this practice center be completely purified
by the Bodhisattva's nectar of compassion.
[BELL]

9. May the Day Be Well ♪

May the day be well and the night be well.
May the midday hour bring happiness too.
In every minute and every second,
may the day and night be well.
By the blessing of the Triple Gem,
may all things be protected and safe.
May all beings born in each of the four ways
live in a land of purity.
May all in the Three Realms be born upon Lotus Thrones.
May countless wandering souls
realize the three virtuous positions of the Bodhisattva Path.
May all living beings, with grace and ease,

fulfill the Bodhisattva Stages.
The countenance of the World-Honored One, like the full moon
or like the orb of the sun, shines with the light of clarity.
A halo of wisdom spreads in every direction,
enveloping all with love and compassion,
joy and equanimity.

Namo Shakyamunaye Buddhaya
Namo Shakyamunaye Buddhaya
Namo Shakyamunaye Buddhaya
[BELL, BELL]

10. Invocation of the Buddhas and Bodhisattvas ♪

[THIS IS CHANTED AS THE BODY OF THE DECEASED AND THE COFFIN
ARE SPRINKLED WITH CONSECRATED WATER. AS THE CHANTING
CONTINUES, THE ASSEMBLED COMMUNITY IS INVITED TO CIRCUMAMBULATE
IN A CLOCKWISE DIRECTION AROUND THE COFFIN, PAYING THEIR LAST
RESPECTS AND OFFERING FLOWERS AND GIFTS. THE CHANTING IS CONCLUDED
WHEN EVERYONE HAS HAD THE CHANCE TO PAY THEIR FINAL RESPECTS,
AND THE COFFIN IS THEN CLOSED. IF THE BODY IS BEING WASHED
AND DRESSED, THE CHANTING CONTINUES DURING THIS TIME AND
CONCLUDES ONCE THE BODY HAS BEEN LAID INTO THE COFFIN.]

Introductory Verse
[CHANTED BY HEAD OF CEREMONY]
The river of attachment carries living beings
away to the sea of suffering,
where waves of afflictions rise by the thousands to submerge us.
In order to transcend the wheel of samsara,
with one-pointed concentration we invoke the names of Buddha.

Recitation
[ALL CHANT EACH NAME THREE TIMES]
Namo Shakyamunaye Buddhaya
[Homage to Shakyamuni Buddha, the Fully Awakened One]
[BELL]

Namo Amitabhaya Buddhaya
[Homage to the Buddha of Infinite Light]
[BELL]

Namo Manjushriye Bodhisattvaya
[Homage to Manjushri, Bodhisattva of Great Understanding]
[BELL]

Namo Samantabhadraya Bodhisattvaya
[Homage to Samantabhadra, Bodhisattva of Great Action]
[BELL]

Namo Avalokiteshvaraya Bodhisattvaya
[Homage to Avalokiteshvara, Bodhisattva of Great Compassion]
[BELL]

Namo Kshitigarbhaya Bodhisattvaya
[Homage to Kshitigarbha, Bodhisattva of Great Aspiration]
[BELL]

11. THE THREE REFUGES ♪

I take refuge in the Buddha,
the one who shows me the way in this life.
I take refuge in the Dharma,
the way of understanding and of love.
I take refuge in the Sangha,
the community that lives in harmony and awareness.
[BELL]

Dwelling in the refuge of Buddha,
I clearly see the path of light and beauty in the world.
Dwelling in the refuge of Dharma,
I learn to open many doors on the path of transformation.
Dwelling in the refuge of Sangha,
shining light that supports me, keeping my practice free of obstruction.
[BELL]

Taking refuge in the Buddha in myself,
I aspire to help all people recognize their own awakened nature,
realizing the Mind of Love.
Taking refuge in the Dharma in myself,
I aspire to help all people fully master the ways of practice
and walk together on the path of liberation.
Taking refuge in the Sangha in myself,
I aspire to help all people build Fourfold Communities,
to embrace all beings and support their transformation.
[BELL, BELL]

12. SHARING THE MERIT *Pure Land Version* ♪

Reciting the sutras, practicing the way of awareness
gives rise to benefits without limit.
We vow to share the fruits with all beings.
We vow to offer tribute to parents, teachers, friends,
and numerous beings
who give guidance and support along the path.
[BELL]

May we be born now in the Pure Land
within the heart of a lotus flower.
In the moment when the lotus blooms,
we touch the reality of no-birth and no-dying.
May Buddhas and Bodhisattvas be our companions
on the wonderful path of practice.
[BELL]

May we end all afflictions
so that understanding can arise,
the obstacles of unwholesome acts be dissolved,
and the fruit of awakening be fully realized.
[BELL]

13. WORDS OF GRATITUDE
[AT THIS TIME, A RELATIVE OR FRIEND OF THE DECEASED IS INVITED
TO COME MINDFULLY BEFORE THE COMMUNITY TO OFFER A FEW WORDS
OF GRATITUDE TO EVERYONE WHO PARTICIPATED IN THE CEREMONY.]

14. INVITATION TO BURIAL OR CREMATION
[THE HEAD OF CEREMONY THEN INVITES THE COMMUNITY TO CONTINUE
WITH THE BURIAL CEREMONY ON PAGE 237 OR CREMATION CEREMONY
ON PAGE 242.]

Burial Ceremony

[FOR THIS CEREMONY, THE GRAVE SHOULD BE PREPARED BEAUTIFULLY. AT THE HEAD THERE SHOULD BE A FLOWER ARRANGEMENT AND AN INCENSE HOLDER. THREE STICKS OF INCENSE AND SOME MATCHES SHOULD ALSO BE AVAILABLE.]

1. Introductory Words
[ADAPT AS APPROPRIATE.]

Dear Brothers and Sisters, the community has gathered at [PLACE OF BURIAL] to join together in a ceremony of burial for [NAME OF DECEASED], whose children, relatives, and friends are here to take part in the ceremony.

Parents and grandparents, whether they are still alive or have left this life, are present in their children and grandchildren. The life of children and grandchildren is the life of the parents and the grandparents. The life of the ancestors continues in the life of the children and grandchildren. According to the teaching of the Buddha, the peace and joy of the children and grandchildren are the peace and joy of the parents, grandparents, and all ancestors. Let us listen with a calm and peaceful mind in order to make possible the calmness, clarity, and peace of those who have left this life.

2. Consecration of Burial Site

Incense perfumes the atmosphere
with the fragrance of great understanding and deep compassion.
One wisp of this smoke fills the Ten Directions
with mindfulness, concentration, and insight,
putting an end to countless sorrows and misperceptions.
It has the power to purify and to make things fresh and new.
Homage to the Bodhisattva Who Refreshes the Earth.
[BELL]

With flowers and incense, we turn to the source of compassion,
cooling and refreshing the world.
Listening deeply and offering help to countless beings,
ending the suffering of all species,
great love and compassion are unshakable;
helping freedom and uprightness to manifest,
responding wherever there is a need,

no appeal for help to true compassion fails to succeed.
With right faith and a calm mind,
we call upon the source of compassion within us
to make itself present in our offering of incense and flowers,
protecting and caring for this sacred Earth,
where the body of our beloved is being laid to rest.
[BELL, BELL]

3. CONTEMPLATION ON NO-COMING, NO-GOING ♪

This body is not me.
I am not limited by this body.
I am life without boundaries.
I have never been born,
and I have never died.

Look at the ocean and the sky filled with stars,
manifestations from my wondrous True Mind.

Since before time, I have been free.
Birth and death are only doors through which we pass,
sacred thresholds on our journey.
Birth and death are a game of hide-and-seek.

So laugh with me,
hold my hand,
let us say good-bye,
say good-bye, to meet again soon.
We meet today.
We will meet again tomorrow.
We will meet at the source every moment.
We meet each other in all forms of life.
[BELL]

4. BURIAL
[ADAPT AS APPROPRIATE.]

Dear Brothers and Sisters, now is the time to lower the casket into the Earth.
Aware of our breathing, we remember the presence of [NAME OF DECEASED],

knowing that he/she remains alive in many generations of children and grandchildren in the future.

[THE CASKET IS LOWERED INTO THE GRAVE WHILE COMMUNITY MEMBERS SILENTLY OBSERVE THEIR BREATHING, FOCUSING ON THE PRESENCE OF THE BELOVED IN THEIR OWN HEARTS.]

May this Earth, blessed and purified with great understanding and deep compassion, protect and nurture the virtues and wholesome seeds that [NAME OF DECEASED] has transmitted to his/her children, relatives, friends, and countless other beings. May these seeds grow to fruition in each of us, so that [NAME OF DECEASED] may rest peacefully in the garden of awakening.

[THE HEAD OF CEREMONY INVITES THE CLOSEST RELATIVES TO OFFER THE FIRST SPADE OR HANDFULS OF EARTH TO COVER THE COFFIN OF THE DECEASED. DURING THIS PART OF THE CEREMONY, THE HEAD OF CEREMONY WATCHES CAREFULLY, INITIATING A SIMPLE SONG OR CHANT OR SPEAKING WORDS OF SUPPORT WHEN NEEDED. AS THE LAST PARTICIPANTS OFFER THEIR CONTRIBUTION OF EARTH, THE HEAD OF CEREMONY MAY BEGIN THE "INVOCATION OF THE BUDDHAS AND BODHISATTVAS" TO CONCLUDE THE CEREMONY.]

5. INVOCATION OF THE BUDDHAS AND BODHISATTVAS ♪

Introductory Verse
[CHANTED BY HEAD OF CEREMONY]
The river of attachment carries living beings
away to the sea of suffering,
where waves of afflictions rise by the thousands to submerge us.
In order to transcend the wheel of samsara,
with one-pointed concentration we invoke the names of Buddha.

Recitation
[CHANT EACH NAME THREE TIMES]
Namo Shakyamunaye Buddhaya
[Homage to Shakyamuni Buddha, the Fully Awakened One]
[BELL]

Namo Amitabhaya Buddhaya
[Homage to the Buddha of Infinite Light]
[BELL]

Namo Manjushriye Bodhisattvaya
[Homage to Manjushri, Bodhisattva of Great Understanding]
[BELL]

Namo Samantabhadraya Bodhisattvaya
[Homage to Samantabhadra, Bodhisattva of Great Action]
[BELL]

Namo Avalokiteshvaraya Bodhisattvaya
[Homage to Avalokiteshvara, Bodhisattva of Great Compassion]
[BELL]

Namo Kshitigarbhaya Bodhisattvaya
[Homage to Kshitigarbha, Bodhisattva of Great Aspiration]
[BELL, BELL]

6. SHARING THE MERIT ♪

Reciting the sutras, practicing the way of awareness
gives rise to benefits without limit.
We vow to share the fruits with all beings.
We vow to offer tribute to parents, teachers, friends,
and numerous beings
who give guidance and support along the path.
[BELL, BELL, BELL]

7. HUGGING MEDITATION AND CONDOLENCES*
[SPOKEN BY HEAD OF CEREMONY]

Dear Sangha, throughout this ceremony we have been reminded that the peace and joy we have now is the peace and joy of the one who has passed away. To express their loyalty and gratitude to the deceased, relatives and friends are invited to turn and look at each other deeply, showing their true

* For instructions on Hugging Meditation practice, please see page 21.

love, acceptance, and forgiveness for each other. Please take each other by the hand or hug each other. Breathe deeply three times and be fully mindful as you do this. Your peace and joy are the basis for the peace and joy of the deceased.

May we all remain established in mindfulness to give spiritual support to the relatives and friends of the deceased as they practice this.

CREMATION CEREMONY ॐ

1. INTRODUCTORY WORDS
[ADAPT AS APPROPRIATE.]

Dear Brothers and Sisters, the community has gathered at [PLACE OF CREMATION] to join together in a ceremony of cremation for [NAME OF DECEASED], whose children, relatives, and friends are here to take part in the ceremony.

Parents and grandparents, whether they are still alive or have left this life, are present in their children and grandchildren. The life of children and grandchildren is the life of the parents and the grandparents. The life of the ancestors continues in the life of the children and grandchildren. According to the teaching of the Buddha, the peace and joy of the children and grandchildren are the peace and joy of the parents, grandparents, and all ancestors. Let us listen with a calm and peaceful mind in order to make possible the calmness, clarity, and peace of those who have left this life.

2. CONSECRATION OF CREMATORIUM

Incense perfumes the atmosphere
with the fragrance of great understanding and deep compassion.
One wisp of this smoke fills the Ten Directions
with mindfulness, concentration, and insight,
putting an end to countless sorrows and misperceptions.
It has the power to purify and to make things fresh and new.
Homage to the Bodhisattva Who Refreshes the Earth.
[BELL]

With flowers and incense, we turn to the source of compassion,
cooling and refreshing the world.
Listening deeply and offering help to countless beings,
ending the suffering of all species,
great love and compassion are unshakable.
Helping freedom and uprightness to manifest,

responding wherever there is a need,
no appeal for help to true compassion fails to succeed.
With right faith and a calm mind,
we call upon the source of compassion within us
to make itself present in our offering of incense and flowers,
protecting and caring for this sacred Earth,
where the body of our beloved is being laid to rest.
[BELL, BELL]

3. CONTEMPLATION ON NO-COMING, NO-GOING ♪

This body is not me.
I am not limited by this body.
I am life without boundaries.
I have never been born,
and I have never died.

Look at the ocean and the sky filled with stars,
manifestations from my wondrous True Mind.

Since before time, I have been free.
Birth and death are only doors through which we pass,
sacred thresholds on our journey.
Birth and death are a game of hide-and-seek.

So laugh with me,
hold my hand,
let us say good-bye,
say good-bye, to meet again soon.

We meet today.
We will meet again tomorrow.
We will meet at the source every moment.
We meet each other in all forms of life.
[BELL]

4. CREMATION
[ADAPT AS APPROPRIATE.]

Dear Brothers and Sisters, now is the time for cremation. Aware of our breathing, we remember the presence of [NAME OF DECEASED], knowing that he/she remains alive in many generations of children and grandchildren in the future.

May these flames, blessed and purified with great understanding and deep compassion, protect and nurture the virtues and wholesome seeds that [NAME OF DECEASED] has transmitted to his/her children, relatives, friends, and countless other beings. May these seeds grow to fruition in each of us, so that [NAME OF DECEASED] may live with freedom in the garden of awakening.

[THE CASKET IS THEN CREMATED. ONCE THE COFFIN BEGINS TO ENTER THE FURNACE, THE HEAD OF CEREMONY CAN GIVE SUPPORT BY CHANTING OR SPEAKING. WHEN THE HEAD OF CEREMONY WISHES TO CONCLUDE THE CEREMONY, HE OR SHE MAY BEGIN THE FOLLOWING CHANTS.]

5. INVOCATION OF THE BUDDHAS AND BODHISATTVAS ♪
Introductory Verse
[CHANTED BY HEAD OF CEREMONY]

The river of attachment carries living beings
away to the sea of suffering,
where waves of afflictions rise by the thousands to submerge us.
In order to transcend the wheel of samsara,
with one-pointed concentration we invoke the names of Buddha.

Recitation
[CHANT EACH NAME THREE TIMES]

Namo Shakyamunaye Buddhaya
[Homage to Shakyamuni Buddha, the Fully Awakened One]
[BELL]

Namo Amitabhaya Buddhaya
[Homage to the Buddha of Infinite Light]
[BELL]

Namo Manjushriye Bodhisattvaya
[Homage to Manjushri, Bodhisattva of Great Understanding]
[BELL]

Namo Samantabhadraya Bodhisattvaya
[Homage to Samantabhadra, Bodhisattva of Great Action]
[BELL]

Namo Avalokiteshvaraya Bodhisattvaya
[Homage to Avalokiteshvara, Bodhisattva of Great Compassion]

Namo Kshitigarbhaya Bodhisattvaya
[Homage to Kshitigarbha, Bodhisattva of Great Aspiration]
[BELL, BELL]

6. Sharing the Merit ♪

Reciting the sutras, practicing the way of awareness
gives rise to benefits without limit.
We vow to share the fruits with all beings.
We vow to offer tribute to parents, teachers, friends,
and numerous beings
who give guidance and support along the path.
[BELL, BELL, BELL]

7. Hugging Meditation and Condolences*
[SPOKEN BY HEAD OF CEREMONY]

Dear Sangha, throughout this ceremony we have been reminded that the peace and joy we have now is the peace and joy of the one who has passed away. To express their loyalty and gratitude to the deceased, relatives and friends are invited to turn and look at each other deeply, showing their true love, acceptance, and forgiveness for each other. Please take each other by the hand or hug each other. Breathe deeply three times and be fully mindful as you do this. Your peace and joy are the basis for the peace and joy of the deceased.

May we all remain established in mindfulness to give spiritual support to the relatives and friends of the deceased as they practice this.

* For instructions on Hugging Meditation practice, please see page 21.

CEREMONY FOR THE DECEASED ॐ

[THIS CEREMONY CAN BE USED WHEN WE HEAR OF THE DECEASE OF A LOVED ONE, OR WHEN WE WISH TO COMMEMORATE THE ANNIVERSARY OF THE DECEASE OF A LOVED ONE. TRADITIONALLY, THIS CEREMONY IS ALSO USED ON THE ONE-HUNDREDTH DAY AFTER DECEASE.

A PHOTOGRAPH OF THE DECEASED SHOULD BE PLACED ON THE ANCESTRAL ALTAR WITH A SMALL PLACARD ON WHICH ARE WRITTEN HIS/HER NAME AND THE DATES OF BIRTH AND PASSING AWAY. ALSO, AN OFFERING OF FOOD SHOULD BE MADE TO THE DECEASED AND PLACED ON THE ANCESTRAL ALTAR IN FRONT OF HIS/HER PHOTOGRAPH. THE FOOD SHOULD BE SOMETHING THAT THE DECEASED ENJOYED DURING HIS/HER LIFETIME.

CEREMONIES FOR THE DECEASED SHOULD BE GUIDED BY A DHARMA TEACHER AND ADAPTED TO SUIT THE CIRCUMSTANCES AS WELL AS LOCAL CUSTOMS AND TRADITIONS.]

1. OPENING THE CEREMONY

Incense Offering [page 87]
Touching the Earth [page 88]

2. OPENING VERSE ♪

[BELL, BELL, BELL]

Namo Tassa Bhagavato Arahato Samma Sambuddhassa
Namo Tassa Bhagavato Arahato Samma Sambuddhassa
Namo Tassa Bhagavato Arahato Samma Sambuddhassa
[BELL]

The Dharma is deep and lovely.
We now have a chance to see, study, and practice it.
We vow to realize its true meaning.
[BELL]

3. THE HEART OF PERFECT UNDERSTANDING ♪

The Bodhisattva Avalokita,
while moving in the deep course of Perfect Understanding,
shed light on the Five Skandhas and found them equally empty.
After this penetration, he overcame ill-being.
[BELL]

Listen, Shariputra,
form is emptiness, and emptiness is form.
Form is not other than emptiness, emptiness is not other than form.
The same is true with feelings, perceptions, mental formations, and consciousness.
[BELL]

Listen, Shariputra,
all dharmas are marked with emptiness.
They are neither produced nor destroyed,
neither defiled nor immaculate,
neither increasing nor decreasing.
Therefore in emptiness there is neither form, nor feelings, nor perceptions,
nor mental formations, nor consciousness.
No eye, or ear, or nose, or tongue, or body, or mind.
No form, no sound, no smell, no taste, no touch, no object of mind.
No realms of elements (from eyes to mind consciousness),
no interdependent origins and no extinction of them
(from ignorance to death and decay).
No ill-being, no cause of ill-being, no end of ill-being, and no path.
No understanding and no attainment.
[BELL]

Because there is no attainment,
the Bodhisattvas, grounded in Perfect Understanding,
find no obstacles for their minds.
Having no obstacles, they overcome fear,
liberating themselves forever from illusion, realizing perfect nirvana.
All Buddhas in the past, present, and future,
thanks to this Perfect Understanding,
arrive at full, right, and universal enlightenment.
[BELL]

Therefore one should know
that Perfect Understanding is the highest mantra, the unequaled mantra,
the destroyer of ill-being, the incorruptible truth.
A mantra of Prajñaparamita should therefore be proclaimed:

Gate gate paragate parasamgate bodhi svaha
Gate gate paragate parasamgate bodhi svaha
Gate gate paragate parasamgate bodhi svaha
[BELL, BELL]

4. INTRODUCTORY WORDS
[ADAPT AS APPROPRIATE.]

Today the community has gathered to recite and practice the sutras, to invoke the Buddhas' and Bodhisattvas' names, to make offerings, and to transfer the merits to [NAME OF DECEASED] on the ___ anniversary of the day of their decease. The children, relatives, and friends of [NAME OF DECEASED] are here to take part in the ceremony.

We ask the community to listen with a quiet mind. Parents and grandparents, whether they are still alive or have left this life, are present in their children and grandchildren. The life of children and grandchildren is the life of the parents and the grandparents. The life of the ancestors carries on in the life of the children and grandchildren. According to the teaching of the Buddha, the peace and joy of the children and grandchildren are the peace and joy of the parents, grandparents, and all ancestors. With a feeling of calm, clarity, and peace, we will make possible the calm, clarity, and peace of those who have left this life.

Please will the children, grandchildren, and close relatives of [NAME OF DECEASED] stand before the Three Jewels, join your palms and touch the Earth to the Buddhas and Bodhisattvas.

5. TOUCHING THE EARTH ♪
[RECITED BY HEAD OF CEREMONY AS RELATIVES TOUCH THE EARTH]

Offering light in the Ten Directions,
the Buddha, the Dharma, and the Sangha,
to whom we bow in gratitude.
[BELL]

Teaching and living the way of awareness
in the very midst of suffering and confusion,
Shakyamuni Buddha, the Fully Enlightened One,
to whom we bow in gratitude.
[BELL]

Cutting through ignorance, awakening our hearts and our minds,
Manjushri, the Bodhisattva of Great Understanding,
to whom we bow in gratitude.
[BELL]

Working mindfully, working joyfully for the sake of all beings,
Samantabhadra, the Bodhisattva of Great Action,
to whom we bow in gratitude.
[BELL]

Seed of awakening and loving kindness
in children and all beings,
Maitreya, the Buddha to-be-born,
to whom we bow in gratitude.
[BELL]

Seeing the Buddha in everyone,
Sadaparibhuta, the Bodhisattva of Constant Respect,
to whom we bow in gratitude.
[BELL]

Showing the way fearlessly and compassionately,
the stream of all our Ancestral Teachers,
to whom we bow in gratitude.
[BELL, BELL]

6. Contemplation on No-Coming, No-Going ♪

This body is not me.
I am not limited by this body.
I am life without boundaries.
I have never been born,
and I have never died.

Look at the ocean and the sky filled with stars,
manifestations from my wondrous True Mind.

Since before time, I have been free.
Birth and death are only doors through which we pass,

sacred thresholds on our journey.
Birth and death are a game of hide-and-seek.

So laugh with me,
hold my hand,
let us say good-bye,
say good-bye, to meet again soon.

We meet today.
We will meet again tomorrow.
We will meet at the source every moment.
We meet each other in all forms of life.
[BELL]

7. Invocation of the Buddhas and Bodhisattvas ♪

Introductory Verse
[CHANTED BY HEAD OF CEREMONY]

The river of attachment carries living beings
away to the sea of suffering,
where waves of afflictions rise by the thousands to submerge us.
In order to transcend the wheel of samsara,
with one-pointed concentration we invoke the names of Buddha.

Recitation
[ALL CHANT EACH NAME THREE TIMES]

Namo Shakyamunaye Buddhaya
[Homage to Shakyamuni Buddha, the Fully Awakened One]
[BELL]

Namo Amitabhaya Buddhaya
[Homage the Buddha of Infinite Light]
[BELL]

Namo Manjushriye Bodhisattvaya
[Homage to Manjushri, Bodhisattva of Great Understanding]
[BELL]

Namo Samantabhadraya Bodhisattvaya
[Homage to Samantabhadra, Bodhisattva of Great Action]
[BELL]

Namo Avalokiteshvaraya Bodhisattvaya
[Homage to Avalokiteshvara Bodhisattva of Great Compassion]
[BELL]

Namo Kshitigarbhaya Bodhisattvaya
[Homage to Kshitigarbha, Bodhisattva of Great Aspiration]
[BELL, BELL]

8. Beginning Anew

With great respect, we turn towards the conqueror of afflictions,
offering heartfelt words of repentance.
We have lived in forgetfulness for a long time.
As we have not had the opportunity to encounter the Dharma,
our habit energies have led us into suffering.
We have made many mistakes out of unskillfulness.
We have been blinded by our wrong perceptions
for a very long time.
Our heart's garden is sown with attachment, hatred, and pride.
In us are seeds of killing, stealing, sexual misconduct, and lies.
Our everyday deeds and words do damage.
All these wrong actions are obstacles to our peace and joy.
Let us begin anew.
[BELL]

We see that we have been thoughtless,
straying from the path of mindfulness.
We have stored up afflictions and ignorance,
which have brought about so much aversion and sorrow.
There are times we have been weary of life
because we are so full of anxiety.
Because we do not understand others,
we are angry and resentful.
First we try to reason with each other, then we blame.
Every day the suffering increases, making the rift greater.

There are days when we are unwilling to speak to each other,
unwilling to look each other in the face.
And we create internal formations, which last for a long time.
Now we turn to the Three Jewels.
Sincerely recognizing our errors, we bow our heads.
[BELL]

We know so well that in our consciousness
are buried all the wholesome seeds —
seeds of love and understanding and seeds of peace and joy.
But because we do not know how to water them,
the wholesome seeds do not sprout fresh and green.
We continue to allow sorrow to overwhelm us
until there is no light in our lives.
When we chase after a distant happiness,
life becomes but a shadow of the reality.
Our mind is occupied by the past,
or worrying about this or that in the future.
We cannot let go of our anger,
and we consider of no value the precious gifts of life
which are already in our hands,
thereby trampling on real happiness.
As month follows month, we are sunk in sorrow.
So now in the precious presence of the Buddha,
fragrant with sandalwood incense,
we recognize our errors and begin anew.
[BELL]

With all our heart we go for refuge,
turning to the Buddhas in the Ten Directions
and all the Bodhisattvas, noble disciples, and self-achieved Buddhas.
Very sincerely we recognize our errors
and the mistakes of our wrong judgments.
Please bring the balm of clear water
to pour on the roots of our afflictions.
Please bring the raft of the true teachings
to carry us over the ocean of sorrows.
We vow to live an awakened life,
to practice smiling and conscious breathing,

and to study the teachings, authentically transmitted.
Diligently, we shall live in mindfulness.
[BELL]

We come back to live in the wonderful present,
to plant our heart's garden with good seeds,
and to make strong foundations of understanding and love.
We vow to train ourselves in mindfulness and concentration,
practicing to look and understand deeply
to be able to see the nature of all that is,
and so to be free of the bonds of birth and death.
We learn to speak lovingly, to be affectionate,
to care for others whether it is early morn or late afternoon,
to bring the roots of joy to many places,
helping people to abandon sorrow,
to respond with deep gratitude
to the kindness of parents, teachers, and friends.
With deep faith we light up the incense of our heart.
We ask the Lord of Compassion to be our protector
on the wonderful path of practice.
We vow to practice diligently,
cultivating the fruits of this path.
[BELL, BELL]

9. THE REFUGE CHANT ♪

Incense perfumes the atmosphere.
A lotus blooms and the Buddha appears.
The world of suffering and discrimination
is filled with the light of the rising sun.
As the dust of fear and anxiety settles,
with open heart, one-pointed mind,
I turn to the Three Jewels.
[BELL]

The Fully Enlightened One, beautifully seated, peaceful and smiling,
a living source of understanding and compassion,
to the Buddha I go for refuge.
[BELL]

The path of mindful living,
leading to healing, joy, and enlightenment, the way of peace,
to the Dharma I go for refuge.
[BELL]

The loving and supportive community of practice,
realizing harmony, awareness, and liberation,
to the Sangha I go for refuge.
[BELL]

I am aware that the Three Gems are within my heart.
I vow to realize them,
practicing mindful breathing and smiling,
looking deeply into things.
I vow to understand living beings and their suffering,
to cultivate compassion and loving kindness,
to practice joy and equanimity.
[BELL]

I vow to offer joy to one person in the morning,
to help relieve the grief of one person in the afternoon,
living simply and sanely with few possessions,
keeping my body healthy.
I vow to let go of all worries and anxiety
in order to be light and free.
[BELL]

I am aware that I owe so much
to my parents, teachers, friends, and all beings.
I vow to be worthy of their trust, to practice wholeheartedly
so that understanding and compassion will flower,
helping living beings be free from their suffering.
May the Buddha, the Dharma, and the Sangha
support my efforts.
[BELL, BELL]

10. The Three Refuges ♪

I take refuge in the Buddha,
the one who shows me the way in this life.
I take refuge in the Dharma,
the way of understanding and of love.
I take refuge in the Sangha,
the community that lives in harmony and awareness.
[BELL]

Dwelling in the refuge of Buddha,
I clearly see the path of light and beauty in the world.
Dwelling in the refuge of Dharma,
I learn to open many doors on the path of transformation.
Dwelling in the refuge of Sangha,
shining light that supports me, keeping my practice free of obstruction.
[BELL]

Taking refuge in the Buddha in myself,
I aspire to help all people recognize their own awakened nature,
realizing the Mind of Love.
Taking refuge in the Dharma in myself,
I aspire to help all people fully master the ways of practice
and walk together on the path of liberation.
Taking refuge in the Sangha in myself,
I aspire to help all people build Fourfold Communities,
to embrace all beings and support their transformation.
[BELL, BELL]

11. Mindfulness of the Deceased

Brothers and Sisters, it is time to bring to mind [NAME OF DECEASED] and to
send the energy of loving kindness and compassion to him/her. Let us sit
and enjoy our breathing for a moment, allowing [NAME OF DECEASED] to be
present with us now.
[ENJOY TEN BREATHS IN SILENCE]

Brothers and Sisters, please listen. The peace and joy of the entire world, including the worlds of the living and the dead, depend upon our own peace

and joy in this moment. With all our heart and one-pointed mind, let us
begin anew for the benefit of ourselves and our beloved ones.

12. SHARING THE MERIT *Pure Land Version* ♪

Reciting the sutras, practicing the way of awareness
gives rise to benefits without limit.
We vow to share the fruits with all beings.
We vow to offer tribute to parents, teachers, friends,
and numerous beings
who give guidance and support along the path.
[BELL]

May we be born now in the Pure Land
within the heart of a lotus flower.
In the moment when the lotus blooms,
we touch the reality of no-birth and no-dying.
May Buddhas and Bodhisattvas be our companions
on the wonderful path of practice.
[BELL]

May we end all afflictions
so that understanding can arise,
the obstacles of unwholesome acts be dissolved,
and the fruit of awakening be fully realized.
[BELL, BELL, BELL]

13. WORDS OF GRATITUDE
[AT THIS TIME, A RELATIVE OR FRIEND OF THE DECEASED
IS INVITED TO COME MINDFULLY BEFORE THE COMMUNITY
TO REMEMBER THE VIRTUES AND ACHIEVEMENTS OF THE DECEASED
AND TO OFFER A FEW WORDS OF GRATITUDE TO EVERYONE WHO
PARTICIPATED IN THE CEREMONY.]

Ceremony for the Deceased
on the Seventh and Forty-Ninth Days

[ACCORDING TO THE BELIEF IN AN INTERMEDIATE STATE, THOSE WHO HAVE PASSED AWAY CAN BE REBORN IN THE PURE LAND AS SOON AS THEY LEAVE THIS LIFE, OR THEY CAN PASS A PERIOD OF TIME FROM ONE TO SEVEN WEEKS BEFORE BEING BORN IN THE PURE LAND OR TAKING REBIRTH. DURING THAT TIME, THE BODY OF THE INTERMEDIATE STATE PASSES THROUGH SEVEN DIFFERENT TRANS-FORMATIONS. WE CAN GENERATE A GREAT DEAL OF ENERGY AND ACTIVE SUPPORT FOR THESE TRANSFORMATIONS THROUGH THE PRACTICES OF MINDFULNESS, CHANTING, PUTTING INTO PRACTICE THE SUTRA, MAKING OFFERINGS, PRACTIC-ING GENEROSITY, AND OTHER MERITORIOUS ACTS ON THE PART OF RELATIVES AND FRIENDS OF THE PERSON WHO HAS PASSED AWAY. THUS, EVERY SEVEN DAYS, CHANTING OF THE SUTRA, INVOKING THE NAMES OF BUDDHAS AND BODHI-SATTVAS, RELEASING BIRDS AND FISH FROM CAPTIVITY, AND MAKING OFFERINGS ARE ORGANIZED.

THE FINAL SEVEN-DAY OFFERING TO THE DECEASED IS CALLED THE "FINAL SEVEN," AND IT IS THE MOST SOLEMN OF ALL THE SEVEN-DAY OFFERINGS. THE CEREMONY PRESENTED HERE CAN BE SUPPLEMENTED BY THE READING OF ONE OF THE DISCOURSES IN THIS BOOK [SEE PAGES 269–348]. THE RECITATION OF THESE SUTRAS IS OF GREAT BENEFIT TO THE ONE WHO HAS PASSED AWAY AND TO THOSE WHO ARE RECITING.

FOR EACH OF THE SEVEN-DAY CEREMONIES, A PHOTOGRAPH OF THE DECEASED SHOULD BE PLACED ON THE ANCESTRAL ALTAR WITH A SMALL PLACARD ON WHICH ARE WRITTEN HIS/HER NAME AND THE DATES OF BIRTH AND PASSING AWAY. FOR THE "FINAL SEVEN" CEREMONY, AN OFFERING OF FOOD SHOULD BE MADE TO THE DECEASED AND PLACED ON THE ANCESTRAL ALTAR IN FRONT OF HIS/HER PHOTOGRAPH. THIS FOOD SHOULD BE SOMETHING THAT THE DECEASED ENJOYED DURING HIS/HER LIFETIME. AN OFFERING SHOULD ALSO BE PREPARED FOR ALL THE PARTICIPANTS IN THE CEREMONY. THESE GIFTS SHOULD BE SMALL TOKENS OF APPRECIATION AND ARE OFFERED AFTER THE CONCLUSION OF THE CEREMONY.

CEREMONIES FOR THE DECEASED SHOULD BE GUIDED BY A DHARMA TEACHER AND ADAPTED TO SUIT THE CIRCUMSTANCES AS WELL AS LOCAL CUSTOMS AND TRADITIONS.]

1. OPENING THE CEREMONY
Sitting Meditation [12 MINUTES]

2. INCENSE OFFERING *Version Two* ♪

[BELL, BELL, BELL]
The fragrance of this incense
invites the awakened mind
to be truly present with us now.
The fragrance of this incense
fills our practice center,
protects and guards our mind
from all wrong thinking.
The fragrance of this incense
collects us and unites us.
Precepts, concentration, and insight
we offer for all that is.

Namo Bodhisattvebhyah
Namo Mahasattvebhyah
[BELL]

All the Dharma realms are as fragrant as the Earth.
With the incense that has just been lit
a cloud of good omen goes to the Four Directions.
The Buddhas are here in body, speech, and mind.
[BELL]

3. TOUCHING THE EARTH ♪

Offering light in the Ten Directions,
the Buddha, the Dharma, and the Sangha,
to whom we bow in gratitude.
[BELL]

Teaching and living the way of awareness
in the very midst of suffering and confusion,
Shakyamuni Buddha, the Fully Enlightened One,
to whom we bow in gratitude.
[BELL]

Cutting through ignorance, awakening our hearts and our minds,
Manjushri, the Bodhisattva of Great Understanding,
to whom we bow in gratitude.
[BELL]

Working mindfully, working joyfully for the sake of all beings,
Samantabhadra, the Bodhisattva of Great Action,
to whom we bow in gratitude.
[BELL]

Listening deeply, serving beings in countless ways,
Avalokiteshvara, the Bodhisattva of Great Compassion,
to whom we bow in gratitude.
[BELL]

Fearless and persevering through realms of suffering and darkness,
Kshitigarbha, the Bodhisattva of Great Aspiration,
to whom we bow in gratitude.
[BELL]

Seed of awakening and loving kindness
in children and all beings,
Maitreya, the Buddha to-be-born,
to whom we bow in gratitude.
[BELL]

Showing the way fearlessly and compassionately,
the stream of all our Ancestral Teachers,
to whom we bow in gratitude.
[BELL, BELL]

4. Beginning Anew

With great respect, we turn towards the conqueror of afflictions,
offering heartfelt words of repentance.
We have lived in forgetfulness for a long time.
As we have not had the opportunity to encounter the Dharma,
our habit energies have led us into suffering.
We have made many mistakes out of unskillfulness.

We have been blinded by our wrong perceptions
for a very long time.
Our heart's garden is sown with attachment, hatred, and pride.
In us are seeds of killing, stealing, sexual misconduct, and lies.
Our everyday deeds and words do damage.
All these wrong actions are obstacles to our peace and joy.
Let us begin anew.
[BELL]

We see that we have been thoughtless,
straying from the path of mindfulness.
We have stored up afflictions and ignorance,
which have brought about so much aversion and sorrow.
There are times we have been weary of life
because we are so full of anxiety.
Because we do not understand others,
we are angry and resentful.
First we try to reason with each other, then we blame.
Every day the suffering increases, making the rift greater.
There are days when we are unwilling to speak to each other,
unwilling to look each other in the face.
And we create internal formations, which last for a long time.
Now we turn to the Three Jewels.
Sincerely recognizing our errors, we bow our heads.
[BELL]

We know so well that in our consciousness
are buried all the wholesome seeds —
seeds of love and understanding and seeds of peace and joy.
But because we do not know how to water them,
the wholesome seeds do not sprout fresh and green.
We continue to allow sorrow to overwhelm us
until there is no light in our lives.
When we chase after a distant happiness,
life becomes but a shadow of the reality.
Our mind is occupied by the past,
or worrying about this or that in the future.
We cannot let go of our anger,
and we consider of no value the precious gifts of life

which are already in our hands,
thereby trampling on real happiness.
As month follows month, we are sunk in sorrow.
So now in the precious presence of the Buddha,
fragrant with sandalwood incense,
we recognize our errors and begin anew.
[BELL]

With all our heart we go for refuge,
turning to the Buddhas in the Ten Directions
and all the Bodhisattvas, noble disciples, and self-achieved Buddhas.
Very sincerely we recognize our errors
and the mistakes of our wrong judgments.
Please bring the balm of clear water
to pour on the roots of our afflictions.
Please bring the raft of the true teachings
to carry us over the ocean of sorrows.
We vow to live an awakened life,
to practice smiling and conscious breathing,
and to study the teachings, authentically transmitted.
Diligently, we shall live in mindfulness.
[BELL]

We come back to live in the wonderful present,
to plant our heart's garden with good seeds,
and to make strong foundations of understanding and love.
We vow to train ourselves in mindfulness and concentration,
practicing to look and understand deeply
to be able to see the nature of all that is,
and so to be free of the bonds of birth and death.
We learn to speak lovingly, to be affectionate,
to care for others whether it is early morn or late afternoon,
to bring the roots of joy to many places,
helping people to abandon sorrow,
to respond with deep gratitude
to the kindness of parents, teachers, and friends.
With deep faith we light up the incense of our heart.
We ask the Lord of Compassion to be our protector
on the wonderful path of practice.

We vow to practice diligently,
cultivating the fruits of this path.
[BELL, BELL, BELL]

5. CONTEMPLATION ON NO-COMING, NO-GOING ♪

This body is not me.
I am not limited by this body.
I am life without boundaries.
I have never been born,
and I have never died.

Look at the ocean and the sky filled with stars,
manifestations from my wondrous True Mind.

Since before time, I have been free.
Birth and death are only doors through which we pass,
sacred thresholds on our journey.
Birth and death are a game of hide-and-seek.

So laugh with me,
hold my hand,
let us say good-bye,
say good-bye, to meet again soon.

We meet today.
We will meet again tomorrow.
We will meet at the source every moment.
We meet each other in all forms of life.
[BELL]

6. THE REFUGE CHANT ♪

Incense perfumes the atmosphere.
A lotus blooms and the Buddha appears.
The world of suffering and discrimination
is filled with the light of the rising sun.
As the dust of fear and anxiety settles,
with open heart, one-pointed mind,

I turn to the Three Jewels.
[BELL]

The Fully Enlightened One, beautifully seated, peaceful and smiling,
a living source of understanding and compassion,
to the Buddha I go for refuge.
[BELL]

The path of mindful living,
leading to healing, joy, and enlightenment, the way of peace,
to the Dharma I go for refuge.
[BELL]

The loving and supportive community of practice,
realizing harmony, awareness, and liberation,
to the Sangha I go for refuge.
[BELL]

I am aware that the Three Gems are within my heart.
I vow to realize them,
practicing mindful breathing and smiling,
looking deeply into things.
I vow to understand living beings and their suffering,
to cultivate compassion and loving kindness,
to practice joy and equanimity.
[BELL]

I vow to offer joy to one person in the morning,
to help relieve the grief of one person in the afternoon,
living simply and sanely with few possessions,
keeping my body healthy.
I vow to let go of all worries and anxiety
in order to be light and free.
[BELL]

I am aware that I owe so much
to my parents, teachers, friends, and all beings.
I vow to be worthy of their trust, to practice wholeheartedly
so that understanding and compassion will flower,

helping living beings be free from their suffering.
May the Buddha, the Dharma, and the Sangha
support my efforts.
[BELL, BELL]

7. THE THREE REFUGES ♪

I take refuge in the Buddha,
the one who shows me the way in this life.
I take refuge in the Dharma,
the way of understanding and of love.
I take refuge in the Sangha,
the community that lives in harmony and awareness.
[BELL]

Dwelling in the refuge of Buddha,
I clearly see the path of light and beauty in the world.
Dwelling in the refuge of Dharma,
I learn to open many doors on the path of transformation.
Dwelling in the refuge of Sangha,
shining light that supports me, keeping my practice free of obstruction.
[BELL]

Taking refuge in the Buddha in myself,
I aspire to help all people recognize their own awakened nature,
realizing the Mind of Love.
Taking refuge in the Dharma in myself,
I aspire to help all people fully master the ways of practice
and walk together on the path of liberation.
Taking refuge in the Sangha in myself,
I aspire to help all people build Fourfold Communities,
to embrace all beings and support their transformation.
[BELL, BELL]

8. MINDFULNESS OF THE DECEASED

Brothers and Sisters, it is time to bring to mind [NAME OF DECEASED] and to
send the energy of loving kindness and compassion to him/her. Let us sit

and enjoy our breathing for a moment, allowing [NAME OF DECEASED] to be present with us now.
[TEN BREATHS IN SILENCE]

Brothers and Sisters, please listen. The peace and joy of the entire world, including the worlds of the living and the dead, depend upon our own peace and joy in this moment. With all our heart and one-pointed mind, let us begin anew for the benefit of ourselves and our beloved ones.

9. SHARING THE MERIT *Pure Land Version*

Reciting the sutras, practicing the way of awareness
gives rise to benefits without limit.
We vow to share the fruits with all beings.
We vow to offer tribute to parents, teachers, friends,
and numerous beings
who give guidance and support along the path.
[BELL]

May we be born now in the Pure Land
within the heart of a lotus flower.
In the moment when the lotus blooms,
we touch the reality of no-birth and no-dying.
May Buddhas and Bodhisattvas be our companions
on the wonderful path of practice.
[BELL]

May we end all afflictions
so that understanding can arise,
the obstacles of unwholesome acts be dissolved,
and the fruit of awakening be fully realized.
[BELL, BELL, BELL]

10. WORDS OF GRATITUDE
[AT THIS TIME, A RELATIVE OR FRIEND OF THE DECEASED IS INVITED
TO COME MINDFULLY BEFORE THE COMMUNITY TO OFFER A FEW WORDS
OF GRATITUDE TO EVERYONE WHO PARTICIPATED IN THE CEREMONY.]

Discourses

Discourse on Love ♪

"He or she who wants to attain peace should practice being upright, humble, and capable of using loving speech. He or she will know how to live simply and happily, with senses calmed, without being covetous and carried away by the emotions of the majority. Let him or her not do anything that will be disapproved of by the wise ones.

"(And this is what he or she contemplates:)

"May everyone be happy and safe, and may all hearts be filled with joy.

"May all beings live in security and in peace — beings who are frail or strong, tall or short, big or small, invisible or visible, near or faraway, already born, or yet to be born. May all of them dwell in perfect tranquility.

"Let no one do harm to anyone. Let no one put the life of anyone in danger. Let no one, out of anger or ill will, wish anyone any harm.

"Just as a mother loves and protects her only child at the risk of her own life, cultivate boundless love to offer to all living beings in the entire cosmos. Let our boundless love pervade the whole universe, above, below, and across. Our love will know no obstacles. Our heart will be absolutely free from hatred and enmity. Whether standing or walking, sitting or lying, as long as we are awake, we should maintain this mindfulness of love in our own heart. This is the noblest way of living.

"Free from wrong views, greed, and sensual desires, living in beauty and realizing Perfect Understanding, those who practice boundless love will certainly transcend birth and death."

Etena sacca vajjena sotthi te hotu sabbada.

[REPEAT THREE TIMES]

[By the firm determination of this truth, may you ever be well.]

Metta Sutta, Sutta Nipata 1.8*

---

* For commentary, see Thich Nhat Hanh, *Teachings on Love* (Berkeley, CA: Parallax Press, 1998).

Discourse on Happiness

I heard these words of the Buddha one time when the Lord was living in the vicinity of Savatthi at the Anathapindika Monastery in the Jeta Grove. Late at night, a deva appeared whose light and beauty made the whole Jeta Grove shine radiantly. After paying respects to the Buddha, the deva asked him a question in the form of a verse:

"Many gods and men are eager to know
what are the greatest blessings
which bring about a peaceful and happy life.
Please, Tathagata, will you teach us?"

(This is the Buddha's answer:)

"Not to be associated with the foolish ones,
to live in the company of wise people,
honoring those who are worth honoring —
this is the greatest happiness.

"To live in a good environment,
to have planted good seeds,
and to realize that you are on the right path —
this is the greatest happiness.

"To have a chance to learn and grow,
to be skillful in your profession or craft,
practicing the precepts and loving speech —
this is the greatest happiness.

"To be able to serve and support your parents,
to cherish your own family,
to have a vocation that brings you joy —
this is the greatest happiness.

"To live honestly, generous in giving,
to offer support to relatives and friends,

living a life of blameless conduct —
this is the greatest happiness.

"To avoid unwholesome actions,
not caught by alcoholism or drugs,
and to be diligent in doing good things —
this is the greatest happiness.

"To be humble and polite in manner,
to be grateful and content with a simple life,
not missing the occasion to learn the Dharma —
this is the greatest happiness.

"To persevere and be open to change,
to have regular contact with monks and nuns,
and to fully participate in Dharma discussions —
this is the greatest happiness.

"To live diligently and attentively,
to perceive the Noble Truths,
and to realize nirvana —
this is the greatest happiness.

"To live in the world
with your heart undisturbed by the world,
with all sorrows ended, dwelling in peace —
this is the greatest happiness.

"For he or she who accomplishes this,
unvanquished wherever she goes,
always he is safe and happy —
happiness lives within oneself."

Mahamangala Sutta, Sutta Nipata 2.4*

---

* For further commentary, see *Two Treasures: Buddhist Teachings on Awakening ad True Happiness* (Berkeley, CA: Parallax Press, 2007).

Elder Discourse

I heard these words of the Buddha one time when the Lord was staying at the monastery in the Jeta Grove, in the town of Shravasti. At that time there was a monk named Thera (Elder), who always preferred to be alone. Whenever he could, he praised the practice of living alone. He sought alms alone and sat in meditation alone.

One time a group of bhikshus came to the Lord, paid their respect by prostrating at his feet, stepped to one side, sat down at a distance, and said, "Blessed One, there is an elder by the name of Thera who only wants to be alone. He always praises the practice of living alone. He goes into the village alone to seek alms, returns home from the village alone, and sits in meditation alone."

The Lord Buddha told one of the bhikshus, "Please go to the place where the monk Thera lives and tell him I wish to see him."

The bhikshu obeyed. When the monk Thera heard the Buddha's wish, he came without delay, prostrated at the feet of the Buddha, stepped to one side, and sat down at a distance. Then the Blessed One asked the monk Thera, "Is it true that you prefer to be alone, praise the life of solitude, go for alms alone, come back from the village alone, and sit in meditation alone?"

The monk Thera replied, "It is true, Blessed One."

Buddha asked the monk Thera, "How do you live alone?"

The monk Thera replied, "I live alone; no one else lives with me. I praise the practice of being alone. I go for alms alone, and I come back from the village alone. I sit in meditation alone. That is all."

The Buddha taught the monk as follows, "It is obvious that you like the practice of living alone. I do not want to deny that, but I want to tell you that there is a more wonderful and profound way to be alone. It is the way of deep observation in order to see that the past no longer exists and the future has not yet come, and to dwell at ease in the present moment, free from desire. When a person lives in this way, he has no hesitation in his heart. He gives up all anxieties and regrets, lets go of all binding desires, and cuts the fetters which prevent him from being free. This is called 'the better way to live alone.' There is no more wonderful way of being alone than this."

Then the Blessed One recited this gatha:

"Observing life deeply,
it is possible to clearly see all that is.
Not enslaved by anything,
it is possible to put aside all craving,
resulting in a life of peace and joy.
This is truly to live alone."

Hearing the Lord's words, the monk Thera was delighted. He prostrated respectfully to the Buddha and departed.

Samyukta Agama 1071
(The equivalent in the Pali Canon is
Theranamo Sutta, Samyutta Nikaya 21.10*)

---

* For commentary, see Thich Nhat Hanh, *Our Appointment with Life: The Buddha's Teaching on Living in the Present* (Berkeley, CA: Parallax Press, 1990).

Discourse on Knowing
the Better Way To Live Alone

I heard these words of the Buddha one time when the Lord was staying at the monastery in the Jeta Grove, in the town of Savatthi. He called all the monks to him and instructed them, "Bhikkhus!"

And the bhikkhus replied, "We are here."

The Blessed One taught, "I will teach you what is meant by 'knowing the better way to live alone.' I will begin with an outline of the teaching, and then I will give a detailed explanation. Bhikkhus, please listen carefully."

"Blessed One, we are listening."

The Buddha taught:

"Do not pursue the past.
Do not lose yourself in the future.
The past no longer is.
The future has not yet come.
Looking deeply at life as it is
in the very here and now,
the practitioner dwells
in stability and freedom.
We must be diligent today.
To wait till tomorrow is too late.
Death comes unexpectedly.
How can we bargain with it?
The sage calls a person who
dwells in mindfulness
night and day
'the one who knows
the better way to live alone.'

"Bhikkhus, what do we mean by 'pursuing the past'? When someone considers the way her body was in the past, the way her feelings were in the past, the way her perceptions were in the past, the way her mental formations were in the past, the way her consciousness was in the past; when she considers these things and her mind is burdened by and attached to these things which belong to the past, then that person is pursuing the past.

"Bhikkhus, what is meant by 'not pursuing the past'? When someone considers the way her body was in the past, the way her feelings were in the past, the way her perceptions were in the past, the way her mental formations were in the past, the way her consciousness was in the past; when she considers these things but her mind is neither enslaved by nor attached to these things which belong to the past, then that person is not pursuing the past.

"Bhikkhus, what is meant by 'losing yourself in the future'? When someone considers the way his body will be in the future, the way his feelings will be in the future, the way his perceptions will be in the future, the way his mental formations will be in the future, the way his consciousness will be in the future; when he considers these things and his mind is burdened by and daydreaming about these things which belong to the future, then that person is losing himself in the future.

"Bhikkhus, what is meant by 'not losing yourself in the future'? When someone considers the way his body will be in the future, the way his feelings will be in the future, the way his perceptions will be in the future, the way his mental formations will be in the future, the way his consciousness will be in the future; when he considers these things but his mind is not burdened by or daydreaming about these things which belong to the future, then he is not losing himself in the future.

"Bhikkhus, what is meant by 'being swept away by the present'? When someone does not study or learn anything about the Awakened One, or the teachings of love and understanding, or the community that lives in harmony and awareness; when that person knows nothing about the noble teachers and their teachings, and does not practice these teachings, and thinks, 'This body is myself; I am this body. These feelings are myself; I am these feelings. This perception is myself; I am this perception. This mental formation is myself; I am this mental formation. This consciousness is myself; I am this consciousness,' then that person is being swept away by the present.

"Bhikkhus, what is meant by 'not being swept away by the present'? When someone studies and learns about the Awakened One, the teachings of love and understanding, and the community that lives in harmony and awareness; when that person knows about noble teachers and their teachings, practices these teachings, and does not think, 'This body is myself; I am this body. These feelings are myself; I am these feelings. This perception is myself; I am this perception. This mental formation is myself; I am this mental formation. This consciousness is myself; I am this consciousness,' then that person is not being swept away by the present.

"Bhikkhus, I have presented the outline and the detailed explanation of knowing the better way to live alone."

Thus the Buddha taught, and the bhikkhus were delighted to put his teachings into practice.

Bhaddekaratta Sutta, Majjhima Nikaya 131*

* For commentary, see Thich Nhat Hanh, *Our Appointment with Life: The Buddha's Teaching on Living in the Present* (Berkeley. CA: Parallax Press, 1990).

Discourse on the Four Kinds of Nutriments

This is what I heard one time when the Buddha was in the Anathapindika Monastery in the Jeta Grove near to the town of Shravasti.

That day the Buddha told the monks: "There are four kinds of nutriments which enable living beings to grow and maintain life. What are these four nutriments? The first is edible food, the second is the food of sense impressions, the third is the food of volition, and the fourth is the food of consciousness."

"Bhikkhus, how should a practitioner regard edible food? Imagine a young couple with a baby boy whom they look after and raise with all their love. One day they decide to bring their son to another country to make their living. They have to go through the difficulties and dangers of a desert. During the journey, they run out of provisions and fall extremely hungry. There is no way out for them and they discuss the following plan: 'We only have one son whom we love with all our heart. If we eat his flesh we shall survive and manage to overcome this dangerous situation. If we do not eat his flesh all three of us will die.' After this discussion, they killed their son, with tears of pain and gritting their teeth they ate the flesh of their son, just so as to be able to live and come out of the desert."

The Buddha asked: "Do you think that couple ate their son's flesh because they wanted to enjoy its taste and because they wanted their bodies to have the nutriment that would make them more beautiful?"

The monks replied: "No, Venerable Lord." The Buddha asked: "Were the couple forced to eat their son's flesh in order to survive and escape from the dangers of the desert?" The monks replied: "Yes, Venerable Lord."

The Buddha taught: "Monks, every time we ingest edible food, we should train ourselves to look at it as our son's flesh. If we meditate on it in this way we shall have clear insight and understanding which puts an end to misperceptions about edible food and our attachment to sensual pleasures will dissolve. Once the attachment to sensual pleasures is transformed there are no longer any internal formations concerning the five objects of sensual pleasure in the noble disciple who applies himself to the training and the practice. When the internal formations still bind us we have to keep returning to this world.

"How should the practitioner meditate on the food of sense impressions? Imagine a cow which has lost its skin. Wherever it goes the insects and maggots which live in the earth, in the dust and on the vegetation attach themselves to the cow and suck its blood. If the cow lies on the earth, the maggots in the earth will attach themselves to it and feed off of it. Whether lying down or standing up, the cow will be irritated and suffer pain. When you ingest the food of sense impressions, you should practice to see it in this light. You will have insight and understanding which puts an end to misperceptions concerning the food of sense impressions. When you have this insight you will no longer be attached to the three kinds of feeling. When no longer attached to the three kinds of feeling the noble disciple does not need to strive anymore because whatever needs to be done has already been done.

"How should the practitioner meditate on the food of volition? Imagine there is a village or a large town near to a pit of burning charcoal. There are only the smokeless, glowing embers left. Now there is an intelligent man with enough wisdom who does not want to suffer and only wants happiness and peace. He does not want to die and he only wants to live. He thinks: 'Over there the heat is very great, although there is no smoke and there are no flames. Still, if I have to go into that pit there is no doubt that I shall die.' Knowing this he is determined to leave that large town or that village and go somewhere else. The practitioner should meditate like this on the food of volition. Meditating like this he will have insight and understanding which puts an end to misperceptions about the food of volition. When he arrives at that understanding the three kinds of craving will be ended. When these three cravings are ended, the noble disciple who trains and practices will have no more work to do, because whatever needs to be done has already been done.

"How should the practitioner meditate on the food of consciousness? Imagine that the soldiers of the king have arrested a criminal. They bind him and bring him to the king. Because he has committed theft he is punished by people piercing his body with three hundred knives. He is assailed by fear and pain all day and all night. The practitioner should regard the food of consciousness in this light. If he does he will have insight and understanding which puts an end to misperceptions concerning the food of consciousness. When he has this understanding regarding the food of consciousness the noble disciple who trains and practices will not need to strive anymore because whatever needs to be done has been done."

When the Buddha had spoken, the monks were very happy to put the teachings into practice.

Samyukta Agama, Sutra 373*

---

* For commentary on this sutra see, Thich Nhat Hanh, *The Path of Emancipation* (Berkeley, CA: Parallax Press, 2000) pp. 84–91.

Discourse on the Middle Way

I heard these words of the Buddha one time when the Lord was staying at the guest house in a forest of the district of Nala. At that time, the Venerable Kacchayana came to visit him and asked, "The Tathagata has spoken of Right View. How would the Tathagata describe Right View?"

The Buddha told the venerable monk, "People in the world tend to believe in one of two views: the view of being or the view of nonbeing. That is because they are bound to wrong perception. It is wrong perception that leads to the concepts of being and nonbeing. Kaccayana, most people are bound to the internal formations of discrimination and preference, grasping and attachment. Those who are not bound to the internal knots of grasping and attachment no longer imagine and cling to the idea of a self. They understand, for example, that suffering comes to be when conditions are favorable, and that it fades away when conditions are no longer favorable. They no longer have any doubts. Their understanding has not come to them through others; it is their own insight. This insight is called Right View, and this is the way the Tathagata would describe Right View.

"How is this so? When a person who has correct insight observes the coming to be of the world, the idea of nonbeing does not arise in her, and when she observes the fading away of the world, the idea of being does not arise in her mind. Kaccayana, viewing the world as being is an extreme; viewing it as nonbeing is another extreme. The Tathagata avoids these two extremes and teaches the Dharma dwelling in the Middle Way.

"The Middle Way says that this is, because that is; this is not, because that is not. Because there is ignorance, there are impulses; because there are impulses, there is consciousness; because there is consciousness, there is the psyche-soma; because there is the psyche-soma, there are the six senses; because there are the six senses, there is contact; because there is contact, there is feeling; because there is feeling, there is craving; because there is craving, there is grasping; because there is grasping, there is becoming; because there is becoming, there is birth; because there is birth, there are old age, death, grief, and sorrow. That is how this entire mass of suffering arises. But with the fading away of ignorance, impulses cease; with the fading away of impulses, consciousness ceases; …and finally birth, old age, death, grief, and sorrow will fade away. That is how this entire mass of suffering ceases."

After listening to the Buddha, the Venerable Kaccayana was enlightened and liberated from sorrow. He was able to untie all of his internal knots and attain arhatship.

Samyukta Agama 301

Anuradha Discourse

I heard these words of the Buddha one time when the Lord was staying in the gabled house in the Great Forest near the town of Vesali. At that time, the Venerable Anuradha was staying in a hermitage in the forest not far from where the Buddha was. One day a group of recluses came to see the Venerable Anuradha, and after exchanging greetings and courtesies, asked the venerable monk, "Venerable Anuradha, the Tathagata is often praised for having reached the highest fruit of awakening. He must have explained to you his understanding of these four propositions:

    1. "After death, the Tathagata continues to exist.

    2. "After death, the Tathagata ceases to exist.

    3. "After death, the Tathagata both continues and ceases to exist.

    4. "After death, the Tathagata neither continues nor ceases to exist.

"Please tell us which of these propositions is true."

The Venerable Anuradha replied, "Friends, the Tathagata, the World-Honored One, the one who has realized the highest fruit of awakening, has never proposed or spoken about these four propositions."

When they heard the Venerable Anuradha's reply, the recluses said, "It is possible that this monk has just been ordained, or if he was ordained some time ago, he must be of slow wits." Not satisfied with Venerable Anuradha's answer, they left him, thinking that he was either newly ordained or of little intelligence.

When the recluses had gone, the Venerable Anuradha thought, "If recluses continue to ask me these questions, how should I answer so as to speak the truth and not misrepresent the teachings of the Buddha? How should I answer so as to be in harmony with the right Dharma and not to be criticized by the adherents of the Buddha's path?" Then Anuradha went to where the Buddha was staying, bowed to the Buddha, spoke words of greeting, and then told the Buddha what had happened.

The Buddha asked him, "What do you think, Anuradha? Can you find the Tathagata in form?"

"No, World-Honored One."

"Can you find the Tathagata outside of form?"

"No, World-Honored One."

"Can you find the Tathagata in feelings, perceptions, mental formations, or consciousness?"

"No, World-Honored One."

"Can you find the Tathagata outside of feelings, perceptions, mental formations, or consciousness?"

"No, World-Honored One."

"Well then, Anuradha, do you think that the Tathagata transcends form, feelings, perceptions, mental formations, and consciousness?"

"No, World-Honored One."

"Anuradha, if you cannot find the Tathagata even while he is still alive, can you find the Tathagata within these four propositions:

1. "After death, the Tathagata continues to exist.
2. "After death, the Tathagata ceases to exist.
3. "After death, the Tathagata both continues and ceases to exist.
4. "After death, the Tathagata neither continues nor ceases to exist."

"No, World-Honored One."

"Quite so, Anuradha. The Tathagata has only spoken and taught in relation to one thing: suffering and the end of suffering."

Samyutta Nikaya 22.86

Discourse on the Full Awareness of Breathing

I

I heard these words of the Buddha one time when he was staying in Savatthi in the Eastern Park, with many well-known and accomplished disciples, including Sariputta, Mahamoggallana, Mahakassapa, Mahakacchayana, Mahakotthita, Mahakappina, Mahachunda, Anuradha, Revata, and Ananda. The senior bhikkhus in the community were diligently instructing bhikkhus who were new to the practice — some instructing ten bhikkhus, some twenty, some thirty, and some forty; and in this way the bhikkhus who were new to the practice gradually made great progress.

That night the moon was full, and the Pavarana Ceremony was held to mark the end of the rainy-season retreat. Lord Buddha, the Awakened One, was sitting in the open air, and his disciples were gathered around him. After looking over the assembly, he began to speak:

"O bhikkhus, I am pleased to observe the fruit you have attained in your practice. Yet I know you can make even more progress. What you have not yet attained, you can attain. What you have not yet realized, you can realize perfectly. [To engage your efforts,] I will remain here until the next full-moon day."

When they heard that the Lord Buddha was going to remain in Savatthi for another month, bhikkhus throughout the country began traveling there to study with him. The senior bhikkhus continued teaching the bhikkhus new to the practice even more ardently. Some were instructing ten bhikkhus, some twenty, some thirty, and some forty. With this help, the newer bhikkhus were able, little by little, to continue their progress in understanding.

When the next full-moon day arrived, the Buddha, seated under the open sky, looked over the assembly of bhikkhus and began to speak:

"O bhikkhus, our community is pure and good. At its heart, it is without useless and boastful talk, and therefore it deserves to receive offerings and be considered a field of merit. Such a community is rare, and any pilgrim who seeks it, no matter how far he must travel, will find it worthy.

"O bhikkhus, there are bhikkhus in this assembly who have realized the fruit of Arhatship, destroyed every root of affliction, laid aside every burden, and attained right understanding and emancipation. There are also bhikkhus who have cut off the first five internal knots and realized the fruit of never returning to the cycle of birth and death.

"There are those who have thrown off the first three internal knots and realized the fruit of returning once more. They have cut off the roots of greed, hatred, and ignorance, and will only need to return to the cycle of birth and death one more time. There are those who have thrown off the three internal knots and attained the fruit of stream-enterer, coursing steadily to the Awakened State. There are those who practice the Four Establishments of Mindfulness. There are those who practice the Four Right Efforts, and those who practice the Four Bases of Success. There are those who practice the Five Faculties, those who practice the Five Powers, those who practice the Seven Factors of Awakening, and those who practice the Noble Eightfold Path. There are those who practice loving kindness, those who practice compassion, those who practice joy, and those who practice equanimity. There are those who practice the Nine Contemplations, and those who practice the Observation of Impermanence. There are also bhikkhus who are already practicing Full Awareness of Breathing."

II

"O bhikkhus, the Full Awareness of Breathing, if developed and practiced continuously, will be rewarding and bring great advantages. It will lead to success in practicing the Four Establishments of Mindfulness. If the method of the Four Establishments of Mindfulness is developed and practiced continuously, it will lead to success in the practice of the Seven Factors of Awaking. The Seven Factors of Awakening, if developed and practiced continuously, will give rise to understanding and liberation of the mind.

"What is the way to develop and practice continuously the method of Full Awareness of Breathing so that the practice will be rewarding and offer great benefit?

"It is like this, bhikkhus: the practitioner goes into the forest or to the foot of a tree, or to any deserted place, sits stably in the lotus position, holding his or her body quite straight, and practices like this: 'Breathing in, I know I am breathing in. Breathing out, I know I am breathing out.'

1. 'Breathing in a long breath, I know I am breathing in a long breath. Breathing out a long breath, I know I am breathing out a long breath.
2. 'Breathing in a short breath, I know I am breathing in a short breath. Breathing out a short breath, I know I am breathing out a short breath.
3. 'Breathing in, I am aware of my whole body. Breathing out, I am aware of my whole body.' He or she practices like this.
4. 'Breathing in, I calm my whole body. Breathing out, I calm my whole body.' He or she practices like this.

5. 'Breathing in, I feel joyful. Breathing out, I feel joyful.' He or she practices like this.
6. 'Breathing in, I feel happy. Breathing out, I feel happy.' He or she practices like this.
7. 'Breathing in, I am aware of my mental formations. Breathing out, I am aware of my mental formations.' He or she practices like this.
8. 'Breathing in, I calm my mental formations. Breathing out, I calm my mental formations.' He or she practices like this.
9. 'Breathing in, I am aware of my mind. Breathing out, I am aware of my mind.' He or she practices like this.
10. 'Breathing in, I make my mind happy. Breathing out, I make my mind happy.' He or she practices like this.
11. 'Breathing in, I concentrate my mind. Breathing out, I concentrate my mind.' He or she practices like this.
12. 'Breathing in, I liberate my mind. Breathing out, I liberate my mind.' He or she practices like this.
13. 'Breathing in, I observe the impermanent nature of all dharmas. Breathing out, I observe the impermanent nature of all dharmas.' He or she practices like this.
14. 'Breathing in, I observe the disappearance of desire. Breathing out, I observe the disappearance of desire.' He or she practices like this.
15. 'Breathing in, I observe the no-birth, no-death nature of all phenomena. Breathing out, I observe the no-birth, no-death nature of all phenomena.' He or she practices like this.
16. 'Breathing in, I observe letting go. Breathing out, I observe letting go.' He or she practices like this.

"The Full Awareness of Breathing, if developed and practiced continuously according to these instructions, will be rewarding and of great benefit."

III

"In what way does one develop and continuously practice the Full Awareness of Breathing, in order to succeed in the practice of the Four Establishments of Mindfulness?

"When the practitioner breathes in or out a long or a short breath, aware of his breath or his whole body, or aware that he is making his whole body calm and at peace, he abides peacefully in the observation of the body in the body, persevering, fully awake, clearly understanding his state, gone beyond all attachment and aversion to this life. These exercises of breathing with

Full Awareness belong to the First Establishment of Mindfulness, the body.

"When the practitioner breathes in or out aware of joy or happiness, of the mental formations, or to make the mental formations peaceful, he abides peacefully in the observation of the feelings in the feelings, persevering, fully awake, clearly understanding his state, gone beyond all attachment and aversion to this life. These exercises of breathing with Full Awareness belong to the Second Establishment of Mindfulness, the feelings.

"When the practitioner breathes in or out with the awareness of the mind, or to make the mind happy, to collect the mind in concentration, or to free and liberate the mind, he abides peacefully in the observation of the mind in the mind, persevering, fully awake, clearly understanding his state, gone beyond all attachment and aversion to this life. These exercises of breathing with Full Awareness belong to the Third Establishment of Mindfulness, the mind. Without Full Awareness of Breathing, there can be no development of meditative stability and understanding.

"When the practitioner breathes in or breathes out and contemplates the essential impermanence or the essential disappearance of desire or the no-birth, no-death nature of all phenomena or letting go, he abides peacefully in the observations of the objects of mind in the objects of mind, persevering, fully awake, clearly understanding his state, gone beyond all attachment and aversion to this life. These exercises of breathing with Full Awareness belong to the Fourth Establishment of Mindfulness, the objects of mind.

"The practice of Full Awareness of Breathing, if developed and practiced continuously, will lead to perfect accomplishment of the Four Establishments of Mindfulness."

IV

"Moreover, if they are developed and continuously practiced, the Four Establishments of Mindfulness will lead to perfect abiding in the Seven Factors of Awakening. How is this so?

"When the practitioner can maintain, without distraction, the practice of observing the body in the body, the feelings in the feelings, the mind in the mind, and the objects of mind in the objects of mind, persevering, fully awake, clearly understanding her state, gone beyond all attachment and aversion to this life, with unwavering, steadfast, imperturbable meditative stability, she will attain the First Factor of Awakening, namely mindfulness. When this factor is developed, it will come to perfection.

"When the practitioner can abide in meditative stability without being distracted and can investigate every dharma, every object of mind that arises, then the Second Factor of Awakening will be born and developed in her, the factor of investigating dharmas. When this factor is developed, it will come to perfection.

"When the practitioner can observe and investigate every dharma in a sustained, persevering, and steadfast way, without being distracted, the Third Factor of Awakening will be born and developed in her, the factor of energy. When this factor is developed, it will come to perfection.

"When the practitioner has reached a stable, imperturbable abiding in the stream of practice, the Fourth Factor of Awakening will be born and developed in her, the factor of joy. When this factor is developed, it will come to perfection.

"When the practitioner can abide undistractedly in the state of joy, she will feel her body and mind light and at peace. At this point the Fifth Factor of Awakening will be born and developed, the factor of ease. When this factor is developed, it will come to perfection.

"When both body and mind are at ease, the practitioner can easily enter into concentration. At this point the Sixth Factor of Awakening will be born and developed in her, the factor of concentration. When this factor is developed, it will come to perfection.

"When the practitioner is abiding in concentration with deep calm, she will cease discriminating and comparing. At this point the Seventh Factor of Awakening is released, born, and developed in her, the factor of letting go. When this factor is developed, it will come to perfection.

"This is how the Four Establishments of Mindfulness, if developed and practiced continuously, will lead to perfect abiding in the Seven Factors of Awakening."

V

"How will the Seven Factors of Awakening, if developed and practiced continuously, lead to the perfect accomplishment of true understanding and complete liberation?

"If the practitioner follows the path of the Seven Factors of Awakening, living in quiet seclusion, observing and contemplating the disappearance of desire, he will develop the capacity of letting go. This will be a result of following the path of the Seven Factors of Awakening and will lead to the perfect accomplishment of true understanding and complete liberation."

VI

This is what the Lord, the Awakened One, said; and everyone in the assembly felt gratitude and delight at having heard his teachings.

Anapanasati Sutta, Majjhima Nikaya 118*

* For commentary, see Thich Nhat Hanh, *Breathe! You Are Alive: Sutra on the Full Awareness of Breathing,* Revised Edition (Berkeley, CA: Parallax Press, 1995) and *Path of Emancipation* (Berkeley, CA: Parallax, 2000).

Discourse on the Four Establishments of Mindfulness

I

I heard these words of the Buddha one time when he was living at Kammassadhamma, a market town of the Kuru people. The Buddha addressed the bhikkhus, "O bhikkhus."

And the bhikkhus replied, "Venerable Lord."

The Buddha said, "Bhikkhus, there is a most wonderful way to help living beings realize purification, overcome directly grief and sorrow, end pain and anxiety, travel the right path, and realize nirvana. This way is the Four Establishments of Mindfulness.

"What are the Four Establishments?

1. "Bhikkhus, a practitioner remains established in the observation of the body in the body, diligent, with clear understanding, mindful, having abandoned every craving and every distaste for this life.

2. "He remains established in the observation of the feelings in the feelings, diligent, with clear understanding, mindful, having abandoned every craving and every distaste for this life.

3. "He remains established in the observation of the mind in the mind, diligent, with clear understanding, mindful, having abandoned every craving and every distaste for this life.

4. "He remains established in the observation of the objects of mind in the objects of mind, diligent, with clear understanding, mindful, having abandoned every craving and every distaste for this life."

II

"And how does a practitioner remain established in the observation of the body in the body?

"She goes to the forest, to the foot of a tree, or to an empty room, sits down cross-legged in the lotus position, holds her body straight, and establishes mindfulness in front of her. She breathes in, aware that she is breathing in. She breathes out, aware that she is breathing out. When she breathes in a long breath, she knows, 'I am breathing in a long breath.' When she breathes out a long breath, she knows, 'I am breathing out a long breath.' When she breathes in a short breath, she knows, 'I am breathing in a short breath.' When she breathes out a short breath, she knows, 'I am breathing out a short breath.'

"She uses the following practice: 'Breathing in, I am aware of my whole body. Breathing out, I am aware of my whole body. Breathing in, I calm my body. Breathing out, I calm my body.'

"Just as a skilled potter knows when he makes a long turn on the wheel, 'I am making a long turn,' and knows when he makes a short turn, 'I am making a short turn,' so a practitioner, when she breathes in a long breath, knows, 'I am breathing in a long breath,' and when she breathes in a short breath, knows, 'I am breathing in a short breath,' when she breathes out a long breath, knows, 'I am breathing out a long breath,' and when she breathes out a short breath, knows, 'I am breathing out a short breath.'

"She uses the following practice: 'Breathing in, I am aware of my whole body. Breathing out, I am aware of my whole body. Breathing in, I calm my body. Breathing out, I calm my body.'

"Moreover, when a practitioner walks, he is aware, 'I am walking.' When he is standing, he is aware, 'I am standing.' When he is sitting, he is aware, 'I am sitting.' When he is lying down, he is aware, 'I am lying down.' In whatever position his body happens to be, he is aware of the position of his body.

"Moreover, when the practitioner is going forward or backward, he applies full awareness to his going forward or backward. When he looks in front or looks behind, bends down or stands up, he also applies full awareness to what he is doing. He applies full awareness to wearing the sanghati robe or carrying the alms bowl. When he eats or drinks, chews, or savors the food, he applies full awareness to all this. When passing excrement or urinating, he applies full awareness to this. When he walks, stands, lies down, sits, sleeps or wakes up, speaks or is silent, he shines his awareness on all this.

"Further, the practitioner meditates on her very own body from the soles of the feet upwards and then from the hair on top of the head downwards, a body contained inside the skin and full of all the impurities which belong to the body: 'Here is the hair of the head, the hairs on the body, the nails, teeth, skin, flesh, sinews, bones, bone marrow, kidneys, heart, liver, diaphragm, spleen, lungs, intestines, bowels, excrement, bile, phlegm, pus, blood, sweat, fat, tears, grease, saliva, mucus, synovial fluid, urine.'

"Bhikkhus, imagine a sack which can be opened at both ends, containing a variety of grains — brown rice, wild rice, mung beans, kidney beans, sesame, white rice. When someone with good eyesight opens the bags, he will review it like this: 'This is brown rice, this is wild rice, these are mung beans, these are kidney beans, these are sesame seeds, this is white rice.' Just so the practitioner passes in review the whole of his body from the soles of the feet to the hair on the top of the head, a body enclosed in a layer of skin and full of all the impurities which belong to the body: 'Here is the hair of the head, the hairs on the body, nails, teeth, skin, flesh, sinews, bones, bone marrow, kidneys, heart, liver, diaphragm, spleen, lungs, intestines, bowels, excrement, bile, phlegm, pus, blood, sweat, fat, tears, grease, saliva, mucus, synovial fluid, urine.'

"Further, in whichever position her body happens to be, the practitioner passes in review the elements which constitute the body: 'In this body is the earth element, the water element, the fire element, and the air element.'

"As a skilled butcher or an apprentice butcher, having killed a cow, might sit at the crossroads to divide the cow into many parts, the practitioner passes in review the elements which comprise her very own body: 'Here in this body are the earth element, the water element, the fire element, and the air element.'

Further, the practitioner compares his own body with a corpse which he visualizes thrown onto a charnel ground and lying there for one, two, or three days — bloated, blue in color, and festering, and he observes, 'This body of mine is of the same nature. It will end up in the same way; there is no way it can avoid that state.'

"Further, the practitioner compares his own body with a corpse which he visualizes thrown onto a charnel ground, pecked at by crows, eaten by hawks, vultures, and jackals, and infested with maggots and worms, and he observes, 'This body of mine is of the same nature, it will end up in the same way, there is no way it can avoid that state.'

"Further, the practitioner compares his own body with a corpse which he visualizes thrown onto a charnel ground; it is just a skeleton with a little flesh and blood sticking to it, and the bones are held together by the ligaments.

"Further, the practitioner compares his own body with a corpse which he visualizes thrown onto a charnel ground; it is just a skeleton, no longer adhered to by any flesh, but still smeared by a little blood, the bones still held together by the ligaments.

"Further, the practitioner compares his own body with a corpse which he visualizes thrown onto a charnel ground; it is just a skeleton, no longer adhered to by any flesh nor smeared by any blood, but the bones are still held together by the ligaments.

"Further, the practitioner compares his own body with a corpse which he visualizes thrown onto a charnel ground; all that is left is a collection of bones scattered here and there; in one place a hand bone, in another a shin bone, a thigh bone, a pelvis, a spinal column, a skull.

"Further, the practitioner compares his own body with a corpse which he visualizes thrown onto a charnel ground; all that is left is a collection of bleached bones, the color of shells.

"Further, the practitioner compares his own body with a corpse which he visualizes thrown onto a charnel ground; it has been lying there for more than one year and all that is left is a collection of dried bones.

"Further, the practitioner compares his own body with a corpse which he visualizes thrown onto a charnel ground; all that is left is the dust which comes from the rotted bones, and he observes, 'This body of mine is of the same nature, it will end up in the same way. There is no way it can avoid that state.'

"This is how the practitioner remains established in the observation of the body in the body, observation of the body from within or from without, or both from within or from without. He remains established in the observation of the process of coming-to-be in the body or the process of dissolution in the body or both in the process of coming-to-be and the process of dissolution. Or he is mindful of the fact, 'There is a body here,' until understanding and full awareness come about. He remains established in the observation, free, not caught in any worldly consideration. That is how to practice observation of the body in the body, O bhikkhus."

III

"Bhikkhus, how does a practitioner remain established in the observation of the feelings in the feelings?

"Whenever the practitioner has a pleasant feeling, she is aware, 'I am experiencing a pleasant feeling.' The practitioner practices like this for all the feelings, whether they are pleasant, painful, or neutral, observing when they belong to the body and when they belong to the mind.

"This is how the practitioner remains established in the observation of the feelings in the feelings, observation of the feelings from within or from without, or observation of the feelings both from within and from without. She remains established in the observation of the process of coming-to-be in the feelings or the process of dissolution in the feelings or both in the process of coming-to-be and the process of dissolution. Or she is mindful of the fact, 'There is feeling here,' until understanding and full awareness come about. She remains established in the observation, free, not caught in any worldly consideration. That is how to practice observation of the feelings in the feelings, O bhikkhus."

IV

"Bhikkhus, how does a practitioner remain established in the observation of the mind in the mind?

"When his mind is desiring, the practitioner is aware, 'My mind is desiring.' When his mind is not desiring, he is aware, 'My mind is not desiring.' He is aware in the same way concerning a hating mind, a confused mind, a collected mind, a dispersed mind, an expansive mind, a narrow mind, the highest mind, and a concentrated and liberated mind.

"This is how the practitioner remains established in the observation of the mind in the mind, observation of the mind from within or from without, or observation of the mind both from within and from without. He remains established in the observation of the process of coming-to-be in the mind or the process of dissolution in the mind or both in the process of coming-to-be and the process of dissolution. Or he is mindful of the fact, 'There is mind here,' until understanding and full awareness come about. He remains established in the observation, free, not caught in any worldly consideration. This is how to practice observation of the mind in the mind, O bhikkhus."

V

"Bhikkhus, how does a practitioner remain established in the observation of the objects of mind in the objects of mind?

"First of all, she observes the objects of mind in the objects of mind with regard to the Five Hindrances. How does she observe this?

"When sensual desire is present in her, she is aware, 'Sensual desire is present in me.' Or when sensual desire is not present in her, she is aware, 'Sensual desire is not present in me.' When sensual desire begins to arise, she is aware of it. When sensual desire that has already arisen is abandoned, she is aware of it. When sensual desire that has already been abandoned will not arise again in the future, she is aware of it.

"She practices in the same way concerning anger, dullness and drowsiness, agitation and remorse, and doubt.

"Further, the practitioner observes the objects of mind in the objects of mind with regard to the Five Aggregates of Clinging. How does she observe this?

"She observes like this: 'Such is form. Such is the arising of form. Such is the disappearance of form. Such is feeling. Such is the arising of feeling. Such is the disappearance of feeling. Such is perception. Such is the arising of perception. Such is the disappearance of perception. Such are mental formations. Such is the arising of mental formations. Such is the disappearance of mental formations. Such is consciousness. Such is the arising of consciousness. Such is the disappearance of consciousness.

"Further, bhikkhus, the practitioner observes the objects of mind in the objects of mind with regard to the six sense organs and the six sense objects. How does she observe this?

"She is aware of the eyes and aware of the form, and she is aware of the internal formations which are produced in dependence on these two things. She is aware of the birth of a new internal formation and is aware of abandoning an already produced internal formation, and she is aware when an already abandoned internal formation will not arise again.

"She is aware in the same way of the ears and sound, the nose and smell, the tongue and taste, the body and touch, the mind and objects of mind.

"Further, bhikkhus, the practitioner remains established in the observation of the objects of mind in the objects of mind with regard to the Seven Factors of Awakening.

"How does he remain established in the practice of observation of the Seven Factors of Awakening?

"When the factor of awakening, mindfulness, is present in him, he is aware, 'Mindfulness is present in me.' When mindfulness is not present in him, he is aware, 'Mindfulness is not present in me.' He is aware when not-yet-born mindfulness is being born and when already-born mindfulness is perfectly developed.

"In the same way, he is aware of the factors of investigation, diligence, joy, ease, concentration, and equanimity.

"Further, bhikkhus, a practitioner remains established in the observation of objects of mind in the objects of mind with regard to the Four Noble Truths.

"How, bhikkhus, does the practitioner remain established in the observation of the Four Noble Truths?

"A practitioner is aware 'This is suffering,' as it arises. She is aware, 'This is the cause of the suffering,' as it arises. She is aware, 'This is the end of

---

* For commentary, see Thich Nhat Hanh, *Transformation and Healing: Sutra on the Four Establishments of Mindfulness*, Revised Edition (Berkeley, CA: Parallax Press, 2006).

suffering,' as it arises. She is aware, 'This is the path which leads to the end of suffering,' as it arises.

"This is how the practitioner remains established in the observation of the objects of mind in the objects of mind either from within or from without, or both from within and from without. She remains established in the observation of the process of coming-to-be in any of the objects of mind or the process of dissolution in the objects of mind or both in the process of coming-to-be and the process of dissolution. Or she is mindful of the fact, 'There is an object of mind here,' until understanding and full awareness come about. She remains established in the observation, free, not caught in any worldly consideration. That is how to practice observation of the objects of mind in the objects of mind, O bhikkhus."

VI

"Bhikkhus, he who practices the Four Establishments of Mindfulness for seven years can expect one of two fruits — the highest understanding in this very life or, if there remains some residue of affliction, he can attain the fruit of no-return.

"Let alone seven years, bhikkhus, whoever practices the Four Establishments of Mindfulness for six, five, four, three, two years or one year, for seven, six, five, four, three, or two months, one month or half a month, can also expect one of two fruits — either the highest understanding in this very life or, if there remains some residue of affliction, he can attain the fruit of no-return.

"That is why we said that this path, the path of the four grounds for the establishment of mindfulness, is the most wonderful path, which helps beings realize purification, transcend grief and sorrow, destroy pain and anxiety, travel the right path, and realize nirvana."

The bhikkhus were delighted to hear the teaching of the Buddha. They took it to heart and began to put it into practice.

Satipatthana Sutta, Majjhima Nikaya 10*

Discourse on the Five Ways of Putting an End to Anger

I heard these words of the Buddha one time when he was staying in the Anathapindika Monastery in the Jeta Grove near the town of Shravasti.

One day the Venerable Shariputra said to the monks, "Friends, today I want to share with you five ways of putting an end to anger. Please listen carefully and put into practice what I teach."

The bhikshus agreed and listened carefully.

The Venerable Shariputra then said, "What are these five ways of putting an end to anger?

"This is the first way. My friends, if there is someone whose bodily actions are not kind but whose words are kind, if you feel anger toward that person but you are wise, you will know how to meditate in order to put an end to your anger.

"My friends, say there is a bhikshu practicing asceticism who wears a patchwork robe. One day he is going past a garbage pile filled with excrement, urine, mucus, and many other filthy things, and he sees in the pile one piece of cloth still intact. Using his left hand, he picks up the piece of cloth, and he takes the other end and stretches it out with his right hand. He observes that this piece of cloth is not torn and has not been stained by excrement, urine, sputum, or other kinds of filth. So he folds it and puts it away to take home, wash, and sew into his patchwork robe. My friends, if we are wise, when someone's bodily actions are not kind but his words are kind, we should not pay attention to his unkind bodily actions, but only be attentive to his kind words. This will help us put an end to our anger.

"My friends, this is the second method. If you become angry with someone whose words are not kind but whose bodily actions are kind, if you are wise, you will know how to meditate in order to put an end to your anger.

"My friends, say that not far from the village there is a deep lake, and the surface of that lake is covered with algae and grass. There is someone who comes near that lake who is very thirsty, suffering greatly from the heat. He takes off his clothes, jumps into the water, and using his hands to clear away the algae and grass, enjoys bathing and drinking the cool water of the lake. It is the same, my friends, with someone whose words are not kind but whose bodily actions are kind. Do not pay attention to that person's words. Only be attentive to his bodily actions in order to be able to put an end to your anger. Someone who is wise should practice in this way.

"Here is the third method, my friends. If there is someone whose bodily actions and words are not kind, but who still has a little kindness in his heart, if you feel anger toward that person and are wise, you will know how to meditate to put an end to your anger.

"My friends, say there is someone going to a crossroads. She is weak, thirsty, poor, hot, deprived, and filled with sorrow. When she arrives at the crossroads, she sees a buffalo's footprint with a little stagnant rainwater in it. She thinks to herself, 'There is very little water in this buffalo's footprint. If I use my hand or a leaf to scoop it up, I will stir it up and it will become muddy and undrinkable. Therefore, I will have to kneel down with my arms and knees on the earth, put my lips right to the water, and drink it directly.' Straightaway, she does just that. My friends, when you see someone whose bodily actions and words are not kind, but where there is still a little kindness in her heart, do not pay attention to her actions and words, but to the little kindness that is in her heart so that you may put an end to your anger. Someone who is wise should practice in that way.

"This is the fourth method, my friends. If there is someone whose words and bodily actions are not kind, and in whose heart there is nothing that can be called kindness, if you are angry with that person and you are wise, you will know how to meditate in order to put an end to your anger.

"My friends, suppose there is someone on a long journey who falls sick. He is alone, completely exhausted, and not near any village. He falls into despair, knowing that he will die before completing his journey. If at that point, someone comes along and sees this man's situation, she immediately takes the man's hand and leads him to the next village, where she takes care of him, treats his illness, and makes sure he has everything he needs by way of clothes, medicine, and food. Because of this compassion and loving kindness, the man's life is saved. Just so, my friends, when you see someone whose words and bodily actions are not kind, and in whose heart there is nothing that can be called kindness, give rise to this thought: 'Someone whose words and bodily actions are not kind and in whose heart is nothing that can be called kindness, is someone who is undergoing great suffering. Unless he meets a good spiritual friend, there will be no chance for him to transform and go to realms of happiness.' Thinking like this, you will be able to open your heart with love and compassion toward that person. You will be able to put an end to your anger and help that person. Someone who is wise should practice like this.

"My friends, this is the fifth method. If there is someone whose bodily actions are kind, whose words are kind, and whose mind is also kind, if you are angry with that person and you are wise, you will know how to meditate in order to put an end to your anger.

"My friends, suppose that not far from the village there is a very beautiful lake. The water in the lake is clear and sweet, the bed of the lake is even, the banks of the lake are lush with green grass, and all around the lake, beautiful fresh trees give shade. Someone who is thirsty, suffering from heat, whose body is covered in sweat, comes to the lake, takes off his clothes, leaves them on the shore, jumps down into the water, and finds great comfort and enjoyment in drinking and bathing in the pure water. His heat, thirst, and suffering disappear immediately. In the same way, my friends, when you see someone whose bodily actions are kind, whose words are kind, and whose mind is also kind, give your attention to all his kindness of body, speech, and mind, and do not allow anger or jealousy to overwhelm you. If you do not know how to live happily with someone who is as fresh as that, you cannot be called someone who has wisdom.

"My dear friends, I have shared with you the five ways of putting an end to anger."

When the bhikshus heard the Venerable Shariputra's words, they were happy to receive them and put them into practice.

Madhyama Agama 25
(Corresponds with Aghata Vinaya Sutta
[Discourse on Water as an Example], Anguttara Nikaya 5.162)

Discourse on the White-Clad Disciple

I heard these words of the Buddha one time when he was staying at the monastery in the Jeta Grove near Shravasti that had been donated by the layman Anathapindika. On that day, Anathapindika came with five hundred other lay students of the Buddha to the hut where Shariputra resided. They bowed their heads in reverence to Shariputra and sat down respectfully to one side. Venerable Shariputra offered them skillful teachings, bringing them joy and confidence in the Three Jewels and the practice of the true Dharma. Then, Shariputra and the five hundred laymen and women went together to the hut of the Buddha, where Shariputra, Anathapindika, and the other five hundred laymen and women prostrated at the Buddha's feet and sat down to one side.

When he observed that everyone was seated, the Buddha addressed Shariputra, saying, "Shariputra, if lay students of the Buddha, those who wear white robes, study and practice the Five Mindfulness Trainings and the Four Contemplations, they will realize without hardship the capacity to abide happily in the present moment. They know they will not fall into the realms of hell, hungry ghosts, animals, and other suffering paths.

"Such men and women will have attained the fruit of stream-enterer, and they will have no fear of descending into dark paths. They are on the way of right awakening. They will only need to return to the worlds of gods or men seven more times before attaining perfect liberation and the end of suffering.

"Shariputra, how do lay students of the Buddha, those who wear white robes, study and practice the Five Mindfulness Trainings and the Four Contemplations?

"Lay students of the Buddha refrain from killing, put an end to killing, rid themselves of all weapons, learn humility before others, learn humility in themselves, practice love and compassion, and protect all living beings, even the smallest insects. They uproot from within themselves any intention to kill. In this way, lay students of the Buddha study and practice the first of the Five Mindfulness Trainings.

"Lay students of the Buddha refrain from taking what has not been given, put an end to taking what has not been given. They find joy in being generous without expecting anything in return. Their minds are not obscured by greed or craving. They constantly guard their own honesty and uproot from within themselves any intention to take what has not been given. In this way, lay students of the Buddha study and practice the second of the Five Mindfulness Trainings.

"Lay students of the Buddha refrain from sexual misconduct, put an end to sexual misconduct, and protect everyone — those under the care of their father, mother, or both father and mother; their elder sister or elder brother; their parents-in-law or other in-laws; those of the same sex; the wife, daughter, husband or son of another; and those who have been raped, assaulted, or sexually abused, or who have been prostitutes. Lay students of the Buddha uproot from within themselves any intention to commit sexual misconduct. In this way, lay students of the Buddha study and practice the third of the Five Mindfulness Trainings.

"Lay students of the Buddha refrain from saying what is not true, put an end to saying what is not true. They say only what is true, and they find great joy in saying what is true. They always abide in truth and are completely reliable, never deceiving others. They have uprooted from within themselves any intention to say what is not true. In this way, lay students of the Buddha study and practice the fourth of the Five Mindfulness Trainings.

"Lay students of the Buddha refrain from drinking alcohol, put an end to drinking alcohol. They uproot from within themselves the habit of drinking alcohol. In this way, lay students of the Buddha study and practice the fifth of the Five Mindfulness Trainings.

"Shariputra, how do lay students of the Buddha attain the Four Contemplations and abide happily in the present moment with ease and without hardship? They practice being aware of the Buddha, meditating on the one who has come from Suchness and returns to Suchness; as one who is truly and fully awakened, without any attachments; as one whose understanding and practice are perfect; as the Well-Gone One; as one who knows and fully understands the world; as one who has attained the very highest; as one who has tamed what needs to be tamed; as a teacher of humans and gods; as an Awakened One; and as a World-Honored One. When they meditate in this way, all unwholesome desires come to an end, and impure, sorrowful, or anxious elements no longer arise in their hearts. As a result of contemplating the Buddha, their thoughts are clear, they feel joy, and they arrive at the first of the Four Contemplations, abiding happily in the present moment, with ease and without any hardships.

"Shariputra, the lay students of the Buddha practice being aware of the Dharma, meditating as follows: the Dharma is taught by the Lord Buddha with great skill; it can lead to complete liberation; it can lead to a state of no afflictions; it is cool and refreshing; its value is timeless. When lay students of the Buddha meditate on and observe the Dharma in this way, all unwholesome desires come to an end, and impure, sorrowful, or anxious elements no longer arise in their hearts. As a result of contemplating the Dharma, their thoughts are clear, they feel joy, and they arrive at the second of the Four Contemplations, abiding happily in the present moment, with ease and without any hardship.

"Shariputra, the lay students of the Buddha practice being aware of the Sangha, meditating as follows: the noble community of the Tathagata is advancing in a good direction; it is on an upright path; it is oriented toward the Dharma; it lives the teachings in the way they are meant to be lived. In that community, there are the Four Pairs and the Eight Grades — realized arhats and those who are realizing the fruit of arhatship, non-returners and those who are realizing the fruit of non-returning, once-returners and those who are realizing the fruit of once-returning, and stream-enters and those who are realizing the fruit of stream-entry. The noble community of the Tathagata has successfully realized the practice of the mindfulness trainings *(shila)*, the practice of concentration *(samadhi)*, and the practice of insight *(prajña)*. It has liberation and liberated vision. It is worthy of respect, honor, service, and offerings. It is a beautiful field of merit for everyone. As a result of contemplating the Sangha, their thoughts are clear, they feel joy, and they arrive at the third of the Four Contemplations, abiding happily in the present moment, with ease and without any hardship.

"Shariputra, the lay students of the Buddha practice being mindful of the mindfulness trainings, meditating as follows: the mindfulness trainings have no drawbacks, flaws, impurities, or unsound points; and they help us abide in the land of the Tathagata. The Mindfulness Trainings are not of the nature to deceive. They are always praised, accepted, practiced, and guarded by the holy ones. As a result of contemplating these Trainings, the students' thoughts are clear, they feel joy, and they arrive at the fourth of the Four Contemplations, abiding happily in the present moment, with ease and without any hardship.

"Shariputra, remember that white-clad disciples of the Buddha who practice in this way will not descend into hell realms, hungry ghost realms, animal realms, or any other realms of suffering. They have experienced the fruit of stream-entry, which means not falling into paths of hardship or wrongdoing. Having entered the stream, they cannot help but go in the direction of right awakening. They will only need to return to the world of gods or humans seven more times before they arrive at complete liberation and the end of sorrow."

Thus spoke the Buddha. The Venerable Shariputra, the other monks and nuns, the layman Anathapindika, and the other five hundred laymen and laywomen heard these words and were delighted to put them into practice.

Upasaka Sutra, Madhyama Agama 128*

* For commentary, see Thich Nhat Hanh, *For a Future to Be Possible*, Revised Edition (Berkeley, CA: Parallax Press, 1998).

Discourse on Measuring and Reflecting

I heard these words of the Buddha one time when he was staying with the Bhagga people in Sumsumaragiri, in the Deer Park in the Bhesakala Grove. The Venerable Mahamoggallana addressed the bhikkhus, "My friends."

"Yes, friend," they replied to the Venerable Mahamoggallana.

The Venerable Mahamoggallana spoke as follows:

"My friends, suppose there is a bhikkhu who says to the other bhikkhus: 'Please talk to me, Reverend Bhikkhus. I want you to offer me guidance.' If he is difficult to talk to, endowed with qualities that make him difficult to deal with, impatient, intolerant, not good at accepting constructive criticism or the words of advice and instruction from friends in the practice, then those who practice the path of sublime conduct with him will think, 'He is not one to be spoken to, he is not one to be instructed, he is not someone to have confidence in.' What are the qualities that make someone difficult to approach?

"My friends, a bhikkhu who is attached to wrong desires and is controlled by wrong desires is difficult to approach and talk to.

"These are other reasons that make it difficult to approach and talk to him: a person praises himself and despises others; he is easily angered and mastered by his anger; because he is angry, he bears a grudge; because he is angry, he is bad-tempered; because he is angry, he speaks in a bad-tempered way; he accuses one who has corrected him; he disparages one who has corrected him; he corrects in turn one who has corrected him; he evades the criticism by asking another question; he changes the subject; he manifests ill-temper, anger, and sulkiness; he does not succeed in explaining his behavior when corrected; he is unmindful and ill-willed; he is jealous and greedy; he is hypocritical and deceitful; he is stubborn and arrogant; or he is worldly and clings to things that belong to this world and finds it difficult to let go. These, my friends, are the habit energies that make it difficult to approach and talk to him.

"My friends, suppose there is a bhikkhu who requests of other bhikkhus: 'Please talk to me, Reverend Bhikkhus. I want you to offer me guidance.' If he is easy to talk to, endowed with qualities that make him easy to deal with, patient, tolerant, open and able to accept constructive criticism or the words of advice and instruction from friends in the practice, then those who practice the path of sublime conduct with him will think, 'He is someone we can talk to, someone we can instruct, someone we can have confidence in.' What are the qualities that make someone easy to approach?

"My friends, a bhikkhu who is not caught in wrong desires and is not controlled by wrong desires is easy to approach and talk to. He does not praise himself and despise others; he is not easily angered or mastered by his anger; because he is not angry, he does not bear a grudge; because he is not angry, he is not bad-tempered; because he is not angry, he does not speak in a bad-tempered way; he does not accuse one who has corrected him; he does not disparage one who has corrected him; he does not correct in turn one who has corrected him; he does not evade the criticism by asking another question; he does not change the subject; he does not manifest ill-temper, anger, and sulkiness; he succeeds in explaining his behavior when corrected; he is not jealous and greedy; he is not hypocritical and deceitful; he is not stubborn and arrogant; he is not worldly nor does he cling to things that belong to this world and he does not find it difficult to let go. These, my friends, are the qualities that make it easy to approach and talk to him.

"My friends, one should infer one's own state by considering the state of others in the following way: 'That person has wrong desires and is controlled by his wrong desires; therefore, I do not find him easy to approach. If I had wrong desires and were controlled by those wrong desires, others would not find me easy to approach.' When one sees this clearly, one should make the following determination: 'May I not be attached to wrong desires or be controlled by those wrong desires.'

"This method of reflection needs to be practiced in other cases, such as praising oneself and despising others, being easily angered and mastered by anger, and so on.

"My friends, this is how a bhikkhu should reflect on himself: 'At this moment, am I attached to wrong desires and controlled by wrong desires?' If when a bhikkhu reflects in this way, he knows, 'At this moment, I am attached to wrong desires and controlled by wrong desires,' then he should practice diligently to put an end to these unwholesome mental formations. If, on the other hand, when he reflects, he knows, 'At this moment, I am not attached to wrong desires and not controlled by wrong desires,' then a bhikkhu should live with a feeling of happiness, and he should practice diligently to nourish and increase these wholesome mental formations.

"This method of reflection needs to be practiced in other cases, such as praising oneself and despising others, becoming easily angered and mastered by anger, and so on.

"If, my friends, when he reflects, a bhikkhu sees clearly that he has not yet given up all these unbeneficial qualities, then he should practice diligently to give them all up. If, when he reflects, a bhikkhu sees clearly that he has given up all these unwholesome mental formations, then he should live with a feeling of happiness, and he should practice diligently to nourish and increase these wholesome mental formations.

"It is like when a young person who is fond of adorning himself contemplates his face in the mirror or a bowl of clear water. If he sees dirt or a blemish on his face, he tries to clean it. If he does not see dirt or a blemish, he thinks to himself, 'It is good, my face is clean.'

"So, my friends, if a bhikkhu reflects and sees that all these unwholesome mental formations have not yet been given up, then he practices diligently to give them all up. If he sees that he has given them all up, he feels happy about this and knows that he needs to practice diligently in order to nourish and increase these wholesome mental formations."

The Venerable Mahamoggallana had spoken. The bhikkhus were delighted, had confidence in, and accepted their teacher's words.

Anumana Sutta, Majjhima Nikaya 15

Discourse on the Teachings to Be Given to the Sick

I heard these words of the Buddha one time when the Lord was staying in the monastery in the Jeta Grove in Anathapindika's park, near Shravasti. At that time the householder Anathapindika was seriously ill. When the Venerable Shariputra was told this, he immediately went to Ananda and said, "Brother Ananda, let us go and visit the layman Anathapindika." The Venerable Ananda replied, "Yes, let us go now."

The Venerable Ananda put on his robe, took his bowl, and went into the town of Shravasti with the Venerable Shariputra to make the almsround. Ananda walked behind Shariputra, stopping at every house until they came to the house of the layman Anathapindika, and they went in to visit him. After he had sat down, the Venerable Shariputra asked the layman Anathapindika, "How is your illness? Is it getting better or worse? Is the physical pain easing at all or is it getting greater?" The householder Anathapindika replied, "Venerable monks, it does not seem to be getting better. The pain is not easing. It is getting greater all the time." Shariputra said, "Friend Anathapindika, now is the time to practice the meditation on the Three Jewels, the Buddha, the Dharma, and the Sangha.

"The Buddha has gone to Suchness, is fully and truly awakened, has perfected understanding and action, has arrived at true happiness, understands the nature of the world, is unequaled in understanding, has conquered the afflictions of human beings, is a teacher of gods and humans, and is the Awakened One, the one who liberates the world.

"The Dharma is the teaching of love and understanding that the Tathagata has expounded. It is deep and lovely, worthy of the highest respect, and very precious. It is a teaching that cannot be compared to ordinary teachings. It is a path of practice for the Noble Ones.

"The Sangha is the community of practice, guided by the teachings of the Awakened One. The community is in harmony, and within it all aspects of the practice can be realized. The community is respected and precious. It practices the precepts and realizes concentration, insight, and liberation. Offerings made to the Sangha are very beneficial.

"Friend Anathapindika, if you meditate in this way on the Buddha, the Dharma, and the Sangha, the beneficial effects are beyond measure. Meditating in this way, you can destroy the obstacles of wrong deeds and the afflictions. You can harvest a fruit that is as fresh and sweet as the balm of compassion. A woman or a man practicing an upright way of life who knows how to meditate on the Three Jewels will have no chance of falling into the three lower realms but will be reborn as a human or a god.

"Friend Anathapindika, now is the time to practice the meditation on the Six Sense Bases:

"These eyes are not me. I am not caught in these eyes.
"These ears are not me. I am not caught in these ears.
"This nose is not me. I am not caught in this nose.
"This tongue is not me. I am not caught in this tongue.
"This body is not me. I am not caught in this body.
"This mind is not me. I am not caught in this mind.

"Now continue your meditation with the Six Sense Objects:

"These forms are not me. I am not caught in these forms.
"These sounds are not me. I am not caught in these sounds.
"These smells are not me. I am not caught in these smells.
"These tastes are not me. I am not caught in these tastes.
"These contacts with the body are not me. I am not caught in these contacts with the body.
"These thoughts are not me. I am not caught in these thoughts.

"Now continue your meditation on the Six Sense Consciousnesses:

"Sight is not me. I am not caught in sight.
"Hearing is not me. I am not caught in hearing.
"Consciousness based on the nose is not me. I am not caught in the consciousness based on the nose.
"Consciousness based on the tongue is not me. I am not caught in consciousness based on the tongue.
"Consciousness based on the body is not me. I am not caught in consciousness based on the body.
"Consciousness based on the mind is not me. I am not caught in consciousness based on the mind.

"Now continue your meditation on the Six Elements:

"The earth element is not me. I am not caught in the earth element.
"The water element is not me. I am not caught in the water element.
"The fire element is not me. I am not caught in the fire element.
"The air element is not me. I am not caught in the air element.
"The space element is not me. I am not caught in the space element.
"The consciousness element is not me. I am not caught in the
   consciousness element.

"Now continue your meditation on the Five Aggregates:

"Form is not me. I am not limited by the form aggregate.
"Feelings are not me. I am not limited by the feeling aggregate.
"Perceptions are not me. I am not limited by the perception aggregate.
"Mental formations are not me. I am not limited by the mental
   formation aggregate.
"Consciousness is not me. I am not limited by the consciousness
   aggregate.

"Now continue your meditation on the Three Times:

"The past is not me. I am not limited by the past.
"The present is not me. I am not limited by the present.
"The future is not me. I am not limited by the future.

   "Friend Anathapindika, everything that arises is due to causes and conditions. Everything that is has the nature not to be born and not to die, not
to arrive and not to depart. When eyes arise, they arise, but they do not come
from anywhere. When eyes cease to be, they cease to be, but they do not go
anywhere. Eyes are neither nonexistent before they arise, nor are they ex-
istent after they arise. Everything that is comes to be because of a combination of causes and conditions. When the causes and conditions are
sufficient, eyes are present. When the causes and conditions are not sufficient, eyes are absent. The same is true of ears, nose, tongue, body, and mind;
form, sound, smell, taste, touch, and thought; sight, hearing, and the consciousnesses based on the nose, tongue, body, and mind; the Six Elements,
the Five Aggregates, and the Three Times.
   "In the Five Aggregates, there is nothing that we can call 'I,' a 'person,'
or a 'soul.' Ignorance is the inability to see this truth. Because there is ignorance, there are mistaken impulses. Because there are mistaken impulses,

there is mistaken consciousness. Because there is mistaken consciousness, there is the distinction between the perceiver and the perceived. Because there is the distinction between the perceiver and the perceived, there is the distinction between the six organs and the six objects of sense. Because there is the distinction between the six organs and the six objects of sense, there is contact. Because there is contact, there is feeling. Because there is feeling, there is thirst. Because there is thirst, there is grasping. Because there is grasping, there is being. Because there is becoming, there are birth, death, and the subsequent pain and grief.

"Friend Anathapindika, you have meditated that everything that arises is due to causes and conditions and does not have a separate self. That is called 'the meditation on emptiness.' It is the highest and the most profound meditation."

When he had practiced to this point, the layman Anathapindika began to cry. Venerable Ananda asked him, "Friend, why are you crying? Has your meditation not been successful? Do you have some regret?" The layman Anathapindika replied, "Venerable Ananda, I do not regret anything. The meditation has been most successful. I am crying because I am so deeply moved. I have been fortunate to have been able to serve the Buddha and his community for many years, yet I have never heard a teaching so wonderful and precious as the teaching transmitted by the Venerable Shariputra today."

Then the Venerable Ananda said to the layman Anathapindika, "Do you not know, friend, that the Buddha often gives this teaching to bhikshus and bhikshunis?" The layman Anathapindika replied, "Venerable Ananda, please tell the Buddha that there are also laypeople with the capacity to listen, understand, and put into practice these deep and wonderful teachings."

After hearing Shariputra's instructions and meditating accordingly, Anathapindika felt free and at ease. The Venerables Shariputra and Ananda bade him farewell and went back to the monastery, and Anathapindika passed away and was born in the thirty-third heaven.

Ekottara Agama 51. 8
(In consultation with Majjhima Nikaya 143
and Madhyama Agama 26)

Discourse on Taking Refuge in Oneself

I heard these words of the Buddha one time when the Lord was staying in the Mango Grove in the cool shade of the mango trees along the bank of a river in the land of Magadha. The elders Shariputra and Maudgalyayana had recently passed away. It was the full-moon day of the Uposatha Ceremony and the precepts were recited.

The Buddha spread out his sitting mat and sat facing the community. After looking out at those gathered, he said, "As I look at our community, I see a large space left by the Venerables Shariputra and Maudgalyayana. In our Sangha, these venerables were the monks who were the most eloquent in giving Dharma talks, encouraging and instructing all the other monks, nuns, and laypeople.

"O monks, people seek two kinds of riches — material riches and the riches of the Dharma. In their search for material riches, they can go to worldly people. In their search for the riches of the Dharma, they could always go to the Venerables Shariputra and Maudgalyayana. The Tathagata is someone who is not searching for anything, whether it is material or the Dharma.

"O monks, do not be sad or anxious because Shariputra and Maudgalyayana have passed into nirvana. On large trees, filled with leaves, sumptuous fruits, and flowers, the largest branches always die or are broken first. On jeweled mountains, don't the highest peaks always erode before the smaller ones? In the Sangha of the Tathagata, the Venerables Shariputra and Maudgalyayana were the greatest students. So it is natural that these venerables would enter nirvana first. Do not give rise to feelings of sorrow or anguish.

"All phenomena that are born, exist, and are subject to the influence of other phenomena, in other words, all phenomena that are composite, must abide by the law of impermanence and eventually cease to exist. They cannot exist eternally, without someday being destroyed. Everything we cherish and hold dear today, we will have to let go of and be separated from in the future. In not too long a time, I will also pass away. Therefore, I urge you to practice being an island unto yourself, knowing how to take refuge in yourself, and not taking refuge in anyone or anything else.

"Practice taking refuge in the island of the Dharma. Know how to take refuge in the Dharma, and do not take refuge in any other island or person. Meditate on the body in the body, nourishing Right Understanding and mindfulness to master and transform your cravings and anxieties. Observe the elements outside the body in the elements outside the body, nourishing Right Understanding and mindfulness to master and transform your cravings and anxieties. That is the way to take refuge in the island of self, to return to yourself in order to take refuge in the Dharma, and not to take refuge in any other island or thing."

When the bhikshus heard the Buddha offer this teaching, they were all very happy to put it into practice.

Samyukta Agama 639
Taisho Revised Tripitaka 99

Discourse on Knowing
the Better Way to Catch a Snake

I heard these words one time when the Buddha was staying at the Anatha-pindika Monastery in the Jeta Grove, near Shravasti. At that time, the Bhik-shu Arittha, who before being ordained had been a vulture trainer, had the wrong view that according to the teachings of the Buddha, sense pleasures are not an obstacle to the practice. After hearing this, many bhikshus went to Arittha and asked, "Brother Arittha, do you really believe that the Bud-dha teaches that sense pleasures are not an obstacle to the practice?"

Arittha replied, "Yes, friends, it is true that I believe the Buddha does not regard sense pleasures as an obstacle to the practice."

The bhikshus scolded him, "Brother Arittha, you misrepresent the Bud-dha's teachings and even slander him. The Lord has never said that sense pleasures are not an obstacle to the practice. In fact, he uses many examples to teach that sense pleasures are an obstacle to the practice. You should aban-don your wrong view." Although the bhikshus counseled Arittha in this way, he was not moved to change his view. Three times they asked him to abandon his wrong view, and three times he refused, continuing to say that he was right and the others were wrong.

Having advised him like this to no effect, they stood up and left. They went to the Buddha and recounted all that they had seen and heard.

The Buddha summoned Arittha, admonished him, and taught all of the bhikshus, "Monks, it is important to understand my teachings thoroughly before you teach or put them into practice. If you have not understood the meaning of any teaching I give, please ask me or one of the elder brothers in the Dharma or one of the others who is excellent in the practice about it. There are always some people who do not understand the letter or the spirit of a teaching and, in fact, take it the opposite way of what was intended, whether the teachings are offered in the form of verse or prose, predictions, verse summaries, interdependent origination, similes, spontaneous utter-ances, quotations, stories of previous births, wonderful occurrences, detailed commentaries, or clarifications with definitions. There are always some peo-ple who study only to satisfy their curiosity or win arguments, and not for the sake of liberation. With such a motivation, they miss the true spirit of the teaching. They may go through much hardship, endure difficulties that are not of much benefit, and eventually exhaust themselves.

"Bhikshus, a person who studies that way can be compared to a man trying to catch a poisonous snake in the wild. If he reaches out his hand, the snake may bite his hand, leg, or some other part of his body. Trying to catch a snake that way has no advantages and can only create suffering.

"Bhikshus, understanding my teaching in the wrong way is the same. If you do not practice the Dharma correctly, you may come to understand it as the opposite of what was intended. But if you practice intelligently, you will understand both the letter and the spirit of the teachings and will be able to explain them correctly. Do not practice just to show off or argue with others. Practice to attain liberation, and if you do, you will have little pain or exhaustion.

"Bhikshus, an intelligent student of the Dharma is like a man who uses a forked stick to catch a snake. When he sees a poisonous snake in the wild, he places the stick right below the head of the snake and grabs the snake's neck with his hand. Even if the snake winds itself around the man's hand, leg, or another part of his body, it will not bite him. This is the better way to catch a snake, and it will not lead to pain or exhaustion.

"Bhikshus, a son or daughter of good family who studies the Dharma needs to apply the utmost skill to understanding the letter and the spirit of the teachings. He or she should not study with the aim of boasting, debating, or arguing, but only to attain liberation. Studying in this way, with intelligence, he or she will have little pain or exhaustion.

"Bhikshus, I have told you many times the importance of knowing when it is time to let go of a raft and not hold onto it unnecessarily. When a mountain stream overflows and becomes a torrent of floodwater carrying debris, a man or woman who wants to get across might think, 'What is the safest way to cross this floodwater?' Assessing the situation, she may decide to gather branches and grasses, construct a raft, and use it to cross to the other side. But, after arriving on the other side, she thinks, 'I spent a lot of time and energy building this raft. It is a prized possession, and I will carry it with me as I continue my journey.' If she puts it on her shoulders or head and carries it with her on land, bhikshus, do you think that would be intelligent?"

The bhikshus replied, "No, World-Honored One."

The Buddha said, "How could she have acted more wisely? She could have thought, 'This raft helped me get across the water safely. Now I will leave it at the water's edge for someone else to use in the same way.' Wouldn't that be a more intelligent thing to do?"

The bhikshus replied, "Yes, World-Honored One."

The Buddha taught, "I have given this teaching on the raft many times to remind you how necessary it is to let go of all the true teachings, not to mention teachings that are not true."

༅

"Bhikshus, there are six bases for views. This means that there are six grounds of wrong perception that we need to drop. What are the six?

"First, there is form. Whether belonging to the past, the future, or the present, whether it is our own form or the form of someone else, whether subtle or gross, ugly or beautiful, near or far, such form is not mine, is not me, is not the self. Bhikshus, please look deeply so that you can see the truth concerning form.

"Second, there are feelings.

"Third, there are perceptions.

"Fourth, there are mental formations. Whether these phenomena belong to the past, the future, or the present, whether they are our own or someone else's, whether they are subtle or gross, ugly or beautiful, near or far, such phenomena are not mine, are not me, are not the self.

"Fifth, there is consciousness. Whatever we see, hear, perceive, know, mentally grasp, observe, or think about at the present time or any other time is not ours, is not us, is not the self.

"Sixth, there is the world. Some people think, 'The world is the self. The self is the world. The world is me. I will continue to exist without changing even after I die. I am eternal. I will never disappear.' Please meditate so you can see that the world is not mine, is not me, is not the self. Please look deeply so you can see the truth concerning the world."

༅

Upon hearing this, one bhikshu stood up, bared his right shoulder, joined his palms respectfully, and asked the Buddha, "World-Honored One, can fear and anxiety arise from an internal source?"

The Buddha replied, "Yes, fear and anxiety can arise from an internal source. If you think, 'Things that did not exist in the past have come to exist, but now no longer exist,' you will feel sad or become confused and despairing. This is how fear and anxiety can arise from an internal source."

The same bhikshu then asked, "World-Honored One, can fear and anxiety from an internal source be prevented from arising?"

The Buddha replied, "Fear and anxiety from an internal source can be prevented from arising. If you do not think, 'Things that did not exist in the past have come to exist, but now no longer exist,' you will not feel sad or become confused and despairing. This is how fear and anxiety from an internal source can be prevented from arising."

"World-Honored One, can fear and anxiety arise from an external source?"

The Buddha taught, "Fear and anxiety can arise from an external source. You may think, 'This is a self. This is the world. This is myself. I will exist forever.' Then if you meet the Buddha or a disciple of the Buddha who has the understanding and intelligence to teach you how to let go of all views of attachment to the body, the self, and the objects of the self with a view to giving up pride, internal knots (*samyojana*), and energy leaks, and you think, 'This is the end of the world. I have to give up everything. I am not the world. I am not me. I am not the self. I will not exist forever. When I die, I will be completely annihilated. There is nothing to look forward to, to be joyful about, or to remember,' you will feel sad and become confused and despairing. This is how fear and anxiety can arise from an external source."

ॐ

The Buddha asked, "Bhikshus, do you think the Five Aggregates and the self are permanent, changeless, and not subject to destruction?"

"No, reverend teacher."

"Is there anything you can hold onto with attachment that will not cause anxiety, exhaustion, sorrow, suffering, and despair?"

"No, reverend teacher."

"Is there any view of self in which you can take refuge that will not cause anxiety, exhaustion, sorrow, suffering, and despair?"

"No, reverend teacher."

"Bhikshus, you are quite correct. Whenever there is an idea of self, there is also an idea of what belongs to the self. When there is no idea of self, there is no idea of anything that belongs to the self. Self and what belongs to the self are two views that are based on trying to grasp things that cannot be grasped and to establish things that cannot be established." Such wrong perceptions cause us to be bound by internal knots that arise the moment we are caught by ideas that cannot be grasped or established and have no basis in reality. Do you see that these are wrong perceptions? Do you see the consequences of such wrong perceptions in the case of Bhikshu Arittha?"

ॐ

The Buddha continued, "If, when he considers the six bases for wrong views, a bhikshu does not give rise to the idea of 'I' or 'mine,' he is not caught in the chains of this life. Since he is not caught in the chains of this life, he has no fear. To have no fear is to arrive at nirvana. Such a person is no longer troubled by birth and death; the holy life has been lived; what needs to be done has been done; there will be no further births or deaths; and the truth of things as they are is known. Such a bhikshu has filled in the moat, crossed the moat, destroyed the enemy citadel, unbolted the door, and is able to look directly into the mirror of highest understanding.

"Bhikshus, that is the Way of the Tathagata and those who have attained liberation. Indra, Prajapati, Brahma, and the other gods in their entourage, however hard they look, cannot find any trace or basis for the consciousness of a Tathagata. The Tathagata is a noble fount of freshness and coolness. There is no great heat and no sorrow in this state. When recluses and brahmans hear me say this, they may slander me, saying that I do not speak the truth, that the monk Gautama proposes a theory of nihilism and teaches absolute nonexistence, while in fact living beings do exist. Bhikshus, the Tathagata has never taught the things they say. In truth, the Tathagata teaches only the ending of suffering in order to attain the state of non-fear. If the Tathagata is blamed, criticized, defamed, or beaten, he does not care. He does not become angry, walk away in hatred, or do anything in revenge. If someone blames, criticizes, defames, or beats the Tathagata, how does he react? The Tathagata thinks, 'If someone respects, honors, or makes offerings to a Tathagata, the Tathagata would not on that account feel pleased. He would think only that someone is doing this because the Tathagata has attained the fruits of awakening and transformation.' "

Having heard the Buddha speak thus, the bhikshus, with great joy, put the teachings into practice.

Arittha Sutra, Madhyama Agama 220
Alagaddupama Sutta, Majjhima Nikaya 22*

---

* For the complete text and commentary, see Thich Nhat Hanh, *Thundering Silence: Sutra on Knowing the Better Way to Catch a Snake* (Berkeley, CA: Parallax Press, 1993).

Discourse on Youth and Happiness

I heard these words of the Buddha one time when the Lord was staying at the Bamboo Forest Monastery near the town of Rajagriha. At that time there was a bhikshu who, in the very early morning, came to the banks of the river, took off his upper robe and left it on the bank, and went down to the river to bathe. After bathing, he came out of the river, waited until his body was dry, and then put on his upper robe. At that time a goddess appeared, whose body, surrounded by light, lit up the entire bank of the river. The goddess said to the bhikshu, "Venerable, you've recently become a monk. Your hair is still black; you are very young. At this time in your life, shouldn't you be perfumed with oils, adorned with gems and fragrant flowers, enjoying the five kinds of sensual desire? Why have you abandoned your loved ones and turned your back on the worldly life, living alone? You've shaved your hair and beard, donned the monk's robe, and placed your faith in monastic practice. Why have you abandoned the pleasures of this moment to seek pleasures in a distant future?"

The bhikshu replied, "I have not abandoned the present moment in order to seek pleasures in a distant future. I have abandoned pleasures that are untimely for the deepest happiness of this moment."

The goddess asked, "What do you mean?"

And the bhikshu replied, "The World-Honored One has taught: in the joy associated with sensual desire there is little sweetness and much bitterness, tiny benefits, and a great potential to lead to disaster. Now, as I dwell in the Dharma that is available here and now, I've given up the burning fire of afflictions. The Dharma is available here and now. It is outside of time, and it always invites us to come and see it. It is to be realized and experienced by each of us for ourselves. That is what is meant by abandoning untimely pleasures in order to arrive at the deepest happiness of the present moment."

The goddess asked the bhikshu again, "Why does the World-Honored One say that in the untimely pleasure of sensual desire there is little sweetness and much bitterness, its benefit is tiny but its potential to lead to disaster is great? Why does he say that if we dwell in the Dharma that is available here and now we are able to give up the flames of the afflictions that burn us? Why does he say that this Dharma belongs to the present moment, is outside of time, always invites us to come and see it, is available here and now, and is realized and experienced by each of us for ourselves?"

The bhikshu replied, "I have only been ordained for two years. I do not have the skill to explain to you the true teachings and the wonderful precepts that the World-Honored One has proclaimed. The World-Honored One is presently nearby, in the Bamboo Forest. Why don't you go to him and ask your questions directly? The Tathagata will offer you the Right Dharma, and you will be able to receive and practice his guidance as you see fit."

The goddess replied, "Venerable bhikshu, at this moment the Tathagata is surrounded by powerful and influential gods and goddesses. It would be difficult for me to have the chance to approach him and ask about the Dharma. If you would be willing to ask the Tathagata these questions on my behalf, I will accompany you."

The bhikshu replied, "I will help you."

The goddess said, "Venerable, then I will follow you."

The bhikshu went to the place where the Buddha was staying, bowed his head and prostrated before the Buddha, then withdrew a little and sat down to one side. He repeated the conversation he had just had with the goddess, and then said, "World-Honored One, if this goddess had not spoken sincerely, she would not have come here with me." At that moment, there was a sound from afar, "Venerable monk, I am here. I am here."

The World-Honored One immediately offered this gatha:

"Beings produce wrong perceptions
concerning objects of desire.
That is why they are caught in desire.
Because they do not know what desire really is,
they proceed on the path to Death."

The Buddha then asked the goddess, "Do you understand this gatha? If not, please say so."

The goddess addressed the Buddha, "I have not understood, World-Honored One. I have not understood, Well-Gone One."

So the Buddha recited another gatha for the goddess:

"When you know the true nature of desire,
the desiring mind will not be born.
When there is no desire, and no perception based on it,
at that time, no one is able to tempt you."

Then Buddha asked the goddess, "Have you understood this gatha? If not, please say so."

The goddess addressed the Buddha: "I have not understood, World-Honored One. I have not understood, Well-Gone One."

So the Buddha recited another gatha for the goddess:

"If you think you are greater, less than, or equal,
you cause dissension.
When those three complexes have ended,
nothing can agitate your mind."

Then Buddha asked the goddess, "Have you understood this gatha? If not, please say so."

The goddess addressed the Buddha, "I have not understood, World-Honored One. I have not understood, Well-Gone One."

So the Buddha recited another gatha for the goddess:

"Ending desire, overcoming the three complexes,
our mind is stilled, we have nothing to long for.
We lay aside all affliction and sorrow,
in this life and in lives to come."

Then Buddha asked the goddess, "Have you understood this gatha? If not, please say so."

The goddess addressed the Buddha, "I have understood, World-Honored One. I have understood, Well-Gone One."

The Buddha had finished the teaching. The goddess was delighted at what she had heard. Practicing in accord with these teachings, she disappeared. Not a trace of her was to be seen anywhere.

Samiddhi Sutta, Samyukta Agama 1078
(Corresponds to Samyutta Nikaya 1.20. Also Taisho 99)

Discourse on the Dharma Seal

I heard these words of the Buddha one time when the Lord was residing at Vaishali with his community of bhikshus. One day, he told the community, "Do you know of the wonderful Dharma Seal? Today I would like to tell you about it and explain it to you. Please use your pure mind to listen and receive it with care, and make the best effort to remember and practice it." The community of bhikshus replied, "Wonderful, World-Honored One! Please teach us. We will listen carefully."

The Buddha said, "Emptiness is neither being nor nonbeing. It is free from all wrong views. It is neither produced nor destroyed, and it cannot be grasped by views. Why is this so? Because emptiness cannot be located in space. It has no form. It is not an object of perception. It has never been born, and the intellect cannot grasp it. Because it cannot be grasped, it embraces all dharmas and dwells only in non-discursive, nondiscriminative wisdom. This is the only true and right understanding, bhikshus! You should know that not only emptiness, but all dharmas are like that. This is the Dharma Seal.

"The Dharma Seal is also called the Three Doors of Liberation. It is the basic teaching of all Buddhas, the eye of all Buddhas, the destination of all Buddhas. Listen and receive it with care. Memorize it well and practice it right in the heart of reality.

"Bhikshus, find a quiet place to meditate, such as in a forest under a tree. There you can see that form is painful, empty, and impermanent, and as a result, you will not be attached to form. You will reach the nondiscriminative understanding of form. Then do the same for feelings, perceptions, mental formations, and consciousnesses. See that they are painful, empty, and impermanent, and rise above wrong views about them. Realize the nondiscriminative understanding of feelings, perceptions, mental formations, and consciousness. Bhikshus, the Five Aggregates are empty. They are produced from the mind. Once the mind stops operating in its usual way, the aggregates stop operating as well. When you see this, you will be liberated, free from all views. This is emptiness, the First Door of Liberation.

"Bhikshus, dwelling in concentration, see the dissolution of form, and be free from the illusory nature of perception vis-à-vis form. See the dissolution of sound, smell, taste, touch, and mental formations, and be free from the illusory nature of perceptions vis-à-vis sound, smell, taste, touch, and mental formations. This meditation is called signlessness, the Second Door of Liberation. Once you have entered this door, your knowledge will be pure. Because of this purity of understanding, the three defiling qualities of mind — greed, hatred, and delusion — will be uprooted. With these uprooted, you will dwell in the realm of nondiscursive, nondiscriminative knowledge. When you are dwelling in this knowledge, views concerning 'me and mine,' and thus all views, no longer have the bases and the occasions to arise.

"Bhikshus, once you are free from the view 'I am,' you no longer consider what you see, hear, feel, and perceive as realities independent of your own consciousness. Why? Because you know that consciousness also arises from conditions and is impermanent. Because of its impermanent nature, it cannot be grasped either. This meditation is called wishlessness, the Third Door of Liberation. Once you enter this door, you experience fully the true nature of all dharmas, and you no longer cling to any dharma because you have seen the unconditioned nature of all dharmas."

The Buddha told the community of bhikshus, "This is the wonderful Seal of the Dharma, the Three Doors of Liberation. If you learn and practice it, you will certainly attain pure knowledge."

The monks were very happy to hear the teaching of the World-Honored One. They paid respect to him and promised to learn and practice this wonderful teaching.

Taisho Revised Tripitaka 104*

---

* For commentary, see Thich Nhat Hanh, *The Heart of the Buddha's Teaching* (New York, NY: Broadway Books, 1998).

Discourse on the Eight Realizations of the Great Beings

Wholeheartedly, day and night, disciples of the Awakened One should recite and meditate on the Eight Realizations discovered by the Great Beings.

The First Realization is the awareness that the world is impermanent. Political regimes are subject to fall. Things composed of the four elements are empty, containing within them the seeds of suffering. Human beings are composed of Five Aggregates and are without a separate self. They are always in the process of change — constantly being born and constantly dying. They are empty of self and without a separate existence. The mind is the source of all confusion, and the body the forest of all unwholesome actions. Meditating on this, you can be released from the round of birth and death.

The Second Realization is the awareness that more desire brings more suffering. All hardships in daily life arise from greed and desire. Those with little desire and ambition are able to relax, their body and mind free from entanglement.

The Third Realization is the awareness that the human mind is always searching outside itself and never feels fulfilled. This brings about unwholesome activity. Bodhisattvas, on the other hand, know the value of having few desires. They live simply and peacefully, so they can devote themselves to practicing the Way. They regard the realization of perfect understanding to be their only career.

The Fourth Realization is the awareness that indolence is an obstacle to practice. You must practice diligently to transform unwholesome mental states that bind you, and you must conquer the four kinds of Mara in order to free yourself from the prisons of the Five Aggregates and the Three Worlds.

The Fifth Realization is the awareness that ignorance is the cause of the endless round of birth and death. Bodhisattvas always listen to and learn from others so their understanding and skillful means can develop, and so they can teach living beings and bring them great joy.

The Sixth Realization is the awareness that poverty creates hatred and anger, which creates a vicious cycle of negative thoughts and actions. When practicing generosity, bodhisattvas consider everyone — friends and enemies alike — to be equal. They do not condemn anyone's past wrongdoings or hate even those presently causing harm.

The Seventh Realization is the awareness that the five categories of sensual desire — money, sex, fame, overeating, and oversleeping — lead to problems. Although you are in the world, try not to be caught in worldly matters. A monk, for example, has in his possession only three robes and one bowl. He lives simply in order to practice the Way. His precepts keep him free of attachment to worldly things, and he treats everyone equally and with compassion.

The Eighth Realization is the awareness that the fire of birth and death is raging, causing endless suffering everywhere. Take the Great Vow to help all beings, to suffer with all beings, and to guide all beings to the Realm of Great Joy.

These Eight Realizations are the discoveries of great beings, Buddhas and Bodhisattvas who have practiced diligently the way of understanding and love. They have sailed the Dharmakaya boat to the shore of nirvana, and have then returned to the ordinary world, free of the five sensual desires, their minds and hearts directed toward the Noble Way. Using these Eight Realizations, they help all beings recognize the suffering in the world. If disciples of the Buddha recite and meditate on these Eight Realizations, they will put an end to countless misunderstandings and difficulties and progress toward enlightenment, leaving behind the world of birth and death, dwelling forever in peace.

Taisho Revised Tripitaka 779

Flower Garland Discourse: The Ten Great Aspirations of Samantabhadra Bodhisattva

Body, speech and mind, purified, in oneness,
I bow deeply to touch limitless Buddhas
of the past, present, and future
throughout all worlds in the Ten Directions.

The power of Samantabhadra's vow
enables me to be present everywhere.
Where there is a Buddha, I am there.
As Buddhas are countless, so too am I.

In a particle of dust are countless Buddhas,
all of them present with their own assembly.
The strength of my faith penetrates deeply
into every atom of all Dharma realms.

I aspire to use the Great Ocean of Sound,
giving rise to words of wonderful effect
that praise the Buddha's oceans of virtues,
in the past, present, and future.

I bring these beautiful offerings:
garlands of the most beautiful flowers,
incense, music, perfumes, and parasols,
all to adorn the Tathagatas and their lands.

Bringing food, robes, and fragrant flowers,
torches, sandalwood, sitting mats,
the finest adornments here in abundance —
an offering to the Tathagatas.

Inspired by Samantabhadra's vow,
I bring my heart, wide with deep understanding,
with loving faith in the Buddhas of the Three Times,
as an offering to the Tathagatas everywhere.

From beginningless time I have acted unskillfully
with craving, hatred, and ignorance
in actions of body, speech, and mind.
Determined now to begin anew, I repent.

I rejoice in every virtuous action
by anyone, in any direction,
by students and by those who need learn no more,
of Buddhas and Bodhisattvas.

All beings who are Lamps for the world
and those who have just attained enlightenment,
I beg that you will think lovingly of us,
turning the Wheel of the Dharma for all.

With sincerity, I make a humble request
of the Buddhas and those who are about to enter nirvana:
remain with us here, throughout the Three Times,
for the benefit and the welfare of all.

I humbly make offerings inviting all Buddhas
to stay with us and guide all beings to the other shore.
All the merit of joyous praise and repenting
I offer to the Path of Awakening.

This merit is transferred to the Three Jewels,
to their nature and form in the Dharma realms.
The Two Truths are perfectly woven together
into the Samadhi Seal.

The ocean of merit is measureless.
I vow to transfer it and not hold anything for myself.
If any human, out of discrimination and prejudice,
tries to do harm to the Noble Teaching
with their words and their actions,
may their obstacles be fully removed.

In each moment, wisdom envelops the Dharma realms,
welcoming all to the place of non-regression.

Space and living beings are without limit,
the same with afflictions and results of past actions.
These four are fully and truly immeasurable.
So, too, is my offering of merit.

Avatamsaka Sutra 36,
Taisho Revised Tripitaka 279

Discourse on the Lotus of the Wonderful Dharma: Universal Door Chapter

Introductory Gatha
Chanting the Lotus Sutra by night,
the sound shook the galaxies.
The next morning when planet Earth woke up,
her lap was full of flowers.

Discourse
Buddha of ten thousand beautiful aspects,
may I ask you this question:
"Why did they give that bodhisattva
the name Avalokita?"

The World-Honored One, beautifully adorned,
offered this reply to Akshayamati:

"Because actions founded on her deep aspiration
can respond to the needs of any being in any circumstance.

"Aspirations as wide as the oceans
were made for countless lifetimes.
She has attended to billions of Buddhas,
her great aspiration purified by mindfulness.

"Whoever calls her name or sees her image,
if their mind be perfectly collected and pure,
they will then be able to overcome
the suffering of all the worlds.

"When those with cruel intent
push us into a pit of fire,
invoking the strength of Avalokita,
the fire becomes a refreshing lake.

"Adrift on the waters of the great ocean,
threatened by monsters of the deep,
invoking the strength of Avalokita,
we are saved from the storm waves.

"Standing atop Mount Meru,
should someone desire to push us down,
invoking the strength of Avalokita,
we dwell unharmed like the sun hanging in space.

"Chased by a cruel person
down the Diamond Mountain,
invoking the strength of Avalokita,
not even a hair of our body will be in danger.

"Encircled and assaulted by bandits
holding swords to wound and to kill,
invoking the strength of Avalokita,
sword blades shatter into millions of pieces.

"Imprisoned or bound in iron chains,
with hands and feet placed in a yoke,
invoking the strength of Avalokita,
we are released into freedom.

"Poisons, curses, and bewitchings
putting us into danger,
invoking the strength of Avalokita,
harmful things return to their source.

"Attacked by a fierce and cruel yaksha,
a poisonous naga, or unkind spirit,
invoking the strength of Avalokita,
they will do us no harm.

"With wild animals all around
baring their teeth, tusks, and claws,
invoking the strength of Avalokita
will cause them to run far away.

"Confronted with scorpions and poisonous snakes,
breathing fire and smoke of poisonous gas,
invoking the strength of Avalokita,
they depart, the air clears.

"Caught beneath lightning, thunder, and clouds,
with hail pouring down in torrents,
invoking the strength of Avalokita,
the storm ends, the sunlight appears.

"All living beings caught in distress,
oppressed by immeasurable suffering
are rescued in ten thousand ways
by the wonderful power of her understanding.

"Miraculous power with no shortcoming,
wisdom and skillful means so vast —
in the Ten Directions of all the worlds,
there is no place she does not appear.

"The paths to realms of suffering,
the pain of birth, old age, sickness, and death,
hells, hungry spirits, or animals
are all purified, brought to an end.

"Look of truth, look of purity,
look of boundless understanding,
look of love, look of compassion —
the look to be always honored and practiced.

"Look of immaculate light and purity,
the Sun of Wisdom destroying darkness,
master of fire, wind, and disaster
illuminating the whole world.

"Heart of compassion like rolling thunder,
heart of love like gentle clouds,
water of Dharma nectar raining upon us,
extinguishing the fire of afflictions.

"In the courtroom, the place of lawsuits,
on the fields in the midst of war,
invoking the strength of Avalokita,
our enemies become our friends.

"Sound of wonder, noble sound,
sound of one looking deeply into the world,
extraordinary sound, sound of the rising tide,
the sound to which we will always listen.

"With mindfulness, free from doubts,
in moments of danger and affliction,
our faith in the purity of Avalokita
is where we go for refuge.

"We bow in gratitude to the one
who has all the virtues,
regarding the world with compassionate eyes,
an Ocean of Well-Being beyond measure."

Saddharmapundarika Sutra, Chapter 25,
Taisho Revised Tripitaka 262

Store of Precious Virtues Discourse: Practice of the Highest Understanding

Bodhisattvas, who in this life endeavor to remove
all obstacles and afflictions,
giving rise to a peaceful mind with confidence,
dwelling in awakened calm—
rely on the Practice of the Highest Understanding.

All the rivers on Roseapple Island,
producing the healing herbs, fresh fruits and flowers,
derive their power from the Naga King
who dwells in the cool Manasarowara Lake.

If all the hearer-disciples of the Buddha
use skillful means to teach the Dharma,
help people experience joy, taste the fruit of happiness,
and practice the holy life,
it is due to the sacred power of the Tathagata.

The Buddha transmits the Eyes of the Dharma.
His disciples, training according to it,
practice, realize, and teach it to others.
All that is due to the power and strength of the Buddha.

The incomparable understanding is not to be grasped.
It is not an object of realization. There is no awakening.
Someone who hears this without feeling terror
is a bodhisattva who has the capacity to understand the Buddha.

Form, feelings, perceptions, mental formations,
and consciousness are all empty.
The bodhisattva is not the least bit caught in anything.
He does not settle or abide in any dharma
and realizes the unattainable awakened mind.

When the bodhisattva would leave the shelter of afflictions
and shine her insight on the Five Aggregates,
she sees they are without true nature,
she does not seek the peace of nirvana.
That is to realize the wisdom of a bodhisattva.

What is the object realized by this understanding?
It is to shine the light of insight and see that all is empty.
With this insight, there is no longer any terror.
The bodhisattva awakens himself and others.

Treating the Five Aggregates as real
is not to understand their true nature.
The bodhisattva sees the aggregates as empty
and practices without being caught in the form and in the word.

The Five Aggregates are empty.
Because she does not get caught in the form,
her practice is called "signless."
Where there is practice, there is not the highest understanding.
There is nothing that can be called concentration,
signlessness, and nirvana.

If he can practice this silent awakening,
all the Buddhas of the past empower him.
He knows the true nature of causes and conditions.
Neither suffering nor delight can touch him.

If she practices with no object of her practice,
she practices in accord with the wisdom of the Sugata.
If she practices with the spirit of non-practice,
this is the Highest Understanding.

The practice without object cannot be grasped.
Foolish people are caught in the signs "being" and "nonbeing."
Neither "being" nor "nonbeing" can express the truth.
The bodhisattva of Awakened Understanding transcends both.

The bodhisattva, free of signs,
knows that the Five Aggregates are a magic show.
His practice is silent awakening,
which is the Practice of the Highest Understanding.

Taught by good teachers and spiritual friends,
there is no fear of hearing the Mother of
All Buddhas' Discourses.
But with deluded teachers and friends traveling the wrong path,
he is like a clay pot that has not been fired.

Whom do we call a bodhisattva?
She who is no longer caught by sensual desire,
she who aspires to the fruit of awakening
without being caught by it
is thus called a bodhisattva.

Whom do we call a mahasattva?
He who has comprehended the absolute truth
and cuts through all wrong views in the world,
he is thus called a mahasattva, a great being.

With great generosity, great wisdom, and virtuous power,
she sits aboard the highest vehicle of the Buddhas
and gives rise to the awakened mind to save all beings.
Thus she is called a great being.

Like a magician at the crossroads,
giving rise to an illusory crowd and cutting off their heads,
all worlds are just as illusory.
Knowing this, he feels no fear.

The Five Aggregates are ropes that bind.
Knowing they are not real, she needs no more dwelling.
She practices with her awakened mind not caught in anything.
That is why she is called the highest bodhisattva.

Whom do we call a bodhisattva? —
the one who rides on the great vehicle to rescue all beings.

The Great Vehicle is as vast as space.
All beings can ride on it in joy and safety.

The great vehicle cannot be grasped by ideas.
It goes to nirvana, but nirvana is everywhere.
We cannot recognize the destination. It is like a fire gone out.
That is why it is said he "enters nirvana."

The object of her practice cannot be grasped.
It cannot be found in the Three Times.
It is silence of ideas, fearless and beyond speculation.
It is Practice of the Highest Understanding.

When a bodhisattva engages in the Practice of the
Highest Understanding
and gives rise to great love and compassion to help beings,
never does he think in terms of "living beings."
This is the Highest Understanding in action.

When a bodhisattva gives rise to the notion "living beings"
and practices austerities, caught in the sign "suffering,"
she is caught in the signs "self" and "living being."
This is not the Highest Understanding in action.

When he knows clearly his own nature
and that of other living beings,
and knows that all dharmas are of the same nature,
that birth and death are not in opposition,
but are not distinguishable from birthless and deathless,
it is the Highest Understanding in action.

Abandoning all names and words,
abandoning all things that are born and die in the world,
there is the nectar of deathless and incomparable wisdom.
This is the Highest Understanding in action.

When the bodhisattva practices like this,
and knows which skillful means to use,
does not pursue anything,

and knows that these means have no separate existence,
this is the Practice of the Highest Understanding.

If she does not rely on form, feelings, perceptions,
mental formations, and consciousness,
and only relies on the perfect teachings,
this is the Practice of the Highest Understanding.

Permanent and impermanent, suffering and joy,
self and selfless, all are empty.
He does not abide in a world of conditioned
or unconditioned elements.
Like the Buddha, he abides in the practice of signlessness.

If you aspire to attain the career of a hearer,
the self-enlightened one, or Buddha enlightenment;
if you do not have endurance of the above practice,
you cannot arrive.
It is like crossing the great river; you cannot see the other shore.

If you hear these teachings and are determined
to realize the highest awakening, witness the awakened mind,
and see that the nature of all things is your own nature,
that is the great wisdom the Tathagata is describing.

A bodhisattva who practices great wisdom this way
does not train in the way of a hearer or a self-awakened Buddha.
She trains only in the boundless knowledge of the Tathagata.
True learning is the learning of no-learning.

He trains in the non-increase and non-decrease of forms.
He does not train in any other way.
His only joy is to train according to boundless knowledge.
The same is true of feelings, perceptions, mental formations,
and consciousness.

Form is neither wisdom nor the absence of wisdom.
Feelings, perceptions, mental formations, and consciousness
are also like that.

The nature of form is like empty space —
equality, nonduality, and nondiscrimination.

The basic nature of wrong perception is without limits,
as is the basic nature of all living beings.
The nature of space is without obstructions,
so is the wisdom of the one who perfectly understands the world.

The Buddha has said that wisdom is not form.
When clinging to perceptions is released, nirvana is there.
Whoever has given up clinging to perceptions,
her mind and speech are said to dwell in suchness.

For as many lifetimes as there are grains of sand in the Ganges,
he will not hear the Buddha utter the words "living beings."
Living beings are birthless, pure, and silent from the very beginning.
This is the Practice of the Highest Understanding.

Since every word I have ever uttered
contains the meaning of the Highest Understanding,
the last Buddha transmitted to me the prediction
that I would awaken in this very life.

The actions of one who receives and practices this understanding,
are not less than that of the Buddha.
Swords, poison, fire, and water, and all the efforts of Mara
will not touch him.

Prajñaparamita Ratnaguna Samcaya Gatha,
Taisho Revised Tripitaka 229

The Diamond That Cuts through Illusion

*Opening Gatha**
How may we overcome the fear of birth and death
and arrive at the state that is as indestructible as a diamond?
What way can direct us in our practice
to sweep away our thousands of illusions?
If the awakened mind shows its compassion
and opens up for us the treasure store,
then we may bring into our lives
the wonderful diamond teachings.

Discourse
This is what I heard one time when the Buddha was staying in the monastery in Anathapindika's park in the Jeta Grove near Shravasti with a community of 1,250 bhikshus, fully ordained monks.

That day, when it was time to make the almsround, the Buddha put on his sanghati robe and, holding his bowl, went into the city of Shravasti to beg for food, going from house to house. When the almsround was completed, he returned to the monastery to eat the midday meal. Then he put away his sanghati robe and his bowl, washed his feet, arranged his cushion, and sat down.

At that time, the Venerable Subhuti stood up, bared his right shoulder, put his knee on the ground, and, folding his palms respectfully, said to the Buddha, "World-Honored One, it is rare to find someone like you. You always support and show special confidence in the Bodhisattvas.

"World-Honored One, if sons and daughters of good families want to give rise to the highest, most fulfilled, awakened mind, what should they rely on and what should they do to master their thinking?"

The Buddha said to Subhuti, "This is how the Bodhisattva Mahasattvas master their thinking: 'However many species of living beings there are — whether born from eggs, from the womb, from moisture, or spontaneously; whether they have form or do not have form; whether they have perceptions or do not have perceptions; or whether it cannot be said of them that they have perceptions or that they do not have perceptions, we must lead

* Composed by Thich Nhat Hanh.

all these beings to nirvana so that they can be liberated. Yet when this in-numerable, immeasurable, infinite number of beings has become liberated, we do not, in truth, think that a single being has been liberated.'

"Why is this so? If, Subhuti, a bodhisattva holds on to the idea that a self, a person, a living being, or a life span exists, that person is not a true bodhi-sattva.

"Moreover, Subhuti, when a bodhisattva practices generosity, he does not rely on any object — any form, sound, smell, taste, tactile object, or dharma — to practice generosity. That, Subhuti, is the spirit in which a bodhisattva practices generosity, not relying on signs. Why? If a bodhisattva practices generosity without relying on signs, the happiness that results cannot be conceived of or measured. Subhuti, do you think that the space in the East-ern Quarter can be measured?"

"No, World-Honored One."

"Subhuti, can space in the Western, Southern, or Northern Quarters, above or below be measured?"

"No, World-Honored One."

"Subhuti, if a bodhisattva does not rely on any concept while practicing generosity, the happiness that results from that virtuous act is as great as space. It cannot be measured. Subhuti, the bodhisattvas should let their minds dwell in the teachings I have just given.

"What do you think, Subhuti? Is it possible to grasp the Tathagata by means of bodily signs?"

"No, World-Honored One. When the Tathagata speaks of bodily signs, there are no signs being talked about."

The Buddha said to Subhuti, "In a place where there is something that can be distinguished by signs, in that place there is deception. If you can see the signless nature of signs, you can see the Tathagata."

The Venerable Subhuti said to the Buddha, "In times to come, will there be people who, when they hear these teachings, have real faith and confi-dence in them?"

The Buddha replied, "Do not speak that way, Subhuti. Five hundred years after the Tathagata has passed away, there will still be people who appreci-ate the joy and happiness that come from observing the precepts. When such people hear these words, they will have faith and confidence that this is the truth. Know that such people have sown seeds not only during the lifetime of one Buddha, or even two, three, four, or five Buddhas, but have, in fact, planted wholesome seeds during the lifetimes of tens of thousands of Bud-dhas. Anyone who, for even a moment, gives rise to a pure and clear confidence upon hearing these words of the Tathagata, the Tathagata sees and knows that person, and he or she will attain immeasurable happiness because of this understanding. Why?

"Because that person is not caught in the idea of a self, a person, a living being, or a life span. He or she is not caught in the idea of a dharma or the idea of a non-dharma. He or she is not caught in the notion that this is a sign and that is not a sign. Why? If you are caught in the idea of a dharma, you are also caught in the ideas of a self, a person, a living being, and a life span. If you are caught in the idea that there is no dharma, you are still caught in the ideas of a self, a person, a living being, and a life span. That is why we should not get caught in dharmas or in the idea that dharmas do not exist. This is the hidden meaning when the Tathagata says, 'Bhikshus, you should know that all of the teachings I give to you are a raft.' All teachings must be abandoned, not to mention non-teachings."

The Buddha asked Subhuti, "In ancient times when the Tathagata practiced under the guidance of the Buddha Dipankara, did the Tathagata attain anything?"

Subhuti answered, "No, World-Honored One. In ancient times when the Tathagata practiced under the guidance of the Buddha Dipankara, he did not attain anything."

"What do you think, Subhuti? Does a bodhisattva create a serene and beautiful Buddha Field?"

"No, World-Honored One. Why? To create a serene and beautiful Buddha Field is not in fact to create a serene and beautiful Buddha Field. That is why it is called creating a serene and beautiful Buddha Field."

The Buddha said, "So, Subhuti, all the Bodhisattva Mahasattvas should give rise to a pure and clear intention in this spirit. When they give rise to this intention, they should not rely on forms, sounds, smells, tastes, tactile objects, or objects of mind. They should give rise to an intention with their minds not dwelling anywhere."

"So, Subhuti, when a bodhisattva gives rise to the unequaled mind of awakening, he has to give up all ideas. He cannot rely on forms when he gives rise to that mind, nor on sounds, smells, tastes, tactile objects, or objects of mind. He can only give rise to the mind that is not caught in anything.

"The Tathagata has said that all notions are not notions and that all living beings are not living beings. Subhuti, the Tathagata is one who speaks of things as they are, speaks what is true, and speaks in accord with reality. He does not speak deceptively or to please people. Subhuti, if we say that the Tathagata has realized a teaching, that teaching is neither graspable nor deceptive.

"Subhuti, a bodhisattva who still depends on notions to practice generosity is like someone walking in the dark. She will not see anything. But when a bodhisattva does not depend on notions to practice generosity, she is like someone with good eyesight walking under the bright light of the sun. She can see all shapes and colors.

"Subhuti, do not say that the Tathagata has the idea, 'I will bring living beings to the shore of liberation.' Do not think that way, Subhuti. Why? In truth there is not one single being for the Tathagata to bring to the other shore. If the Tathagata were to think there was, he would be caught in the idea of a self, a person, a living being, or a life span. Subhuti, what the Tathagata calls a self essentially has no self in the way that ordinary persons think there is a self. Subhuti, the Tathagata does not regard anyone as an ordinary person. That is why he can call them ordinary persons.

"What do you think, Subhuti? Can someone meditate on the Tathagata by means of the thirty-two marks?"

Subhuti said, "Yes, World-Honored One. We should use the thirty-two marks to meditate on the Tathagata."

The Buddha said, "If you say that you can use the thirty-two marks to see the Tathagata, then the Cakravartin is also a Tathagata?"

Subhuti said, "World-Honored One, I understand your teaching. One should not use the thirty-two marks to meditate on the Tathagata."

Then the World-Honored One spoke this verse:

> "Someone who looks for me in form
> or seeks me in sound
> is on a mistaken path
> and cannot see the Tathagata."

"Subhuti, if you think that the Tathagata realizes the highest, most fulfilled, awakened mind and does not need to have all the marks, you are wrong. Subhuti, do not think in that way. Do not think that when one gives rise to the highest, most fulfilled, awakened mind, one needs to see all objects of mind as nonexistent, cut off from life. Do not think in that way. One who gives rise to the highest, most fulfilled, awakened mind does not say that all objects of mind are nonexistent and cut off from life."

After they heard the Lord Buddha deliver this discourse, the Venerable

Subhuti, the bhikshus and bhikshunis, laymen and laywomen, and gods and asuras, filled with joy and confidence, began to put these teachings into practice.

Vajracchedika Prajñaparamita Sutra,
Taisho Revised Tripitaka 335*

---

* For the complete text and commentary, see Thich Nhat Hanh, *The Diamond That Cuts through Illusion* (Berkeley, CA: Parallax Press, 1992).

Discourse on the Land of Great Happiness

This is what I heard the Buddha say one time when he was staying in the Anathapindika Monastery in the Jeta Grove. At that time the Buddha had with him a Sangha of 1,250 bhikshus, all arhats and the most well-known among his senior disciples, including Shariputra, Mahamaudgalyayana, Mahakashyapa, Mahakatyayana, Mahakaushthila, Revata, Shuddhipanthaka, Nanda, Ananda, Rahula, Gavampati, Pindolabharadvaja, Kalodayin, Mahakapphina, Vakkula, and Aniruddha. There were also present Bodhisattvas of great stature like Manjushri, Ajita, Gandhahastin, Nityodyukta and many other great Bodhisattvas as well as countless heavenly beings including Indra.

At that time the Buddha called Shariputra to him and said: "If you go from here in the western direction and pass through hundreds of thousands of millions of Buddha Worlds you will come to a world called Sukhavati (Great Happiness). In that world there is a Buddha whose name is Amitabha and who is at this very moment teaching the Dharma.

"Shariputra, why is that land called Great Happiness? Because the people who live there do not have to go through any suffering. They are always enjoying many kinds of happiness. And that is why that world is called Great Happiness.

"Shariputra, around Sukhavati there are seven rows of rails, seven rows of spread out netting and seven rows of trees. All are made of the four kinds of precious jewels. That is why the land is called Great Happiness.

"Furthermore Shariputra, in the land of Great Happiness there are many lakes of the seven precious stones, full of the water of the Eight Virtues. The bed of the lake is made wholly of pure golden sand and on the shores are paths of gold, silver, and crystal. Above these paths are countless pavilions which are built of and decorated with gold, silver, crystal, mother-of-pearl, red agate, and carnelians. The lotus flowers in these lakes are as large as cartwheels. The blue lotuses give out a halo of blue light, the golden lotuses a halo of golden light, the red lotuses a halo of red light and the white lotuses a halo of white light. The fragrance of the lotuses is subtle, wonderful, sweet, and pure.

"Shariputra, Sukhavati is adorned with such beauties as these.

"Furthermore Shariputra, in this Buddha Land people can always hear the sound of heavenly music. The earth is made of pure gold. During the six periods of the day, flowers rain down multitudes of mandarava from the sky. In the morning the people of this land like to take flower baskets made of cloth and fill them with these wonderful flowers in order to make offerings to the Buddhas who live in countless other Buddha Lands. When it is time for the midday meal, everyone returns to Sukhavati and after eating does walking meditation. Shariputra, that is how extraordinarily beautiful Sukhavati is.

"Furthermore Shariputra, in Sukhavati you can always see different species of birds of many wonderful colors, like white cranes, peacocks, orioles, egrets, kavalinkara, and jivanjva birds. These birds sing with harmonious, sweet sounds throughout the six periods of the day. In the song of the birds people can hear teachings on different Dharma doors such as the Five Faculties, the Five Powers, the Seven Factors of Awakening, and the Noble Eightfold Path. When the people of this land hear the teachings in the form of bird songs, their minds are in perfect concentration and they come back to practicing mindfulness of Buddha, Dharma, and Sangha.

"Shariputra, do not think that the birds in Sukhavati have been born as the result of past bad actions. Why? Because the three lower realms of hells, hungry ghosts, and animals do not exist in the land of Amitabha Buddha. Shariputra, in this land the names of the lower realms do not even exist, how much less their actuality! These birds are manifestations of the Buddha Amitabha so that the Dharma can be proclaimed widely in his land.

"Shariputra, in this Buddha Land, whenever a light breeze moves the rows of trees and the jeweled netting, people hear a wonderful sound as if a hundred thousand musical instruments are being played together at the same time. When the people hear this sound, they all naturally return to mindful recollection of the Buddha, the Dharma, and the Sangha. Shariputra, that is how beautiful Sukhavati is.

"Shariputra, why do you think that Buddha is called Amitabha (Limitless Light)? Because he is infinite light which is able to illuminate all worlds in the Ten Directions and this light and radiance never comes to an end. That is why he is called Amitabha.

"What is more, Shariputra, the life span of Amitabha as well as the life span of everyone who lives in his Buddha Land is limitless. It lasts for innumerable kalpas, that is why he is called Amitabha.

"Shariputra, from the time when Amitabha Buddha realized enlightenment until now can be reckoned as ten kalpas. Moreover Shariputra, the number of his hearer disciples who have attained the fruit of arhatship is also limitless. It is not possible to calculate them, so great is their number.

The number of bodhisattvas in that land is also limitless.

"Shariputra, the land of Amitabha is made out of such beautiful qualities as these.

"Shariputra, everyone who is born in Sukhavati naturally has the capacity of non-regression. Among the people living there, many will attain Buddhahood in one more lifetime. The number of these bodhisattvas is infinite, and there is no method of calculation to number them. It may only be expressed by the term limitless.

"Shariputra, when living beings everywhere hear Sukhavati spoken about, they should bring forth the great wish to be born in such a land. Why? Because having been born in that land they will be able to live with and be very close to so many noble practitioners.

"Shariputra, one cannot be born in this land with a lack of merit or wholesome roots. Therefore, Shariputra, whenever men or women of good families hear the name of Amitabha Buddha, they should mindfully repeat that name and wholeheartedly practice visualization with a mind that is one-pointed and not dispersed for one, two, three, four, five, six, or seven days. When that person passes from this life, they will see Amitabha Buddha and the Holy Ones of that land right before their eyes. At the time of their passing, their mind will abide in meditative concentration and will not be deluded or dispersed. That is why they can be born in the Land of Great Happiness.

"Shariputra, it is because I have seen the enormous benefit of this land that I want to tell all who are listening now to bring forth the great wish to be born there.

"Shariputra, as I am now commending the inestimably great benefits and virtues of Buddha Amitabha, there are in the east, in the south, in the west, in the north, above and below, Buddhas as numberless as the sands of the Ganges, each one seated in his own Buddha Field, each one with the long tongue of a Buddha which is able to embrace the three chiliocosms, announcing with all sincerity, 'Living beings in all worlds, you should have confidence in this sutra, which all the Buddhas in the entire cosmos wholeheartedly commend and protect by recollection.'

"Shariputra, why do you think this sutra is wholeheartedly commended and protected by the recitation of all Buddhas? The reason is that when sons or daughters of good families hear this sutra or hear the name of the Buddha Amitabha and wholly put it into practice and maintain mindful recitation of Buddha Amitabha's name, they will be protected by the recollection of all the Buddhas, and they will attain the highest fruit of awakening from which they will never regress. So you should have faith in what I am saying and what all other Buddhas are also saying.

"Shariputra, if there is anyone who has already brought forth the great aspiration, is aspiring now or will aspire in the future to be born in Amitabha's land, at the very moment when that person makes the aspiration, they already attain the fruit of the highest awakening from which they will never regress, and they are dwelling already in the Buddha Field of Amitabha. It is not necessary that they have been born or are being born or will be born there in order to be present within the Buddha Field of Amitabha.

"Shariputra, while I am praising the unimaginably great qualities of the Buddhas, the Buddhas are also praising my unimaginably great qualities saying, 'Buddha Shakyamuni is very rare. In the Saha world which is full of the five impurities — the cloudiness of time, the cloudiness of views, the cloudiness of unwholesome mental states, the cloudiness of the idea of living being and life span — he is able to realize the fruit of the highest awakening and is able to communicate to living beings the Dharma doors, which people will find hard to believe if they have had no preparation.'

"Shariputra, understand that to stay in a world which is full of the five kinds of impurity and to be able to attain the fruit of the highest awakening and also to be able to transmit to all beings Dharma doors which people find hard to believe, like this Dharma door of being born in Sukhavati, is something extremely difficult."

When Shariputra as well as all the bhikshus, heavenly beings, bodhisattvas, warrior gods, and others heard the Buddha deliver this sutra, they all had faith in it, joyously accepted the teaching and paid respect to the Buddha before returning to their dwelling places.

Sukhavati-Vyuha Sutra,
Taisho Revised Tripitaka 366*

---

* For commentary see Thich Nhat Hanh, *Finding Our True Home* (Berkeley, CA: Parallax Press, 2003).

The Discourse on Emptiness in the True Sense of the Word

This is what I heard one time when the Buddha was residing with the Kuru people, in the village of Kalmasadamya. The World-Honored One addressed the monks: "I will offer you now the Teaching that is good at the beginning, good at the middle and good at the end; good in its meaning and good in taste, pure, and homogeneous, the Teaching that will help you successfully lead the pure and noble life of a monk. This is the Teaching of Emptiness in the True Sense of the Word. Please listen and reflect skillfully on it.

"What does it mean, 'the Teaching on Emptiness in the True Sense of the Word?' The eye, O monks, when it arises does not come from anywhere, and when it perishes it does not go anywhere. Therefore, the eye arises not as a real entity, and having arisen, it perishes. The action is there, the result of the action is there, but there is no actor. One aggregate, while disintegrating, gives rise to another aggregate; and one can only look upon phenomena as mere designation. The same thing is true with regard to the ear, the nose, the tongue, the body and the consciousness — everything should be looked upon as mere designation.

"What does mere designation mean? It means: 'This being, that is; from the arising of this, that arises, as in the case of the twelve interdependent links. From the arising of ignorance arise formations, from the arising of formation arises consciousness, etc., until the arising of the entire mass of ill-being.' It also means: 'This being not, that is not; since this has ceased, that does not arise anymore, as in the case of the twelve interdependent links. The cessation of ignorance results in the cessation of formations, the cessation of formations results in the cessation of consciousness, etc., until the cessation of the entire mass of ill-being.' That is, O monks, the Teaching called Emptiness in the true sense of the Word."

Thus spoke the World-Honored One. The monks were delighted and joyfully put the teaching into practice.

Samyukta Agama, 335

Discourse on the Absolute Truth

1. He who still abides by a dogmatic view, considering it as the highest in the world, thinking "this is the most excellent" and disparaging other views as inferior, is still considered not to be fee from disputes.

2. When seeing, hearing, or sensing something and considering it as the only thing that can bring comfort and advantage to self, one is always inclined to get caught in it and rule out everything else as inferior.

3. Caught in one's view and considering all other views as inferior — this attitude is considered by the wise as bondage, as the absence of freedom. A good practitioner is never too quick to believe what is seen, heard, and sensed, including rules and rites.

4. A good practitioner has no need to set up a new theory for the world, using the knowledge he has picked up or the rules and rites he is practicing. He does not consider himself as "superior," "inferior," or "equal" to anyone.

5. A good practitioner abandons the notion of self and the tendency to cling to views. He is free and does not depend on anything, even on knowledge. He does not take sides in controversies and does not hold on to any view or dogma.

6. He does not seek for anything or cling to anything, either this extreme or the other extreme, either in this world or in the other world. He has abandoned all views and no longer has the need to seek for comfort or refuge in any theory or ideology.

7. To the wise person, there are no longer any views concerning what is seen, heard, or sensed. How could one judge or have an opinion concerning such a pure being who has let go of all views?

8. A wise person no longer feels the need to set up dogmas or choosing an ideology. All dogmas and ideologies have been abandoned by such a

person. A real noble one is never caught in rules or rites. He or she is advancing steadfastly to the shore of liberation and will never return to the realm of bondage.

Paramatthaka Sutta
Sutta Nipata 4.5

music

DISCOURSE ON LOVE

With drum and bell   Adapted from a traditional Pali chant

He or she who wants to a- ttain peace   should prac-tice being up-

right, hum - ble and ca - pa-ble of u - sing lo-ving speech.

He or she will know how to live sim - ply and ha -

ppi - ly, with sen - ses calmed,   wi - thout being co -

ve - tous a - nd ca - rried a - way

by the e - mo - tions of the ma - jo - ri-ty. Let

him or her not do a - ny-thing tha - t wi - ll be di - sa-pproved of

by the wise ones. (And this is what he or she con -

tem-plates:) May e - v'ry-one be ha - ppy and safe, a - nd ma - y

he - r o - n-ly child at___ the risk of her own life, cul-ti-vate

bound-less love to o - ffer to a - ll li - ving beings

_ in the en - ti - re co - smos. Let our bound -

less love per - vade the whole u - ni - ve - rse, a - bove, be_

_ low, and a - cross.___ Our love will know no ob -

sta - cles. Our heart___ will be ab - so - lute -

- ly___ free___ from ha - tred and en - mi - ty.

Whe - ther sta - n - ding or wal - king, si - tting or ly -

- ing, as long as we are a-wa - ke, we should main - tai - n

this mind - ful - ne - ss of love in our own heart.

This is the no - bl - est way o - f li - - - - ving.__

__ Free from wrong vie - ws, greed, and sen - sua -

l de - si - res, li - ving in beau - ty and rea - li - zing Pe - r -

fect Un - der - sta - n - ding, those who prac - tice bound - less

love will cer - tain - ly_____ tran - scend bi - rth and death.

(By the firm determination of this truth, may you ever be well.)

E - te - na sa - cca va - jje - na___ so - tthi te ho - tu sa - bba - da.__

E - te - na sa - cca va - jje - na___ so - tthi te ho - tu sa - bba - da.__

E - te - na sa - cca va - jje - na___ so - tthi te ho - tu sa - bba da.__

EVENING CHANT: ORIGINAL VERSION

Slowly

Traditional

At the foo - t o - f the Bo - dhi tree,
In pe - - - r - fect mind - ful - ness,
Na - mo_____

sta - ble i - s my po - s - ture.
my bo - - - - dy and mind dwell.
Sha - - - - - - kya - - -

Bo - dy, spee-ch, and mi - nd a - ll are one.
The pa - th i - s i - llu - mi - ned,
mu - na - ye_____

There is no thou - ght of ri - ght and wrong.
the shore of con - fu - sion le - ft be - hind.
Bu - - - - - ddha - ya

EVENING CHANT: VERSION 1

Very slowly, with bell   Adapted from a traditional Vietnamese chant

Sta - bly_____ sea - ted u - - - n - der the_____

Bo - - - - - dhi_ tree._____ Bo - dy, speech, and

mi - - nd a - re one in sti - ll - ness,_____

free_____ from vie - ws of ri - ght a - nd wro - ng.

When we are fo - cused in per - fect mind - fu - l - ness, the pa - th

is i - llu - mi - ned. The sho - - re of con -

fu - sion is le - - - - ft be - hi - nd.

No - ble San - gha, di - li - gent - ly bring your mind in - to me - di - ta - tion.

Call and response three times

Na - mo_____ Sha - kya - mu - na - ye Bu - ddha - ya

Evening Chant: version 2

Very slowly, with bell

Music by Chan Phap Hien

With po- sture u - pright and sta - ble,

we are sea - ted at the foot of the Bo - dhi tree.___

___ Bo - dy, speech, and mi - nd a - re

o - ne i - n still - ness; there is no more thought

of ri - ght and wro - ng. Our mind and bo- dy dwell

in pe - r-fect mind-ful - ness. We re - di - sco - ver our o - ri - gi-nal na -

ture, lea - ving the shore of i - llu - sion be - hi - nd.

No-ble Sang-ha, di-li-gent - ly bring your mind in-to me-di-ta - tion.

Call and response 3 times

Na - mo___ Sha - kya-mu - na - ye Bu - ddha - ya

THE FOUR GRATITIUDES

Chanted flowingly

Music by Chan The Nghiem

In gra-ti-tude to our fa-ther and mo-ther who have gi-ven us life,

we bow dee-ply be-fore the Three Je-wels in the Te-n Di-rec-tions.

In gra-ti-tude to our tea-chers who have shown us the way to love,

un-der-stand, and live dee-ply the pre-sent mo-ment,

we bow dee-ply be-fore the Three Je-wels in the Te-n Di-rec-tions.

In gra-ti-tude to our friends who guide us and

su-pport us in di-ffi-cult mo-ments,

we bow dee-ply be-fore the Three Je-wels in the Te-n Di-rec-tions.

In gra-ti-tude to all be-ings in the a-ni-mal, plant, and mi-ne-ral worlds,

we bow dee-ply be-fore the Three Je-wels in the Te-n Di-rec-tions.

The Four Recollections

Chanted breath by breath

Music by Chan Phap Hien

The No - ble Tea - cher in whom I take re - fuge

is the One who em - bo - dies and re-veals the Ul - ti-mate Re - a - li - ty,

is the One who is wor - thy of all re - spect and o - ffe-rings,

is the One who is en - dowed with per-fec - ted wis - dom,

is the One who is en - dowed with right un - der - stan - ding

and com - pa - ssio - nate ac - tion,

is the One who ha - ppi - ly crossed to the shore of free - dom,

is the One who looked dee - ply to know the wo - rld well,

is the high - est char - i - o - tee - r trai - ning hu - man - kind,

teaching gods and hu-mans, the A-wa-kened One, the World-Ho-nored One.

The Tea-ching gi-ven by my No-ble Tea-cher

is the path I un-der-take, the Tea-ching well-pro-claimed,

is the Tea-ching that can be rea-lized right here and right now,

is the Tea-ching that is i-mme-diate-ly use-ful and e-ffec-tive,

is the Tea-ching in-vi-ting all to come and see di-rect-ly,

is the Tea-ching that is lea-ding to the good, the true, the beau-ti-ful,

ex-tin-gui-shing the fi-re of a-fflic-tions;

it is a tea-ching for all sen-si-ble peo-ple to rea-lize for them-selves.

Prac-ti-cing the Tea-chings,

the No-ble Co-mmu-ni-ty in which I take re-fuge

that re-mains har-mo-ni-ous,   that re-mains flaw-less, that re-mains re-fined;

is   the won-der-ful prac - tice   that   has   the   ca - pa - ci - ty

to   pre-vent   wrong - do - ing   and   to   pre-vent   dan - ger;

is   the won-der-ful prac - tice   that   has   the   ca - pa - ci - ty

to   pro-tect   self   and   o - thers   and   to   re - veal   beau - ty;

is   the won-der - ful prac - tice   that is   lea-ding to con - cen - tra - tion,

lea-ding to peace - ful - ness,   lea-ding to in - sight,   lea-ding to   non - fear;

is   the won-der - ful prac - tice   that   shows   us   the   wa - y

to   to - tal e-man - ci-pa - tion   and long - la - sting ha - ppi - ness.

FROM THE DEPTHS OF UNDERSTANDING

With drum and bell Music by Chan Phap Hien

From the de - pths of un - der - sta - n - ding,

a flow - er o - f great e - loquence blooms:___ The

Bo - dhi - satt - va sta - nds ma - jes - ti - cally___ u - pon the

wa - ves of birth and dea - th, free___ from a - ll a - ffli - c - tions.

Her great com - pa - ssion e - li - mi - nates a - ll

si - ckness, e - ven that once thought of as in - cu - ra - ble.

Her won - drous light swee - ps a - wa - y all

ob - sta - cles and da - n - gers. The wi - llow branch, once

wa - ved re - vea - ls count - less Bu - ddha lands. Her

THE HEART OF PERFECT UNDERSTANDING

Chanted breath by breath   Music by Chan Phap Hien

The Hea - rt of Per - fect Un - der - stand - ing:

The Bo - dhi - satt - va A - va - lo - ki - ta,

while mo - ving in the deep course of Per - fect Un - der - sta - n - ding,

shed li - ght on the Five Skan - dhas and found them e - qua - lly emp - ty.

Af - ter this pe - ne - tra - tion, he o - ver - came ill - be - ing.

Li - sten, Sha - ri - pu - tra, form is emp - ti - ness, and emp - ti - ness is form.

Form is not o - ther than emp - ti - ness,

emp - ti - ness is not o - ther than form.

The same is true with fee - lings, per - cep - tions,

INCENSE OFFERING: VERSION 1

INCENSE OFFERING: VERSION 2

Slowly

Traditional

The fra - grance o - f this i - n - cense
The fra - grance o - f this i - n - cense
The fra - grance o - f this i - n - cense
Na - mo

in - vites the a - wa - - - kened mind
fi - lls our pra - c - tice ce - n - ter,
co - llects us a - nd u - ni - tes us.
Bo - dhi - sa - tt - ve - bhy - ah

to be truly present
pro - te - cts and gua - rds our mind
Pre - cepts, co - n - cen - tra - tion, i - n - sight,
Na - mo

wi - - - - - - th us now.
fro - m a - ll wrong thi - n - king.
we o - - - ffe - r for a - ll that is.
Ma - ha - sa - tt - ve - bhy - ah

INVOCATION OF THE BUDDHAS AND BODHISATTVAS

Moderately, with drum and bell

Music from *Om Namo Bhagavate*, by Praful

Om___ Om Na - mo___ Sha - kya -
[Optional:] ('mi - ta -

Low harmony begins with 3rd invocation.

mu-na - ye___ Bu - ddha - - - - ya___
bha - - ya)

Om Na - mo___ Ma - n - ju - shri - ye___
[Optional:] (Kshi - ti - gar - bha -

High harmony begins with 3rd invocation.

Bo - dhi - sa - ttva - - - ya___
ya)

JOYFULLY SHARING THE MERIT

Chanted flowingly

Music by Chan Phap Hien

Ble-ssed Ones who dwe - ll in the wo - rld, grant to us com-pa - ssion. In this, and count-less li - ves be-fo - re, fro-m be - gi-nning-less ti - - me, our mis-takes have caused much su - ffe-ring to our - selves and o - thers. We have done wro-ng, en-cou-raged o-thers to do wrong, and gi - ven our con-se-nt to acts of ki-lling, stea-ling, de-cei - ving, se-xual mis-con-duct, and o-ther harm-ful ac-tions a - mong the Ten Un-whole-some Deeds. Whe-ther our faults are kno - wn to o - thers or

30

33 whe-ther they are hi - dden, they have brought us to the rea-

37 - - lms of he - ll, hu - n - gry gho-sts, and a - ni-mals, cau-

40 - sing us to be born in pla - ces filled with pain and su -

44 ffe-ring. We have not yet had the chance to rea-lize our full po-ten-tial.

47 To-day we are de - te - r - mined, with o - ne-poi-n-ted co-n-

50 cen-tra - tion, to re - pent the ob - sta - cles of our past

53 un - whole-some ac - tions.____ Ble-ssed Ones,

56 be our wit-ness and look u - pon us with com - pa - ssion.

59 We su-rren - der be - fore____ you and make this a - spi - ra - tion:

____ If at all wi - thin this ve - ry life____ and count-less lives

93

96 — if we have e - ver re - ci - ted a su - tra, e -

99 ven if on - ly one or two___ lines; if we have e - ver

102 been a monk or a nun,___ e - ven if on - ly for one life;

105 if we have e - ver___ su - ppor-ted o-thers on the path of prac-tice,

108 e - ven if on - ly two or three peo - ple; if we have e -

111 ver ob-served the Mind - ful -ness Trai nings, e - ven if im - per-fect -

114 ly; all of this me - rit has slow-ly formed whole-some

117 seeds wi -thin us. To-day we ga - ther them to - ge-ther like a

120 fra-grant flo -wer gar - land and, with grea - t re - spect, we o - ffer it

to all A - wa - kened Ones;___ a con - tri - bu - tion to the

160

163 All Bu-ddhas in the Three Times and the Te - n Di - rec - tions____

166 ____ have o - ffered their me - rit as we are do - ing to -

169 day. Re - pen - ting all our faults, ____ we joy - fu - lly con - tri -

171 bute to the i - mmea - sura - ble o - cean of me - rit

174 and the to - we - ring peaks of the high - est un - der - stan - ding.

176 The Bu - ddhas and the An - ces - tral Tea - chers

178 are the light which shows us the way.

180 In this so - lemn mo - ment, ____ with all my life's

force, I come back to my - self and bow dee - ply with re - spect.

MAY THE DAY BE WELL

Chanted breath by breath   Music by Chan Phap Hien

May the day be well and the night be well.

May the mid - day hour bring ha - ppi - ness too.

In e - ve - ry mi - nute and e - ve - ry se - cond,

may the day and night be well. By the ble - ssing

of the Tri - ple Gem, may all things be pro - tec - ted and safe.

May all be - ings bo - rn in each of the four ways

live in a la - nd of pu___ ri - ty.

May all in the Three Realms be bo - rn u-pon Lo - tus Thrones.

May count-less wan - der-ing souls rea - lize the three

vir - tuous po - si - tions of the Bo - dhi - satt - va Pa - th.

May all li - ving be - ings, with gra - ce and ease,

ful - fill the Bo - dhi - satt - va Sta - ges.

The coun - te-nance of the World - Ho - nored One,

like the fu - ll moon, or like the o - rb of the sun,

shi - - - nes with the light of cla - ri - ty.

A ha - lo of wi - s - dom spreads in e - ve-ry di - rec - tion,

en - ve - lo-ping all with lo - ve and com-pa - ssion,

joy - - - and e - qua - ni - mi - ty.
(jo - y and e - qua - ni - mi - ty.)

Na - mo___ Sha - kya -

mu - na - ye___ Bu - ddha - ya

mu - na - ye___ Bu - ddha - ya

MORNING CHANT: VERSION 1

Morning Chant: version 2

MORNING CHANT: VERSION 3

Very slowly, with bell   Music by Chan Phap Hien

The Dha - r - ma bo - dy is bri - ngi - ng

mo - r - ning li - ght. In co - n - cen - tra - tion,

ou - r hearts are a - t pea-ce, a half-smile is born u-pon our lips.

This is a new day.___ We vow

to go through it in mind-ful -ness.___ The su-n of wis-dom has now

ri - sen, shi - ning i - n e - ve - ry di - rec - tion.

No - ble San-gha, di - li - gent - ly bring your mind in-to me-di-ta-tion.

Call and response 3 times

Na - mo___ Sha - kya-mu-na - ye Bu - ddha - ya

NAMO'VALOKITESHVARAYA

OPENING VERSE: VERSION 1

Moderately   Traditional

Na - mo—— Ta - ssa Bha - ga - va-to—— A - ra-ha-to——

Sa - mma Sam - bu - ddha - ssa

The Dhar - ma is dee - p and lo - ve - ly. We

now have a chance to see, stu-dy, a-nd pra - c-ti - ce it. We vow to

re - a - lize its true—— mea - ning.

OPENING VERSE: VERSION 2

THE REFUGE CHANT

Chanted flowingly · Music by Chan Phap Hien

Solo: In - cense per - fumes the at - mos - phere.

Chorus: A lo - tus blooms and the Bu - ddha a - ppears.

Solo: The world__ of su - ffe-ring and di - scri - mi - na - tion

Chorus: is filled with the light of the ri - sing sun.

Solo: As the dust of fear and an - xi - e - ty se - ttles,

Chorus: with o-pen heart, one poin-ted mind, I turn to the Three__ Je - wels.

With drum and bell The Fu - lly En-ligh - tened One, beau - ti - fu - lly sea - ted,

peace - ful and smi - ling,__ a li - ving sou-rce of un - der - sta-n -

ding and com-pa - ssion,__ to the Bu - - - ddha

I__ go for re - fuge. The path of mi-nd-ful li - ving,__ __ lea - ding to hea - ling, joy, and en-ligh - te -n-ment, the wa - y of peace, to__ the Dha - - - - r-ma I__ go__ __ for re - fuge.__ The lo-ving and su-ppo- r-tive co-mmu - ni - ty o-f pra-c- tice, rea - li-zing har-mo-ny, a - wa - re - ness, and li-ber - a - tion,__ to the Sa - - ng- ha I__ go for re - fuge. I am a - wa-re that the Three__ Gems are wi-thi-n m- y heart. I vow to rea - lize them, pra- __ c - ti-cing mind - ful brea - thing a - nd smi - ling, loo-king dee - ply__ in - to things.__ I vow to un - der-stand li - ving

be - ings and their su - ffe - ring, to cul - ti - vate com -

pa - ssion and lo - ving ki-ndness, to prac-tice joy and e - qua - ni - mi -

ty. I vow to o - ffer jo - y to one pe - r - son in the

mo - rning, to help re - lieve the grie - f of one pe - r - son in the af - ter -

noon, li - ving sim - ply and sa - ne - ly with few po - sse - ssions, kee -

ping my bo - dy heal - thy. I vow to let go___ of all wo - rries

and an - xi - e - ty in or - der to be li - ght and free.

I am a - wa - re that I owe so___ much to my pa - rents, tea -

chers, friends, and all be - ings. I vow to be wo - r - thy of

thei - r trust, to prac-tice who - le - hear - ted - ly so that un - der - sta - n -

ding and com-pa - ssion wi-ll flo - wer,___ hel-ping li-ving be -

ings   be   free___   from their   su - ffe - ring.

May the Bu-ddha, the Dhar-ma, and the Sang-ha su-pport my e - ffo-rts.

SHARING THE MERIT: VERSION 1

Slowly   Traditional

Re - ci - ting the su - tras,   prac - ti - cing the wa - y   of   a -

wa - re - ness   gives   rise   to be - ne-fits   wi - thout li - mit.

We   vow   to share the fruits   with   all   be - ings.

We   vow to o - ffer tri - bute   to   pa-rents, tea - chers,

friends, and   nu - me - rous   be - ings   who give

gui - dance   and   su-pport a - long   the   path.

SHARING THE MERIT: VERSION 2

Slowly, with drum

Music by Chan The Nghiem

Re-ci-ting the su-tras, prac - ti - cing the way o - f

a - wa - re - ness gives ri - se to be - ne - fits wi - thout li - mit.

We vow to share the frui - ts with all be - ings.

We vow to o - ffer tri - bu - te to pa - rents, tea - chers, friends, a - nd

nu - me - rous beings who gi - ve gui-dance and su-pport a-long the path.

THE THREE REFUGES: VERSION 1

Chanted breath by breath

Music by Chan Phap Hien

I take re - fuge in the Bu - ddha,

the one who shows me the wa - y in this life.

I take re - fuge in the Dha - r - ma,

the way of un - der-stan - ding and of love.

I take re - fuge in the Sa - ng - ha, the co-mmu-ni-ty that lives

in har-mo-ny and a - ware-ness. Dwe-lling in the re-fuge of Bu-ddha,

I clear - ly see the path of light and beau - ty in the world.

Dwe - lling in the re - fuge of Dhar - ma,

I learn to o - pen ma-ny doors on the path of trans - for-ma-tion.

THE THREE REFUGES: VERSION 2

TOUCHING THE EARTH: OPENING GATHA
VERSION 1

Chanted flowingly

Music by Dana Maiben

Solo:
The one who bows and the one who is bowed to

Chorus:
a - re both, by na - tu - re, e - mp - ty.

There - fore the co - mmu - ni - ca - tion be - twee - n them
is i - nex - pre - ssi - bly per - fect.

Our prac - tice cen - ter is the Net of In - dra
re - flec - ting all Bu - ddhas e - v'ry - where.

And with my per - son in front of each Bu - ddha,
I go with my whole life for re - fuge.

TOUCHING THE EARTH: PROSTRATIONS
VERSION 1

Chanted flowingly   Adapted from music by Dana Maiben

O - ffe - ring light   in   the   Ten   Di - rec - tions,

the   Bu - ddha,   the Dhar - ma,   and the Sa - ng - ha

to   whom   we   bow   in   gra - ti - tude._____

Tea - ching and li - ving   the   way   of   a - ware - ness

in   the ve - ry   midst   of   su - ffe - ring and con - fu - sion,

Sha - kya   mu - ni Bu - ddha,   the   Fu - lly En - ligh - tened One,

to   whom   we   bow   in   gra - ti - tude._____

Verses:

Cutting through ignorance,
awakening our hearts and our
minds,
Manjushri, the Bodhisattva of
Great Understanding,
to whom we bow in gratitude.

Working mindfully, working
joyfully for the sake of all beings,
Samantabhadra, the Bodhisattva of
Great Action,
to whom we bow in gratitude.

Listening deeply, serving beings in
countless ways,
Avalokiteshvara, the Bodhisattva
of Great Compassion,
to whom we bow in gratitude.

Fearless and persevering through
realms of suffering and darkness,
Kshitigarbha, the Bodhisattva of
Great Aspiration,
to whom we bow in gratitude.

Seed of awakening and loving
kindness in children and all beings,
Maitreya, the Buddha to-be-born,
to whom we bow in gratitude.

[CONTINUE WITH THE FOLLOWING
OPTIONAL VERSES, OR SKIP TO THE
FINAL VERSE BELOW]

Seeing the Buddha in everyone,
Sadaparibhuta, the Bodhisattva of
Constant Respect,
to whom we bow in gratitude.

Convener of the Sangha, the
teacher Mahakashyapa,
to whom we bow in gratitude.

Wise elder brother, the teacher
Shariputra,
to whom we bow in gratitude.

Showing love for parents, the
teacher Mahamaudgalyayana,
to whom we bow in gratitude.

Master of the Vinaya, the teacher
Upali,
to whom we bow in gratitude.

Recorder of the teachings, the
teacher Ananda,
to whom we bow in gratitude.

The first bhikshuni, Mahagotami,
to whom we bow in gratitude.

Showing the way fearlessly and
compassionately,
The stream of all our Ancestral
Teachers,
to whom we bow in gratitude.

Touching the Earth: Opening Gatha
VERSION 2

Chanted flowingly   Music by Chan Phap Hien

Solo: The one who bows and the one who is bowed to

Chorus: a - re both, by na - tu - re, emp - ty.

Solo: There - fore the co-mmu-ni - ca - tion be - tween them

Chorus: is i - nex - pre - ssi - bly per - fect.

Our prac - tice cen - ter is the Net of In - dra

re - flec - ting all Bu - ddhas e - v'ry - where.

Solo: And with my per - son in front of each Bu - ddha,

Chorus: I_____ go with my whole life for re - fuge.

TOUCHING THE EARTH: PROSTRATIONS
VERSION 2

Chanted breath by breath

Music by Chan Phap Hien

O - ffe-ring light in the Ten Di - rec - tions and all a-cross the Three Times,

the Bu - ddha, the Dhar - ma, and the Sang - ha, to whom we bow in gra - ti - tude.

Tea-ching and li - ving the way of a - ware-ness in the ve-ry midst of su-ffe-ring and con-fu-sion,

Sha-kya-mu - ni Bu-ddha, the Fu - lly En - ligh-tened One, to whom we bow in gra - ti - tude.

Cu - tting through ig - no-rance, a - wa - ke - ning our hearts and minds,

Man-ju-shri, the Bo-dhi-satt-va of Great Un-der-stan-ding, to whom we bow in gra-ti-tude.

Wor-king mind - fu-lly and joy - fu-lly for the sake of all be - ings,

Sa-man-ta-bha-dra, the Bo-dhi-satt-va of Great Ac-tion, to whom we bow in gra - ti - tude.

WE ARE TRULY PRESENT

Chanted breath by breath   Music by Chan Phap Hien

With hearts e- sta-blished in mind- ful-ness,   we are tru - ly pre-sent

for si - tting and wal-king me-di - ta - tion,   and for re-ci-ting the su-tras.

May this prac - tice cen - ter, with its Four - fold San - gha,

be su - ppor - ted by the Three Je - wels and Ho - ly Be - ings,

well pro-tec-ted from the eight mis-for-tunes and the three paths of su-ffe-ring.

May pa-rents, tea-chers, friends, and all be-ings wi- thin the three realms

be filled with the most di - vine grace, and may it be found that in the world

there is no place at war. May the winds be fa - vo - ra - ble,

the rains sea - so - na - ble, and the peo - ple's hearts at peace.

May the prac - tice of the no - ble co - mmu - ni - ty,

di - li - gent and stea - dy, a - scend the Ten Bo - dhi - sa - ttva Sta - ges

with ease and e - ner - gy. May the Sang - ha bo - dy live peace - fu - lly,

fresh and full of joy, a re - fuge for all, o - ffe - ring ha - ppi - ness and in - sight.

The wis - dom of the A - wa - kened Mind shines out like the full moon.

The bo - dy of the A - wa - kened One is pure and clear as cry - stal.

In the world the A- wa-kened One re-lieves bi-tter-ness and su-ffe-ring.

In e-v'ry place the A - wa-kened Mind re-veals love and com-pa-ssion.

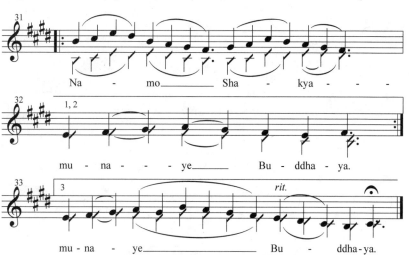

Na - mo_____ Sha - kya - -

mu - na - - - ye_____ Bu - ddha - ya.

mu - na - ye_____ Bu - ddha - ya.

The Five Remembrances

Music by Joseph Emet

INVOKING AVALOKITESHVARA

Adapted from the original text
Music by Chan The Nghiem

THE SONG OF NO-COMING AND NO-GOING

Adapted from a poem by Thich Nhat Hanh
Music by Rashani

sa-cred thre-sholds on our jour - ney. Birth and death are a

hide - and - see - k game._____ So

laugh with me, hold my hand, let us say good-bye, say good-bye to

meet soon a-gain. We meet to-day, we will meet to-mo-rrow.

We shall meet at the source e-v'ry mo-ment. We meet each o - ther in

all forms of life._____ This

bo-dy is not you. You are not caught in this bo-dy._____

THE THREE REFUGES SONG

Quickly

Music by Betsy Rose

I take re-fuge___ in the Budd-ha,_____ the one who
I take re-fuge___ in the Dhar-ma,_____ the way of
I take re-fuge___ in the Sang-ha, the co-mmu-ni-

shows me___ the wa-y in this life. Na-mo Budd-ha-ya, Na-mo
un - de - r - sta - n - ding and love. Na-mo Dhar-ma-ya, Na-mo
ty_____ o-f mind-ful har-mo-ny. Na-mo Sang-ha-ya, Na-mo

Budd-ha-ya, Na-mo Bu - dd-ha-ya.
Dhar-ma-ya, Na-mo Dha - r-ma-ya.
Sang-ha-ya, Na-mo Sa - ng-ha-ya.

THE TWO PROMISES

Music by Betsy Rose

I___ vow to de-ve-lop un-der-sta-n-ding in
I___ vow to de-ve-lop my com-pa-ssion in

or-der to live peace-fu-lly with peo-ple, a-ni-mals, plants, and
or-der to pro-tect the lives of peo-ple, a-ni-mals, plants, and

mi-ne-rals, a-ni-mals, plants, and mi-ne-rals. Mmm ahh, mmm
mi-ne-rals, a-ni-mals, plants, and mi-ne-rals. Mmm ahh, mmm

ahh, mmm ahh.
ahh, mmm ahh.

WATERING SEEDS OF JOY

Adapted from the original text
Music by Chan The Nghiem

and the Pa - tri - a - rchs. I a - m a

con - ti - nu-a - tio - n of all my spi - ri - tual tea-chers.

It i - s my deep a - spi - ra - tio - n to pre-serve, de-

ve-lop, and nou-rish seeds of u - n - der-stan - di - ng, seeds of lo - ve,

seeds of free - dom which they have tran-smi - tted to

me. In my dai - ly life, I al - so want to so - w seeds of love and com-

pa-ssion in my own con-scious-ness and in the heart o - f o-ther people.

I am de-ter-mined not to wa-ter the seeds of cra-ving, a-ver-sion, and

vio- le - nce in me.   I am de-ter-mined not to wa-ter the seeds of

cra-ving, a - ver-sion, and vio-le - nce in o - the - rs.   With re - solve and

with   com - pa - ssio - n,   I give ri - se to

this a-spi-ra - tio - n: May my prac-tice be an o-ff'ring of the heart.

May my prac-tice be an   o - ff'ring of   the heart.

DRINKING TEA

Music by ChiSing

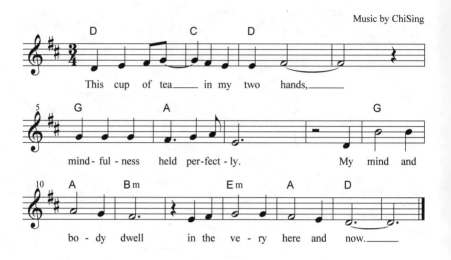

This cup of tea___ in my two hands,___

mind - ful - ness held per-fect - ly. My mind and

bo - dy dwell in the ve - ry here and now.___

ENTERING THE MEDITATION HALL

Music by ChiSing

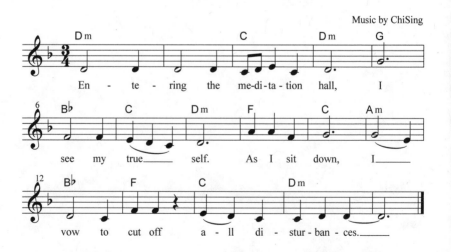

En - te - ring the me-di-ta-tion hall, I

see my true___ self. As I sit down, I___

vow to cut off a - ll di - stur - ban - ces.___

GATHA ON IMPERMANENCE

Chanted flowingly

Adapted from the original text
Music by Jamie Rusek

The day is now en - ded. Our lives are shor - ter.

Let us look care - fu - lly. What have we done?___

No - ble San - gha, with all of our heart,

let us be di - li - gent, en - ga-ging in prac - tice.

Let us live dee - ply, free from our a - fflic - tions,

a - ware of im - per - ma - nence

so that life... so that life does not drift...

does not drift a - way wi - thout mea - ning.

INVITING THE BELL

Music by Chan Mai Nghiem

Bo - dy, spee - ch, and mind held in per - fect one - ness,
I send my hea - rt a-long with the sound__ o - f the bell.__ May the
*May it
hea - rers a - wa - ken from____ for - get - ful - ness,____ tran-scen-ding
pe - ne trate dee - ply____ the u - ni - verse,____ a - wa - ke -
an - xi - e - ty and so - rrow.____
ning be - ings to life. ____

* adapted from other inviting-the-bell gathas

LIGHTING A CANDLE

Music by Chan Chau Nghiem

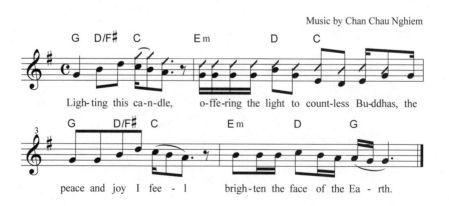

Ligh - ting this ca-n-dle, o-ffe-ring the light to count-less Bu-ddhas, the
peace and joy I fee - l brigh - ten the face of the Ea - rth.

LISTENING TO THE BELL

Chanted flowingly, with bell invited between phrases
[x-note] = bell

Adapted from the original text
Music by Chan The Nghiem

Hea - - ri - ng the___ bell,___

I let go of all my a - fflic - tions.

My heart i - s calm, my so - rro - ws e - n - ded.

No lo - nger bound to a - ny thi - - -

ng. I learn to li - sten to my su - ffe - ring___

and to the su - - - ffri - ng of o - thers.

When un - der - stan - ding i - s born i - n me,___

com - pa - ssion is al - so bo - - - -

rit.

- - - - - rn.

SWEEPING

Music by Chan Chau Nghiem

As I care - fu -lly sweep the ground of en-ligh - ten - ment, a tree of un - der - stan-ding springs up fro - m the Earth.

glossary

Glossary

Akshayamati – Bodhisattva of Infinite Thought.

ashravas – All phenomena can be categorized as *ashrava*, "with leaks," or *anashrava*, "without leaks." When our actions are "ashrava," they don't yet have the nature of true insight and liberation, so they create more seeds of delusion in our mind. When our actions are "anashrava," they produce no unwholesome karmic fruit.

asura – A god or spirit who is fond of fighting and subject to frequent outbursts of anger.

Avalokiteshvara – Bodhisattva of Compassion and Deep Listening.

bell of mindfulness – The sound of a bell or a clock, an electric beeper, or even the ring of a telephone that is used to call an individual or the community back to their breathing and the practice of mindfulness.

bhikkhu (Pali), **bhikshu** (Sanskrit) – One who seeks alms, referring to monks who have received full ordination (as opposed to novice ordination).

bhikkhuni (Pali), **bhikshuni** (Sanskrit) – One who seeks alms, referring to nuns who have received full ordination (as opposed to novice ordination).

bodhicitta – The awakening mind. Sometimes translated as the Mind of Love, because it is our awakened nature that impels us to love beings unconditionally and our understanding that enables us to do this.

Bodhisattva – ("Bodhisattvebhyah" is the dative plural meaning "to the bodhisattvas.") Literally "enlightened being," one committed to enlightening oneself and others so that all may be liberated from suffering.

brahmacarya – A holy life in harmony with the mindfulness trainings; chastity, especially the celibate life of a Buddhist monk or nun.

Buddha – ("Buddhaya" is the dative singular meaning "to the Buddha.") The Awakened One. Refers also to the capacity within every being to be "awake" or "enlightened."

cakravartin – World ruler, universal monarch.

chiliocosm – Inconceivably vast space. Thousand-world universe, each world having a Mount Sumeru, sun, moon, and four continents surrounded by oceans.

Cundi – A form of Avalokiteshvara Bodhisattva, the Bodhisattva of Compassion, depicted with one thousand arms.

deva – Celestial being, angel.

Dharma – ("Dharmaya" is the dative singular meaning "to the Dharma.") The true teachings of the Awakened One, the path of understanding and love.

dharma – Phenomenon, thing, object of mind.

Dharmadhatu – The entire cosmos of dharma elements. The underlying indestructible togetherness of the ultimate and historical dimensions.

Dharmakaya – The body of the Dharma; what remains when the historical Buddha is no longer with us. The true and ultimate reality.

discourse – A teaching given by the Buddha or one of his enlightened disciples ("sutra" in Sanskrit, "sutta" in Pali).

Eight Misfortunes – Obstacles to one's capacity to receive and practice the true teachings. To be (1) in the hell realms, (2) a hungry ghost, (3) an animal, (4) lazy when having excessive comforts, (5) ignorant without favorable conditions for awareness, (6) without hearing, sight, or speech,* (7) caught in arrogant speculation, (8) born before or after a Buddha's lifetime.

Eight Virtues – Eight virtues of water: clear, cool, sweet in taste, light in texture, sparkling bright, calm, eliminates hunger and thirst, and nourishes the practice.

Five Eyes – Physical eyes, deva eyes, Dharma eyes, wisdom eyes, Buddha eyes.

Five Faculties – Faith, energy, mindfulness, concentration, and wisdom.

Five Powers – Same as the Five Faculties, except that as powers they cannot be shaken by their opposites (e.g., energy cannot be swayed by laziness).

Five Skandhas – The five aspects of a person: form, feelings, perceptions, mental formations, and consciousness. Sometimes called Five Aggregates.

Fourfold Sangha – A practicing community of monks, nuns, laymen, and laywomen. *See also* Sangha.

Four Pairs and Eight Kinds of Holy People – Arhat, Non-Returner, Once-Returner, Stream-Enterer. The one who has attained the path heading toward the fruit and the one who has attained the fruit are considered one pair. Individually they are considered the Eight Types of Noble Ones.

Four Quarters – North, South, East, and West.

four ways of birth – From eggs, from a womb, by metamorphosis, and by division.

Four Wisdoms – Great Mirror Wisdom, Wisdom of Equality, Wisdom of Deep Looking, and Wisdom of Perfect Realization.

Gate gate paragate parasamgate bodhi svaha – The mantra from the Heart of the Prajñaparamita, uttered by Avalokiteshvara, meaning: "Gone, gone, gone all the way over, gone with all beings to the other shore, enlightenment, rejoice!"

gatha – A short poem or verse that we can recite during our daily activities to help us dwell in mindfulness.

hungry ghost – *Preta,* a being without faith or belief who ceaselessly craves without satisfaction.

Indra's Net – A limitless net stretching infinitely in all directions, with a jewel in each eye of the net. These jewels are infinite in number, each reflecting in itself all other jewels. This image is taken from the Avatamsaka Sutra and is generally used to illustrate the teachings of interbeing and interpenetration.

kalpa – An inconceivably long time, an eon.

---

* Considered a limitation at the time of the Buddha.

Kshitigarbha – Earth Store Bodhisattva, who vows to save beings in the realms of greatest suffering.

Lotus Throne – Seat of a Buddha.

mahasattva – ("Mahasattvebhyah" is the dative plural meaning "to the Great Beings.") Great Being, one who has realized the highest truths.

mandarava – Flowers that fall from the sky in the Pure Land, Sukhavati.

Manjushri – Bodhisattva of Understanding.

Manasarowara Lake – Also known as Anavatapta Lake, meaning cool, where there exists no heat of the afflictions.

Mara – The tempter, the Evil One, the killer, the opposite of the Buddha nature in each person; sometimes personalized as a deity. The obstacles to our practice, which arise in our own minds.

mindfulness trainings (formerly "precepts") – Guidelines offered by the Buddha to protect us and help us live in mindfulness, in the form of precepts prescribing a particular course of conduct.

mudra of peace – Also known as Seal of Peace, the sign made with the right hand when blessing water. The thumb joins the tip of the bent fourth finger while the second, third, and fifth fingers are held straight.

Naga King – A water deity governing springs, rain, rivers, lakes, and oceans.

Nagapushpa Assembly – The assembly that gathers around the Dragon Flower Tree to hear the teachings of Maitreya, the Buddha-to-be.

Namo – A phrase uttered when paying homage or respect to someone or something.

Namo Tassa Bhagavato Arahato Samma Sambuddhassa – "Homage to him, the World-Honored One, who is worthy of offerings, the One endowed with Perfect Understanding."

nirvana – The extinction of all views and concepts and the suffering based on them, to have no attachments to the realm of birth and death. Refers to the ultimate reality.

Prajñaparamita – Perfection of Wisdom, crossing to the other shore with understanding.

Pure Land – Sukhavati, the land of great happiness where the Buddha Amitabha dwells. An ideal place to practice the path of liberation.

Roseapple Island – Jambudvipa; an ancient name for India, the continent where humans live. From jambu, meaning roseapple tree.

Sadaparibhuta – The Bodhisattva Never Despising, or Never Disparaging.

Samantabhadra – Bodhisattva of Great Action, who made the ten great vows of practice.

samsara – Cycle of birth and death.

Sangha – ("Sanghaya" is the dative singular meaning "to the Sangha.") The Community that endeavors to practice the true teachings in harmony.

Sanghakaya – The collective body of the Sangha.

Shakyamuni – ("Shakyamunaye" is the dative singular meaning "to Shakyamuni.") Literally, "sage of the Shakya clan." Refers to the historical Buddha whose awakening and teachings laid the foundation for the practice of Buddhism.

Six Dark Paths – Gods, humans, asuras, hells, hungry ghosts, animals.

Six Miracles (The Six Miraculous Powers) – (1) To see a great distance, (2) to hear all sounds, (3) to know one's past lives, (4) to perceive others' thoughts, (5) to travel anywhere at will, (6) to take on any form at will.

Six Tastes – Sweet, sour, salty, pungent, bitter, and astringent.

Sugata – Well-Gone One, one who has lived and practiced skillfully; another name for the Buddha.

Tathagata – One who comes from nowhere and goes nowhere, an epithet the Buddha used when referring to himself.

Ten Directions – Eight compass directions plus above and below. Refers to the entire universe.

Ten Stages – Bhumi, the stages through which a bodhisattva passes on the path of awakening.

Ten Unwholesome Deeds – Killing, stealing, sexual misconduct, lying, deceiving, exaggerating, contradicting, coveting, being angry, having wrong views.

Three Actions – Actions of body, speech, and mind.

Three Baskets – Tripitaka: discourses *(sutras)*, precepts *(vinaya)*, and commentaries on the Buddha's teachings *(abhidharma)*.

Three Bodies of Buddha – Dharmakaya (body of true nature), Sambhogakaya (body of bliss or enjoyment), Nirmanakaya (transformation body).

Three Jewels, Three Gems, Triple Gem – Buddha, Dharma, Sangha.

Three Paths of Suffering – Hells, hungry ghosts, animals.

Three Qualities (of food) – *Sattva* (pure), *rajas* (fiery), and *tamas* (heavy).

Three Realms – Form, formlessness, desire.

Three Times – Past, present, future.

Three Virtuous Positions of the Bodhisattva Path – Dwelling firmly in the practice (ten abodes), manifesting right actions (ten actions), and transferring all merit to the liberation of all beings (ten offerings).

Two Truths – The absolute truth and the relative truth. The absolute truth cannot be expressed directly in words and concepts, while the relative truth can. According to the absolute truth,s there is no self. However, the absolute and relative truths inter-are; there cannot be one without the other.

upasaka m., **upasika** f. – Layman or laywoman practitioner. Literally, "one who is close," i.e., practices closely with monks and nuns.

Vulture Peak – Gridhakuta. The mountain near the town of Rajagriha where the Buddha sometimes stayed and taught.

yaksha – A ghost or demon, usually harmful but sometimes a protector of the Dharma.

Index

Index

Following is a listing of verses, gathas, ceremonies, discourses, chants, songs, etc., and the page numbers on which they appear. Many items appear more than once throughout this book, but in most instances only the first occurrence is noted here. The Table of Contents is another useful resource for locating specific gathas, ceremonies, and discourses.

Parallax Press, a nonprofit organization, publishes books on engaged Buddhism and the practice of mindfulness by Thich Nhat Hanh and other authors. All of Thich Nhat Hanh's work is available at our online store and in our free catalog. For a copy of the catalog, please contact:

Parallax Press
www.parallax.org
P.O. Box 7355
Berkeley, CA 94707
Tel: (510) 525-0101

Individuals, couples, and families are invited to practice the art of mindful living in the tradition of Thich Nhat Hanh at retreat communities in France and the United States. For information, please visit www.plumvillage.org or contact:

Plum Village
13 Martineau
33580 Dieulivol, France
info@plumvillage.org

Green Mountain Dharma Center
P.O. Box 182
Hartland Four Corners, VT 05049
mfmaster@vermontel.net
Tel: (802) 436-1103

Deer Park Monastery
2499 Melru Lane
Escondido, CA 92026
deerpark@plumvillage.org
Tel: (760) 291-1003

For a worldwide directory of Sanghas practicing in the tradition of Thich Nhat Hanh, please visit www.iamhome.org.